P9-DUH-264

COSTUMING FOR OPERA

LEO VAN WITSEN

Costuming for OPERA

Who Wears What and Why

INDIANA UNIVERSITY PRESS • BLOOMINGTON

Manufactured in the United States of America

Library of Congress Cataloging in Publication Data
Van Witsen, Leo, 1912–
Costuming for opera.
Bibliography: p.
1. Operas—Stage guides. 2. Costume. 3. Opera—Production and direction. I. Title.
MT955.V36 782.1'07'3 79-3250
ISBN 0-253-13225-8 1 2 3 4 5 85 84 83 82 81

Contents

FOREWORD

Several years ago, during a post-mortem discussion of the *Ring of the Nibelung* in Bayreuth, I had an argument with Wolfgang Wagner, who had staged this particular production. "Why is it," I asked him, "that your conductor and your singers have treated your grandfather's musical wishes with the utmost respect, while in your stage direction you seem to have gone out of your way to repudiate and contradict all of Richard Wagner's theatrical intentions?"

"You are probably not aware," Wolfgang Wagner replied, "that my grandfather was dissatisfied with his own production of the *Ring*. He was not certain how it should be staged, and it was left to us, his successors, to find better solutions."

Leaving aside the bizarre notion that Richard Wagner would have been pleased with the sorry travesty I had witnessed during the preceding week, his grandson's answer illustrates the attitude prevalent among many present-day operatic producers. "The composer is undoubtedly a great musician," they say. "His indications dealing with vocal and instrumental interpretation are of the highest order. But when it comes to the visual realization of his scores, he is neither competent, imaginative, nor creative. Here, he needs our help!"

This point of view has led to a drastic split between the musical and the theatrical side of opera. The conductors continue to obey the composers' precepts; they insist on a faithful adherence to all nuances noted in the scores, and they occupy themselves zealously with the important tasks of setting the right tempi and achieving the best possible synchronization and balance between the stage and the pit. But they seldom have much expertise in matters pertaining to the visual theater, and when they look toward the stage, they do it mostly for the purpose of cuing the singers. In the meantime, the stage directors and scenic designers go their independent way, a way made particularly attractive by the many mechanical improvements and technical innovations that have been installed in most of today's theaters. The ready availability of various types of projectors, platforms, staircases, and steep ramps has made the modern stage much more amenable to innovations, while the use of turntables and elevators has enabled the stage directors to achieve rapid transformations of scenes and to cut down on the length of intermissions.

One innovation led to another. It soon became fashionable to deride "romantic" interpretations of operatic plots and to modernize the stories by giving them up-to-date looks and contemporary locations. The fact that the words uttered by the vocalists did not always jibe with the "new look" was not considered particularly important, since it was well known that the foreign language and the notoriously poor enunciation of singers prevented the audience from noticing too many discrepancies. The desire to out-do their competitors and to express themselves "creatively" drove many present-day producers to the most ridiculous gimmicks and tempted them to indulge in the most unbridled ego trips.

It all began some forty years ago, and, strangely enough, it originated in Bayreuth, where one would have expected to encounter the most faithful adherence to a composer's wishes. Animals, so dear to Richard Wagner, were the first to be banished. Soon many other "realistic" objects were deleted by directors eager to achieve the most antiseptic, nonrepresentational and symbolic look. It did not take long for this "innovate-at-all-costs" mania to infect other operatic companies. In the process, we lost not only animals and objects but also much self-respect. It is embarrassing and demeaning to listen to singers who mention, point to, and address horses, swans, dragons, buildings, books, flowers, or jewels when none of these are visible either to the performers or to the audiences.

Even more disastrous than this destruction of visual elements is the loss of specific musical contexts. It may be true that police states have existed, and still exist, in many countries and epochs. But Puccini in *Tosca* made a valiant effort to show by the Te Deum of the first act, the Gavotte and the Cantata of the second act, and the Shepherd's Song and the bell-ringing of the third act that this opera was to be played in Rome in the year 1800—and not, for instance, in Budapest in the year 1956, where the aforementioned important musical elements are totally out of place. The Minuet and the Perigordino in the opening scene of *Rigoletto* belong in a very specific social environment of elegance and good manners and not in a house of ill repute, where I have seen them danced more than once. And the musical contrast between this scene and the next one is ruined if both are played around the same meaningless and periodless revolving tower. The musical pomp and majesty of *Aïda*'s King of Egypt sound ridiculous if the Pharaoh and his cohorts move among ruins of broken-down walls and temples. Hundreds of similar examples can be cited.

It is possible to argue that the special strength of music lies in the realm of mood and energy values, and that the portrayal of human passions—which is the main dramatic preoccupation of opera—is not related to geography and chronology. "You must admit," producers have pointed out to me, "that Verdi willingly moved his *Ballo in*

Maschera from Stockholm in the year 1792 to Boston of a hundred years earlier, without changing a single note of music." Of course, I refuse to admit anything of the sort! Verdi was not "willing." He was rather brutally forced to submit to this disastrous transformation by the prejudices and fears of an all-powerful clique of politically motivated Italian censors. And it is shameful that we continue to tolerate this insult to Verdi's memory. We should, of course, return the *Ballo* to its rightful milieu, in a land ruled by a francophile Swedish king, and avoid the silliness of conspirators named Samuel and Tom and the anachronism of Galops and Mazurkas danced at a masquerade attended by Puritans and "Creole" guests.

I will gladly admit that much of operatic music has universal validity and significance. But, in return, these musical moods and energies are capable of infinite shades and nuances. The musical anger of Mozart's Count Almaviva is proportionate to *his* upbringing and lordly environment just as Alfio's vocal rage in *Cavalleria Rusticana* is appropriate, a hundred years later, to his social class. Environment, social class, and chronology are evident in music just as much as in behavior, architecture, furniture, and costumes. Which brings me to the purpose of this foreword.

In this day and age, when so much opera teeters between ignorance and vandalism, it is a pleasure to welcome an expert who is neither an unthinking traditionalist nor a determined iconoclast. Leo Van Witsen combines an objective point of view—based on solid knowledge—with a disarming willingness to inform the readers of his personal tastes and preferences. Having spent most of his life with producers and designers as well as with singers, he is keenly aware of the limitations imposed by tight budgets, and the unlimited delicacy needed to deal with the whims of high-strung personalities. And, most importantly of all, he has a real understanding of the way music and the theater complement each other. For this reason alone, this book should be read and studied by every operatic professional, be he a designer, singer, conductor, stage director, or critic.

Boris Goldovsky

ACKNOWLEDGMENTS

The immigrant who decides to write a book in the language of his adopted country is in for a surprise. Regardless of the number of years he has spent in his second fatherland (in my case, forty plus), when it comes to writing a book, the old native syntaxes and turns of phrase will rear their quaint but unsuitable heads. "It is interesting, but not very good English," was the comment I invariably received when I first began to show my literary efforts to my friends. I have to thank my companion Robert W. Hess for his help in turning my Dutch inflections into tolerable English. In addition, he gave me free access to his large library of music books, scores, records, and tapes, while putting up with my varying moods through it all.

Boris Goldovsky has been my operatic mentor since 1945. Through the years he has been an inspiration and a friend and, like a good friend, he has shown me the errors of my ways. I gratefully acknowledge his criticism of my manuscript. I owe him thanks as well for consenting to write the foreword to this book.

To Stella Blum, the Curator of the Costume Institute of the Metropolitan Museum of Art, and her staff, I am indebted for going over my chapters with a fine-tooth comb and weeding out costume-historical gaffes.

Many others, whose names are listed here, have been helpful in the realization of this book in one way or another. I thank them all, and may Monterone's curse descend upon me if I omitted anyone.

Howard C. Baron, M.D.
Zenos Booker
Mathilda Burry
Frank C. Campbell
James J. Coffey
Eric Crozier
Quaintance Eaton
Martha England
Robert Erler
Arthur Gerold
John Gutman
Dr. Burton Hoffmann
Robert Jacobson
Joseph D. Lewis
David Lloyd
Violet Lowens
Jeanne Maroney
Maria F. Rich
David Roberts
Julius Rudel
Arthur Seelen
Carlos and Alison Slienger
Kurt and Elsa Stone
David D. Swarts
Robert L. B. Tobin
Parsons Trotter

INTRODUCTION

I have been involved in the costuming of operas for more than thirty years and have covered every phase of that craft: designing, manufacturing, selecting from rental stock, and teaching. For the last twenty years, in my capacity as head of the opera department of a large theatrical costume establishment, I have been in daily contact with stage directors, designers, and performers. During my conversations with these people, many of whom are my good friends, certain patterns have emerged regarding their opinions, points of view, and attitudes. Speculating on these patterns has led me to some conclusions that I would like to share with my readers. Generalizations are always dangerous, but I believe that my conclusions have validity, whether or not the people I reached them about agree with me. In these observations I will treat members of the production staff as a unit. Opera singers are a breed apart and will be dealt with separately.

Although the fields of endeavor of stage directors and designers are familiar, I have found it useful to redefine their functions here. The stage director is in charge of all the visual aspects of a theatrical production. His concept embraces everything that happens on the stage, and what everything and everybody on stage looks like. If the stage director's powers of visualization are equally well developed in all the phases of theater production, his billing on the program will read "Production conceived (or devised) by——." Even the stage director who possesses such versatility will delegate part of the visual production to certain specialists, who must be considered his expert extensions: the scene, costume, and lighting designers. To them he will impart very precisely his ideas pertaining to their fields of competence. But the stage director gifted with such all-encompassing powers of visualization is the exception rather than the rule. Usually, while the general concept remains the director's, he will rely on the experts with whom he chooses to surround himself to offer specific suggestions, ideas, and solutions that might not have occurred to him.

When the relationship between the various production participants is a harmonious one, meetings moderated by the stage director can stimulate a lively exchange of ideas, to the benefit of the entire production. Designers do not wear blinders and cannot be expected to exclude from their mind's eye everything that does not involve their own field of expertise. This writer, who has never had the slightest urge to be a stage director or scene designer, has frequently contributed ideas about matters that did not pertain to costumes per se. And he will pursue the same course in the following chapters. To that extent, this is more than a "costume book."

When a theatrical production happens to be an opera, the question arises to what extent the musical production staff (the conductor and occasionally the composer) should be involved in its visual aspects. Regardless of the interest they may have in these matters (it varies from a great deal to none at all), the answer must be: as much as possible. The reason for involving them is to eliminate the element of surprise, if not shock, when the dress rehearsal takes place. During the preparations for a performance, all participants, the musical staff included, form some idea, however vague, of what the stage picture will look like. Usually, their concept is based on memories of previous productions, but it may as well be entirely a product of their imagination, particularly in the case of a new opus. When, then, a totally unanticipated look is unveiled at the dress rehearsal, the experience can be profoundly upsetting. I have witnessed thoroughly unwarranted wholesale rejections at the dress rehearsal for that very reason. This is especially true when the conductor happens to be the head of the opera company as well, as is frequently the case. The showing of costume sketches in advance, which might seem the obvious and simple solution to the problem, has not proven helpful at all. Few laymen can "read" a costume sketch. Even seasoned theatrical producers are often seduced by the beautiful rendering of a poor design. They have to be shown the real thing. Performers, particularly those who accept single engagements tend to be at their most vulnerable at dress rehearsal time. Persuading them to come in advance for costume fittings, so that they will have no surprises sprung on them in *that* department at least, invariably pays off and spares everyone a great deal of unhappiness and last-minute frenzy.

Costume designers learn very early in the game that costumes are everybody's business and that everybody claims to be an expert at them. The suitability and look of a costume must be the exclusive concern of the stage director, the designer, and the performer. At times the fact of life has to be made abundantly clear to the performers' well-meaning mates, relatives, friends, coaches, and voice teachers.

Although there can be no doubt about the great importance of theatrical values in opera production, the music must nevertheless take precedence over everything else. Music has an emotional impact unlike anything the spoken word can evoke. Therefore, opera librettos taken on their own merit seem insufficient or even silly. They are merely a framework that the music fleshes out. Music also conjures up visual imagery to those who are susceptible to it. Stage directors and designers who lack this sensitivity should shun involvement in the musical theater. To stage the opening scenes of *La Traviata* and *Rigoletto* as orgies, for instance, demonstrates in my opinion such a lack of sensitivity to the music. The power of music goes further still: music is a dictator. In this world it is the only dictator to which I will bow. Music can state that sometihng *must* be a certain way, that it can be no other way. In that context I recall a conversation I had with a stage director concerning the opening scene of Mozart's *Don Giovanni*. "Is it necessary," I inquired, "to have this silly tug-of-war between Donna Anna and Don Giovanni, when it is so obvious that one push from him would knock her to the ground and enable him to escape?" In response the stage director pulled out the score and said, "Show me where. The way the music is written no such a break is possible." Thus speaks a stage director after my own heart, but the answer need not be so unequivocal. Inventiveness should be able to provide a solution that eliminates the inappropriate stage action without violating the music.

Many stage directors feel the need to motivate everything that happens on the stage. They will have explanations readily at hand for every bit of stage action they invent. To performers, these motivations can be of tremendous help because they deepen their understanding of the character they are portraying. They are supposed to do the same thing for the audience, but that is a miscalculation. It must be remembered that audiences sit back in their seats, look and listen, but do little else. If what happens on the stage makes sense to them, fine and dandy; if not, they will not be too sorely troubled. The listening public can absolutely be relied on not to indulge in guessing games as to the stage director's intentions. In my chapter on *Don Pasquale* I refer to the green carnation I observed in Dr. Malatesta's lapel in one production of the opera. I, as an insider, guessed the stage director's intention, but no one else did. To observe a designer's or stage director's brains at work may be a fascinating sight, but it does not belong on the stage, where everything is supposed to be self-evident. As Goethe put it, "One sees the intention and becomes disturbed." This predilection for obscure motivations is the result of thinking too much and visualizing too little. It is a trap that is very easy to fall into, and I have not always escaped its lure.

There is a pretty foolproof test designers and stage directors might apply to make certain that in their mental convolutions they do not leave the audience behind: any staging ideas that require "program notes" to convey their intentions to the audience should be eliminated. In production meetings, a warning sign—PROGRAM NOTES—should be flashed on at the appropriate moment.

Only the musical side of all these considerations occupies most composers, Mozart among them. Judging from his voluminous correspondence, he had no interest at all in the visual aspects of his operas. Had he been differently oriented he might have included stage directors and designers in his famous dictum, which he expressed in a letter to his father on October 15, 1871. While discussing the text of his opera *Die Entführing aus dem Serail*, which was then in the process of being composed, he wrote: "In opera the poetry must be without reservation the music's obedient handmaiden." Others have expressed the same sentiments in the phrase *Primo la Musica, dopo le Parole*.

If poets do not take naturally to the role of obedient handmaiden to the music, many stage directors and designers seem to abhor the notion. They are talented people brimming over with ideas, ever anxious to breathe new life into the old chestnuts (if I may mix a metaphor). Theirs is the noble intent of making opera more relevant, more up-to-date, and more palatable to modern audiences.

After giving the matter a great deal of thought, I have reached the conclusion that these concerns are rationalizations. Opera stage directors and designers have two strikes against them. First, the audience's apparent apathy as regards the visual aspects of opera productions. Second, the fear that in the shadow of a giant, they will not be noticed. And what giants these are: Mozart, Verdi, Wagner, Puccini, Strauss! It is enough to make anyone feel puny. It is interesting to note that on the legitimate stage it is that giant Shakespeare who is often considered in need of being visually updated. No wonder, also, that the grandsons of Richard Wagner felt (unwittingly perhaps) that they would never have any impact unless they discarded lock, stock, and barrel all the directions Grandpa had so painstakingly set down. It is reasonable to suggest that Wagner's operas could be mounted with satisfactory result today, following the composer's instructions, and still end up looking totally different from the productions in Wagner's own time. Not only has stagecraft advanced notably since then, but also taste and approach ever change. We are all children of our own time and cannot fail to interpret the old themes through the eyes, ears, and senses of today. (That the ear is involved in this evolution as well was keenly brought home to me recently when I listened to a recording of Bach's *Matthäus-Passion* under the direction of Willem Mengelberg. It was considered an authoritative reading of the score in its day, but we certainly don't play Bach that way anymore. Fifty years from now, today's interpretation will sound old fashioned again.)

Stage directors and designers take it upon themselves to make operas more relevant to the listeners, although the public's desire in these matters has never been polled. Such a poll might prove quite revealing. It is my guess that it would indicate that the audience likes well-staged, beautiful, and appropriately staged productions, but that for them also the music takes precedence. I have never heard of people deciding not to attend an opera performance because the visual production was distasteful to them, or of anyone saying, "I am going to attend an opera I hate, and the singing is supposed to be ghastly, but I find the staging and the mise-en-scène irresistible."

For his labors, the most a scene designer can expect is a ripple of applause at the curtain's rising, while the stage director is lucky if he gets a few polite boos at its closing. The costume and lighting designers, it seems, are thrown in for good measure. Add to this attitude from the audience a total lack of professional knowledge in these matters on the part of the opera reviewers, whose judgment is on a par with the audience's. To the visual staff of an opera production these are bitter pills to swallow. They lay their talents on the line against the overwhelming odds of rising costs and dwindling budgets to create an appropriate and pleasing mise-en-scène. They react to this lack of recognition much like the children of overpermissive parents: in their quest for discipline, they behave more outrageously all the time; unfavorable attention is ultimately better than no attention at all. "Now they will sit up and take notice" seems to be their desperate cry. They will even go so far as to insult the audience's intelligence, as will be discussed at some length in the chapter about *Faust*, but even that seems to be of no avail. Opera stage directors and designers might do well to emulate the musicians, who recreate and reinterpret ever anew and seem to be content with the satisfaction that is to be derived from doing so. To take an opera, its music, and its story on its own merits—to give the devil its due, as it were—can be a beautiful and rewarding experience. Within these bounds it is possible to be innovative, creative, and inventive without rocking the boat. Many people involved in opera's visual production have reached that conclusion and rejoice in being its unsung heroes.

"Not rocking the boat" does not imply that changes of time and venue are not occasionally in order. The pros and cons of such a move have to be weighed very carefully, however, and must be considered from every angle, as will be demonstrated in the following chapters. Sometimes the composers themselves expressed the desire for a contemporary setting (in their own time), as was the case with Verdi's *La Traviata* and Puccini's *La Rondine*, but they were overruled by their producers. Sometimes the censor ordained changes of time and place that today are no longer valid. This is especially true for Verdi's *Un Ballo in Maschera*. In the case of *Rigoletto*, however, I feel that the censor unwittingly did the opera a favor by imposing a change, so totally different is the larger-than-life absolute monarch François I from the dallying little King Francis of Victor Hugo's play and Verdi's opera. Even in obeying a composer's wishes, the designer must remain on his guard. To set *La Rondine* in the era of its genesis (1911) is not a happy solution because of the considerable amount of waltzing that takes place in the second act. It is not impossible to waltz in hobble skirts, but it looks a great deal more graceful in the costumes of the somewhat earlier *Merry Widow* era, which I advocate for the opera. The story of *Don Giovanni* might work very well in modern dress. Young men who are insecure about their masculinity continue to pursue women indiscriminately today just as they did in the seventeenth century, in which the opera is usually set. On the other hand, no guest of today is going to dance to the kind of music Don Giovanni's bands provide at the party. To update Rigoletto's sad story to a time when court jesters no longer exist is no more logical than to advance the time of an opera in which lay brothers figure prominently (*The Barber*, *Figaro*). *Die Entführung* could possibly play in one of the OPEC countries today, *Tosca* fits quite well into Mussolini's era, and *Lucia di Lammermoor* fares much better set in Donizetti's own time (with a few adjustments in the text, naturally) than set almost 150 years earlier. The reference in the libretto to "William and Mary," which would logically determine its period, has traditionally been ignored anyway. There is no law against changing the time and place in which a given opera is set, but it should not be done out of boredom, merely for the sake of doing something different, or to focus the audience's attention on the visual production. Such motivations always produce spurious results.

Even without rocking the boat, costume designers have their hands full. Within the theatrical design troika, they hold a special, although unheralded, place, for they deal with articles to which performers have a very personal relationship. It is important to realize that today's "costumes" were yesterday's "clothes," and people have strong emotional feelings toward their clothes. Ergo, performers have those feelings toward their costumes. Little children consider their clothes an extension of themselves and do not know the difference between the two. In our adult lives we retain many vestiges of this attitude. We consider any praise we receive for our clothes as a personal compliment and any criticism as a personal affront. At times we become very attached to an item of apparel and have to be urged to discard it at long last. Then again, we are eager to acquire new attire and often expect that it will bring about magical changes in the way we look and feel. On the other hand, we seem almost frightened by the unfamiliarity of a newly purchased garment and will hang it in the closet for a while to get acquanted with it. If we harbor such strong feelings toward our everyday clothes, how much more strongly will performers react to theatrical costumes, which are more often than not alien in look and cut, overwhelming in dimension, bulky, and uncomfortable. This last condition in particular is irksome to singers, who like above all to be comfortable when they perform. One has only to observe them during rehearsals to gain that conviction. Singers also realize, however, that donning this alien garb is part and parcel of the glamor of being an opera singer. They know that historical costumes can be immensely flattering, aside from being a great help in their characterization of a role.

There is a difference in the way legitimate actors and opera singers relate to costumes. Actors choose their profession in part because they like to impersonate people other than themselves, and because they enjoy appearing before an audience who will reward them with applause for this display. Impersonation can be defined as "crawling into someone else's skin," a feat that offers some technical problems and is translated instead into the far more practical solution of putting a second skin on top of one's own, in the form of a costume. It goes without saying that good impersonation requires much more than a costume, but the attire is a start. For this reason, the use of nudity on the stage is so limited. It is well nigh impossible to impersonate anyone when one is stark naked. Primitive societies recognized this very early and resorted to the wearing of masks for the purpose of impersonation.

Whatever causes singers to embark on an operatic career, the urge to display their person is rarely the reason. What they want to show off and win approval for is a beautiful voice, but only the recording artist can do so without appearing before an audience. Opera singers react to this necessity for bodily display in the same way as any person who is forced through circumstances to appear before a large assemblage: they want to make a good impression and look their best. "Make me beautiful" is the opera singer's cantus firmus to the costume designer. Singers make this request with such regularity that I have come to anticipate it. I was a little taken aback just the same when a famous opera star who had taken the plunge into musical comedy uttered the magic words when he arrived to be costumed as Tevye in *Fiddler on the Roof*. When I pointed out to him that he was playing the part of a very poor, middle-aged goat's milk seller, he replied, "Never mind the verismo." Opera singers do not only want to be beautiful; they want to be so in terms they understand. The terms they understand are the fashions of the day. A knowledge of costume history or an understanding of historical styles cannot be expected of opera students, and the chances of teaching these matters to them are nil. There are not enough hours in the day to teach them all that is required to be opera singers, let alone such fringe benefits as costume history, theatrical makeup, hairstyles, or even the different stances and behavior people affected in times gone by. (I have managed to teach some opera singers something about makeup with a modicum of success.) The sense of style that will cause performers to wear period costumes with some kind of panache is rare even among actors. The French regale us on occasion with a stylish Molière production and the English are adept in presenting Restoration comedies that prove to be exercises in modes and manners, but by and large actors and singers alike will behave no differently in period costumes than they do in modern dress. I know only one opera singer who has such a sense of style. She will change before one's eyes with the period of the costume she puts on. It is wondrous to behold.

Regardless of the changes that occur in fashion from season to season, the accent for a long time now has been on a "slim" look for men and women alike. Consequently, singers too want to look slim, particularly on the stage, when everybody is watching them. This understandable desire to look slim may pose some problems; for a variety of reasons that will be explored later, many singers are not slim, and nothing short of surgery will give them the slender silhouette they so ardently crave. True, there are certain tricks of the trade, based on optical illusion, that will make people seem more slender than they really are: dark colors are more slenderizing than light ones; breaking up large surfaces into vertical sections (when designing for opera singers, think vertical) and shading-in contours or disguising them all together are useful for this purpose. Optical illusion can make short and stout people look taller and slimmer, so long as they are alone on the stage. Put a tall, skinny person next to them and all illusion flies out the window.

Very few fashions of the past boast the slim silhouette that is worn today, and when one attempts to bring period costumes in line with our present fashion picture, they become distorted beyond all recognition. Fashions of the past have a great charm of their own. Designers and particularly performers fare much better when exploiting their attraction rather than opposing it. Since only stars are in a position to demand that the silhouette of their costumes be drastically altered, a situation may arise in which the entire cast is suitably costumed according to period and silhouette, while a few principals, or possibly only one, stick out like a sore thumb. A sad example of such a condition exists at the present production of Massenet's *Werther* at the Metropolitan Opera. It is a handsome and stylish production in most respects, with the properly bouffant, late eighteenth-century silhouette for all the women, except the leading female character, Charlotte, whose skirts are pulled so tightly over the hips that they resemble the bustle styles of about a hundred years later. It is not just her skirts that have received this purportedly slenderizing treatment. The rest of her costumes fit her so tightly that one fears that she will burst out of them when she takes a deep breath. This situation is the result of a general misconception among clothes-wearing human beings that tight-fitting clothes make people look slimmer. TIGHT-FITTING CLOTHES MAKE ONLY SLIM PEOPLE LOOK SLIMMER. THEY MAKE EVERYBODY ELSE LOOK LIKE STUFFED SAUSAGES. I would like to shout this from the rooftops, put it on large billboards all over the world, and have it broadcast every hour on the hour. It is the bane of a costume designer's existence. It is almost impossible to convince singers that the charm of a tight-fitting bodice comes across only when it is contrasted with a billowing skirt.

Opera singers may be a breed apart, but they share with all other mortals the ability to perceive themselves through heavily tinted, rose-colored glasses. The amount of self-deception that man is capable of in this respect is truly astounding. Think of how many people we encounter daily who are decked out in ways that make it clear that they never look at themselves in the mirror. Actually, nothing could be further from the truth. They look in the mirror all right, but only behold what they want to see. This phenomenon is not restricted to seeing alone; many people only hear what they want to hear. My readers and I may be no different in this regard, but we do not expose ourselves to public scrutiny by appearing on the stage. Performers will occasionally look at themselves through other people's eyes, particularly during costume fittings, but it is usually only a temporary aberration from which they recover quickly to return to their former state of self-deception. A very pretty singer on the Metropolitan roster came to me not long ago and, looking at herself in the mirror, possibly seeing herself through my eyes, suddenly asked, "Leo, am I fat?" Before I had a chance to either confirm or deny, she cried, "No!!!" With the infinite tact for which I am known, I told her that there was nothing wrong with her that losing seventy-five pounds would not fix. Luckily, she was so pleased with the costume I had supplied for her that she let my remark pass. Others avoid any confrontation with reality by simply not coming for costume fittings. One day I met in a restaurant (where he was shoveling it in) a singer of international stature whom I had costumed many times but never fitted. I introduced myself, complimented him on his vocal accomplishments, and assured him that I would be able to do a much better job for him if he would only show up for a fitting every once in a while. His answer was: "Mr. Van Witsen, you are doing just fine. Please do not ask me to come for fittings. I hate it so." If I had his dimensions, I would hate it too.

"I know exactly what I look like, I know exactly what I can wear, I know exactly what becomes me," performers tell the costume designers with boring regularity. Unless the speakers have viewed themselves on film, or, as is increasingly possible, on television, such statements are patently incorrect. Very few people can see themselves objectively in real life, much less perceive what their image will look like when it is projected across the footlights to an audience. On occasion, even those professionals who are trained to deal with such contingencies are tricked. A famous soprano who saw herself in a television broadcast, "live from the Met," went on a diet forthwith, which has not diminished her vocal powers in the least but has greatly improved her looks.

Evidently it is not possible to discuss opera costumes without touching on the delicate subject of singers' avoirdupois. Singers need not be fat to sing well, as has been proven again and again. Singing in general, and opera singing in particular, is physically taxing. Singers have to be strong. Contending with the strain of excess weight cannot but be a deterrent to good singing; it can never be a help. However, many singers are big people. Whatever determines the size of the cavities in their heads, which make such wonderful resonance chambers, also determines the size of the bodies to which those heads belong. Most of the time it is all pretty much in proportion.

There are many reasons why singers tend to overeat. Singers are the only music-producing human beings who carry their instrument inside the body. They cannot send it to a repair shop when it needs fixing. All they can do is "take good care of it," which consists quite logically, if symbolically, of feeding the face that produces the sound. Opera singing is not only physically taxing; it is also emotionally exhausting. After a performance a singer may feel depleted and be tempted to replenish the void by sitting down to a hearty meal.

That the career of being an opera singer has its rewards is certain, or no one would pursue it, but it also has its decided drawbacks. It can be a lonely life with much time spent in hotel rooms. Unlike actors, who may enjoy a run of weeks or even months in one city, the singer's life becomes a string of one-night stands, with a minimum amount of rehearsal time thrown in for good measure. Opera singers are shunted from city to city, if not from country to country. Jet lag has not contributed to the opera singer's happiness. Unhappy people tend to overeat. Da Ponte had a singular flash of psychological insight when he gave Ferrando in *Così fan tutte* the line that says, in essence, "The heart that is nourished on love has no need of other food." Singers are lucky that of all the addictions they might succumb to, overeating is the least harmful, and one for which the audiences will not reject them, so long as they continue to sing beautifully. Like all addictions, overeating fills an emotional need. A singer who decides to go on a diet without filling that need in some other way will suffer withdrawal symptoms and be a deprived and unhappy person. Deprived and unhappy people do not sing very well. It is then that singers will state that losing weight was bad for their voice. Additional weight may also give a singer a sense of solidity and stability, which they may feel in need of.

The status of carrying one's instrument inside the body has certain advantages. Singers never have to fear leaving their voice behind in a taxi as other instrumentalists have been known to do. The voice is always *with them*, but is it always *there*? Sooner or later all singers worry about that. It is the stuff nightmares are made of. One of the world's most renowned opera singers, whose personality all but oozes self-assurance, admitted recently on a nationwide TV talk show that he occasionally wakes up in the middle of the night and wonders "whether it is still there."

It might seem that all this has very little to do with the costume designer's task, but it does. People who feel good about themselves are much easier to deal with than people who are full of doubts.

Singers who are vocally secure are much easier to costume than those who worry a lot about their voices. The latter can be counted on to externalize their insecurity. It took me a while to figure out why singers who had adored their costumes during fittings and who seemed reluctant to part with them after the performance considered them the objects of such scorn during the dress rehearsal. It eventually dawned on me that a costume is a convenient scapegoat, the one item that will not talk back. Singers who hate the conductor's tempi and disagree with the stage director's instructions, who feel musically ill prepared and vocally out of sorts, need not keep those feelings bottled up but can vent their spleen freely upon the poor costumes. The costumes will not give them any lip but supply a wonderful safety valve. The costume designer is therefore well advised to take all these gripes at dress rehearsal time with a grain of salt. Stage directors and designers must learn to distinguish between legitimate complaints and those that are occasioned by rattled nerves.

Few people in other professions would put up with the demands that are made on opera singers. They are frequently required, at a moment's notice, to perform without previous rehearsal. They will be expected to be musically letter perfect, to be able to follow the conductor without seeming glued to his baton, remember stage directions, negotiate steps and platforms on an unfamiliar stage, and operate at maximum efficiency dressed in costumes with long trains (which their colleagues will step on), trailing sleeves (which get caught on the furniture) and, worst of all, headgear that prevents them from hearing the orchestra and their associates. Only total dedication and ambition could induce anyone to put up with that kind of nonsense. That is what distinguishes successful opera singers from the many talented vocalists who sooner or later fall by the wayside. There are easier ways to make a living.

Ideally, performers should be able to rehearse in costume, for then they would be thoroughly adjusted to them come the performance. But this is a very imperfect world and the reality of opera productions is such that one is lucky to obtain the use of rehearsal petticoats, paniers, or farthingales. It is not much, but every little thing helps.

Costume designers are the servants of two masters. Their first allegiance must be to the work that is being produced, via the stage director's interpretation. Second, it is their duty to costume the performers as suitably as the part demands, make them look as beautiful as the role permits, and make them as happy and comfortable as possible. Their task is not made easier by the circumstance that in opera casting the vocal suitability for a role remains the determining factor.

It is then up to the costume designer to reconcile as much as feasible the discrepancy between the singer's physical appearance and the ideal look for the character to be portrayed. There are definite limitations to what can be achieved in this area; in a recent *Falstaff* performance the heavily padded knight did not reach the proportions of the totally unpadded but comfortably endowed Dame Quickly, while in a production of Kurt Weill's *Mahagonny*, the character of Jacob Schmidt, who eats himself to death, was much more slender than the romantic male lead, who should have had a lean and hungry look.

The many adjustments and compromises the opera-costume designer has to make render his job a very challenging one. "You do not know what it means to feel that you are well costumed in a performance," many opera singers have told me. Some of them will go so far as to use costumes as security blankets, especially when they venture forth into foreign territory. They have taken my costumes with them to the far corners of the earth. "Isn't that carrying coals to Newcastle?" I asked a mezzo who took my *Carmen* costumes with her to Barcelona. "Thank God I had them with me," was her belated reply upon her return. Though I have always been happy to comply with requests of this genre and thereby contribute to singers' feeling of well being, I do not really approve of the practice. The number of performers who are allowed to provide their own wardrobe has diminished considerably with the increase of visually integrated productions. Those who can throw enough weight around to insist on wearing their own costumes do so at the peril of ruining a production's overall look. On the other hand, it is exactly because of the amount of weight they have to throw around that I have on occasion heaved a sigh of relief when word reached me that diva so-and-so was bringing her own costumes.

Through the many years that I have costumed operas and opera singers I have practiced what I preach in this book. Evidently I have managed to get the message across to my clients that I have no ax to grind; I want only to be the "obedient handmaiden" to the work at hand, while doing as well as possible by the performers. As a result they have accepted my judgment regarding what is stylistically permissible within a given period, as well as what I considered esthetically suitable for them. My relationships with stage directors, performers, and my fellow costume designers has been a very cordial one. Their friendship and esteem have amply rewarded me for my labors.

CHAPTER *1*

VERDI'S *Aïda*

THE SPHERE OF ACTION of many operas is set in a historical period that does not coincide with the time in which the music was conceived. In such an event the opera's designer has the task of reconciling the divergent elements. When this difference in time spans several thousand years, however, as is the case with *Aïda*, the problem becomes academic. Verdi had to rely entirely on his imagination in order to evoke an atmosphere that might suggest Egyptian music, whereas the costumer has a vast amount of authentic material to draw upon, which he must adapt to suit Verdi's music.

The costumes for the opera's world premiere in Cairo were executed in Paris under the personal supervision of Auguste Mariette, or Mariette Bey as he was usually called, the French Egyptologist who was also the spiritual father of the *Aïda* story. Despite his emphasis on authenticity, the costumes and indeed the entire mise-en-scène necessarily had an 1871 air about them. This period look increased notably in the process of translating the sketches into actual costumes. The women's costumes had all but a bustle silhouette. While Verdi's music cannot be entirely divorced from the time of its genesis, it transcends its period sufficiently so that that element can be overlooked in its re-creation. The producers who have attempted in our day to revive that 1871 atmosphere have done the opera a disservice.

The costume designs for the first *Aïda* production necessarily had an 1871 air about them.

Aïda is not a period piece but an enduring masterwork that deserves to be re-created ever anew.

Verdi did not personally participate in the Cairo production and had no idea what it looked like. When the same designs were sent to him for use in the Milan production, Verdi commented on their beauty but also suggested some specific changes: he wanted the Moorish dancers less nude and Amneris's last-act costume less "happy." Evidently he cared about and had some judgment in these matters. The Italians insisted that they executed the designs better than the Parisians had. Maybe they omitted the bustles.

The actual costumes all but acquired the fashionable bustle silhouette.

As for the costume-historical background of *Aïda*, the culture of ancient Egypt dates from 3407 B.C. until 50 B.C. The story of *Aïda* is placed during the New Kingdom (1596 B.C.–525 B.C.), and specifically in the XX dynasty (1207 B.C.–1101 B.C.) during the reign of Ramses III, who is identified in the opera as "the king" and the father of Amneris.

Changes in fashion throughout the entire Egyptian culture were remarkably few, although some evolution inevitably took place, and, as a result of trade and conquest, foreign influences made themselves felt. This consistency of style over a very long time span enables the designer to avail himself with impunity of elements from all periods

Towering headdresses: not helpful to the expression of human emotions but suitable for characters whose function is mostly decorative.

of this culture, thereby increasing his opportunity to differentiate between diverse categories of people.

The plot of *Aïda*, with its conflict of divided loyalties, is timeless. The characters and the emotions they express are those with which a modern audience can readily identify. Without going to the extreme of costuming them in modern dress, the designer must yet make the performers look like real people. To try, for instance, to reproduce the peculiar stance of Egyptian two-dimensional pictures is foolish, because this form of representation is the result of the Egyptian inability to draw anything foreshortened. Their three-dimensional statuary shows no such distortion. The towering headdresses seen in Egyptian representations should also be dealt with gingerly. They are all right for characters whose function is mostly decorative—ministers and palace officials, maybe even the Pharaoh himself. They are not apt to aid the performer's expression of human emotions.

A wealth of information is available regarding the costumes of ancient Egyptians of all stations, from deities and royalty to humble slaves and captives. Of course, the dress of the figures portrayed in wall paintings or stone carvings is always highly stylized. It is the designer's task to translate the stylizations into wearable clothes without losing the allure of the original. A case in point is the Egyptians' penchant for pleated and gauffered garments. In the pictures, fabric treated in this manner often falls in impossible directions, so that the costumer may well be tempted to forego the pleats and merely drape and pull the fabric. Unfortunately, this "solution" causes the garment to lose all the character that strikes us as typically Egyptian. It is better to obtain the pleated effect either by painting it on or by applying narrow braid. The pleats can then go in any direction one desires.

In their stylized pictures the Egyptians invariably present themselves as very slender people—hardly a realistic appraisal. Their garments consisted of rectangular pieces of fabric, occasionally rounded at the corners, which they wore in a variety of wraparound ways, often pulled quite tightly. There are suggestions that some of these fabrics had a stretch to them. Most likely the Egyptians knew the art of knitting. The hazards of tight-fitting clothes on the generously endowed are discussed at length in my introduction. It is helpful to re-create such wraparound garments in soft, crepelike fabrics, cut on the bias.

No fabric treated in this manner could possibly fall in such directions.

Initially Egyptians used cotton fabrics almost exclusively; later they used linen as well. They wove the linen threads on very wide looms into fabrics of great refinement and transparency. Pictures of high-class persons show an almost "Art Nouveau"–like grace and fluidity of line in their dress, qualities that suggest in our day the use of the softest silk crepe and chiffon. The common man's wraparound kilts were, by contrast, quite rigid and frequently had additional stiffening in the apronlike front panel.

The elaboration, refinement, and colorfulness that mark the costumes of the New Kingdom also characterize the music Verdi composed for *Aïda*. Yet the range of colors used was quite restricted, a factor that largely determines the distinctive look of Egyptian representations. Besides an abundance of white, the colors most often seen are black (never used for a complete garment); shades from beige to ochre; yellow; shades from terra cotta to brown; light, slate, and Prussian blue; turquoise; light, medium, and olive green; red and brownish red; lavender pink; and pervanche. Few of these colors are ever used for anything except decorations. If they are applied to an entire garment it is because it has an all-over pattern.

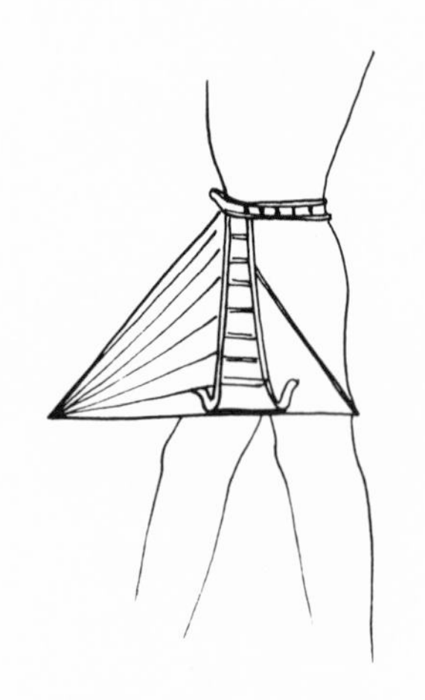

Wraparound kilts with stiffening in the apronlike front panel.

Ancient Egyptians were often scantily clad. Sheer garments over nude bodies were the order of the day, and for women bare breasts were the rule rather than the exception. These are not the accepted norms of our society, and it is the costumer's task to adapt the authentic Egyptian dress to a form that is acceptable on our stage without losing the intrinsic Egyptian style.

Some nudity can be quite appropriate in *Aïda*, particularly in the

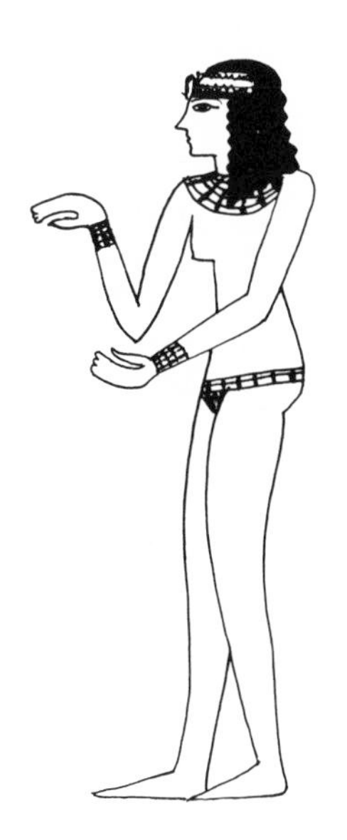

Scantily clad Egyptians.

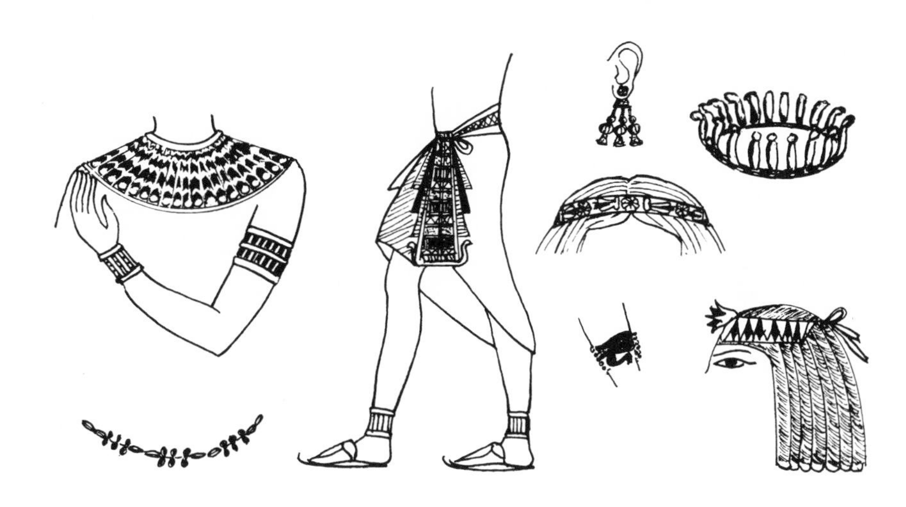

Jeweled pieces: collars, armbands, wristlets, necklaces, aprons, anklets, earrings, tiaras, headbands, and bracelets.

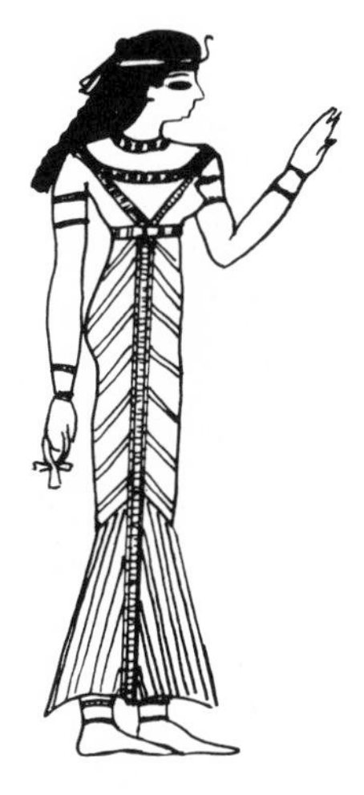

are breasts: the rule rather than e exception.

ballets, and it can be suggested effectively with the aid of body stockings and nude fabrics. Brassieres, however, are strictly a twentieth-century invention and do not belong in the Egyptian wardrobe, no matter how cleverly decorated or disguised.

No chapter on *Aïda* is complete without a discussion of jewelry, wigs, headdresses, skin color, and makeup, which are, incidentally, also the items that make *Aïda* a costly opera to produce. *Aïda* on a shoestring is a contradiction in terms.

The jeweler's craft of the New Kingdom reached a height of refinement unequaled in any other culture. The jeweled pieces were mainly collars, armbands, bracelets, anklets, necklaces, headdresses, crowns, tiaras, headbands, pectorals, and the unique decorative aprons. The latter were used by men only, but a designer might want to take some theatrical liberties and use them for women too. They are wonderful "hip slimmers." Jewelry consisted mostly of precious and semi-precious stones and beads, set in gold. Collars were everyday wear for both sexes. Slaves, however, did not wear them, and, naturally, only the elite wore the ones made of precious stuff.

The ancient Egyptians shaved off their hair or wore it closely cropped. Only women in mourning let their hair grow out. Important people wore elaborate headdresses and wigs; those at the bottom of

Instead of bald wigs, skullcaps and short wigs.

the social ladder contented themselves with skullcaps that covered the entire cranium but left the ears free. Only priests showed their shorn heads. In *Aïda* there is a sizable number of these gentlemen around, which implies the need for many bald wigs. (Nobody is going to shave off his hair, voluntarily or otherwise.) Bald wigs, alas, are as costly as they are impossible to apply successfully. They are not recommended unless one is assured of a vast auditorium and an audience sworn not to use their opera glasses. Instead of bald wigs, the skullcaps that were described before are suggested, suitably decorated with a headband and a raised symbol mounted in front. The familiar Sphinx's headdress, called "Khat," is another possibility. Often made of a striped material, it can be produced in many varieties of shape and fabric. The Khat headdress and the skullcap should take care of the headgear of all the male civilians in the opera. All the others wear various military or ceremonial headdresses, which all have one feature in common: the wearer's hair is entirely covered. Radames is the only male Egyptian who will require a wig when he is not completely in military attire, as in the Consecration Scene, the Nile Scene, and the Tomb Scene. This does not mean that other civilians could not have wigs as well, but they can wear headdresses instead, whereas Radames, once he removed his military headgear, would be bald.

For important people: elaborate headdresses and wigs.

The familiar Egyptian headdress, the "Khat," can be produced in many variations.

Women's hairdos give a very formalized impression. For theatrical purposes, wigs can be made out of tubular black braid or braided "rattail." The hair was invariably parted in the middle and never went below the shoulders (although hair length varied greatly otherwise). Flower wreaths or headbands, which went from the very simple to the very elaborate, were always worn low on the forehead.

In any discussions of skin colors it must be understood at the outset that the designations "white," "black," or "yellow" in this context are misnomers. They are the accepted terms but should not be taken literally when one chooses makeup. The Egyptians' skin color is portrayed as a light terra cotta, while the Ethiopians are black. The authenticity of both these colors is somewhat doubtful, but they are in this instance theatrically effective and hence warranted. Consequently, the entire cast of *Aïda* has to apply body makeup. It is a terrible nuisance but cannot be helped. As alternatives, tights and leotards might be used for the chorus and supers and body stockings for the ballet, but these are not happy solutions because even the best stretch fabrics imitate the human skin poorly. If leotards are used, great care must be taken to match the color of the face and hands to the color of the leotard. The dividing line between skin and leotard had best be masked with collars and wrist ornaments.

The annals of operatic history abound with examples of individual singers who claim immunity from the rules that have been laid down regarding the visual aspects of a production and who will wear on the stage what they feel suits them best. If some strides have been made in this respect as far as costumes are concerned, male singers remain tenaciously attached to their beards and moustaches, and no amount of proof that they are committing gross anachronisms can persuade them to rid themselves of these fashionable facial adornments. Whereas this irrationality must be considered an outrage, it is also a fact of life. It plagued Mariette Bey no less in 1871 than it does the producer of *Aïda* today. Only Mariette received assurance from the opera management in Cairo that they had the power to demand that male singers shave off their facial shrubbery if the role required it.

While information about the costumes of the ancient Egyptians has reached us in almost overwhelming abundance, thanks to the excavations, hardly anything is known of their frequent adversaries, the Ethiopians. It is very likely that when both the Egyptian and Ethiopian empires were at their zenith, they occupied the territories that now constitute Nubia and the Sudan and were therefore indeed neighbors, whose cultures were closely akin. Regardless of any conjecture in that respect, theatrical reality demands that these opposing nations should look as different from each other as possible. Because the Ethiopians appear as captives, they can be expected to look "down on their luck." Some stage directors may want them totally in rags. Whatever state of distress they are in, they must within the framework of the production form a cohesive unit in color and design.

Grand operas like *Aïda* present the costumer with a problem that is very much his concern, although it is to a considerable degree beyond his control: the use of extra choruses and large numbers of supernumeraries. At times the conductor's craving for "sound," the stage director's vision of vast triumphant armies and hordes of defeated captives, plus the choreographer's yearnings for spectacular ballets may collectively become self-defeating. The economics of mounting an opera that demands the use of masses of people presents problems that are not easily solved. Choristers and especially supers often seem maddeningly unaware of their stage appearance. If they feel, maybe rightly so, that it is not their concern, others on the production staff had better make it theirs, lest the final result be a parody. On the stage, alas, "more" does not necessarily mean "better," and in opera there is no "safety in numbers." Short of obtaining the expensive services of assistant stage directors to train a mob of people, it is important to appoint within each group some responsible members who can be coached in supervising the looks and demeanor of the entire crowd. It is also a good idea to post wardrobe personnel at strategic spots backstage and near dressing-room doors for last minute checking, or else the costumer will get blamed for such visual disasters as sloppy costumes, wrinkled tights, ill-fitting wigs, and crooked headgear. Individually such mishaps may seem minor; cumulatively they may ruin the entire stage picture. These problems are peculiar to all grand operas, but in *Aïda* they seem compounded because of the combined use of wigs, body makeup, tights, collars, etc., etc. The voice of bitter experience speaks: "Visually there is an awful lot that can go wrong in an *Aïda* production."

AÏDA

Aïda is one in a long list of operatic heroines who occupy a socially low position. This puts the onus on the costumer, who must make certain that she will be singled out according to her importance in the opera without standing out socially. What complicates Aïda's situation is the circumstance that she is a princess in disguise, which somehow should come across to the audience as well. It is important, first of all, that among Amneris's slaves Aïda be the only Ethiopian. Thus her black skin and African hairdo will set her apart from the Egyptian women, while her noble bearing will betray her royal status to an insider only. It is to be expected that Amneris would issue clothes to her palace slaves; these should all be identical in cut and related in color, while Aïda's, though in a shade that harmonizes with the others, stands out. Aïda was, until love intervened, Amneris's favorite slave, and it is entirely possible that her mistress presented her with a collar or a headband that will set her apart from the others. Collars are very Egyptian but they do not always flatter a short neck, frequently a soprano's hallmark.

In designing the slave's costumes, the first consideration must be to make Aïda look as attractive and desirable as possible: it must be credible that a young general would betray his country and sacrifice his life for this woman. A sheath of silk crepe beginning below the breast with one or two tapering halters over the shoulders, a vertical ornamental band over one shoulder down to the hem, or a sheer matching overgarment with dolman sleeves are just a few possibilities that might work for a specific Aïda's figure and yet stay entirely within the realm of adaptation of an authentic Egyptian costume.

There is no need, nor is there any occasion, for Aïda to change costumes between scenes 1 and 2 of the second act. If it is deemed desirable, she might wear a different costume in act 1, scene 1, which should be a more subdued verison of the second-act garment, but this addition is by no means vital.

For important women like Amneris, scalelike and patterned fabrics and horizontal borders.

For the Nile Scene a change of costume *is* essential, and it must support the different moods that Aïda displays in this scene. Before her unexpected encounter with Amonasro, she pours out her heart as a hapless exile despairing of ever seeing her homeland again. In her encounter with Amonasro she eventually becomes the repentant daughter; with Radames she is the reluctant seductress. If the libretto had not indicated that Aïda is "veiled" in this scene, the designer would have had to invent such a device. Only it would be more serviceable to develop it into something more substantial than a mere veil—a garment more along the line of a sheer mantle, which "accidentally" comes off as she rushes up to Radames. At that moment the gown underneath is revealed to sustain the change of mood. Because Aïda is not a wanton seductress but rather does this under duress, the seductive features of her costume must be very subtle. It is essentially the removal of the veil that has to do the trick.

In the Tomb Scene both Aïda and Radames should give the impression that they are no longer of this earth. To use Gustav Mahler's phrase, ". . . . der Welt abhanden gekommen." In order to be visible in the dimly lit tomb, Aïda should wear a very simple, light-colored gown. A sheer, dark, dolman-sleeved mantle may perform a slenderizing function if needed.

AMNERIS

Amneris's first-act costume is the type an average Egyptian princess wears around the palace on an ordinary weekday. She is not in a cheerful mood for very long, and her duplicity toward Aïda, her suspected rival for Radames's affection, should find expression in her costume. How to treat the sheathlike garment that is the basis of the Egyptian woman's dress depends entirely on the figure of the wearer and therefore defies detailed description. It should be in a rich fabric, possibly with an all-over scalelike pattern in gold embroidery and a wide decorative border at the hem. A jeweled collar and matching arm and wrist bracelets are standard equipment. To ensure that the armband will stay in place without being so tight as to make the flesh bulge, it helps to mount it on a sleeve of sheer nude fabric.

As noted earlier, the decorative apron that is actually part of the Egyptian man's costume can be used effectively for women as well. A successful slenderizing device consists of prolonging the middle-front section of the collar in a vertical band that tapers toward the waist, where it joins the decorative apron. A similar panel attached to the collar in back but hanging loose, spreading toward the hem, and trailing on the floor can be very effective. A metallic, sunburst-pleated cape, which in front only covers the arms to the wrist and from there tapers downward toward a train, should be attached underneath the collar. It will give Amneris the appropriate regal appearance.

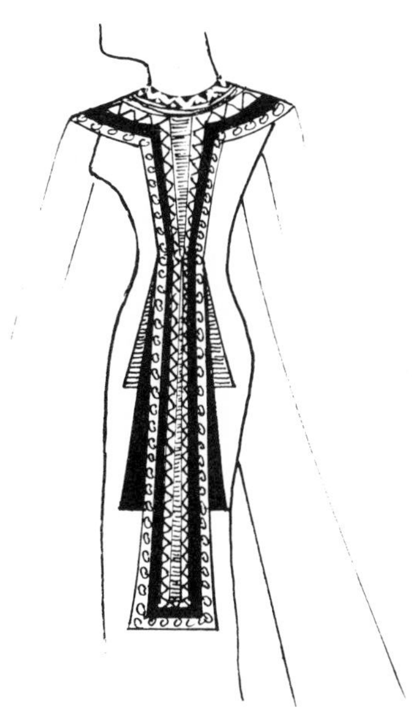

As a slenderizing device, the collar and apron may be joined.

Amneris's wig should be simple and elegant. The golden hawk's-wing headdress is particularly fitting here.

The only happy moment for this rejected, vengeful princess occurs in the first scene of the second act, before Aïda's entrance. Here she has to look most alluring and feminine. She wears a substantial but lightweight negligee that might, for example, be made entirely out of lotus-blossom-leaf motives, gradated in color and size from neck to bottom.

Scenes with the dressing and undressing of high-born persons by their servants require careful rehearsal and should be performed as a sort of ritual. The servants must seem aware of the honor and the responsibility of their task. A princess's negligee is not to be treated like an old rag that is tossed casually over one arm, but rather as a precious piece of clothing carried with some awe by several persons. Barring stage directions to the contrary, the person being dressed should convey an impression of uninvolvement in these proceedings. In reality she should be quite aware of what is going on and can,

The golden hawk's-wing headdress is particularly fitting for Amneris, but the famous tapered Nefertiti headdress has some disadvantages.

through a light movement of the arms or a small step forward, greatly facilitate her dressers' task. Measured, deliberate action on the part of the dressers produces the speediest results. Quick, nervous motions and, above all, fumbling should be avoided at all cost.

The sheath Amneris wears underneath the negligee should also be the basis of her Triumphal Scene costume. It could be similar to her first-act dress but now in shades of gold on gold. Over that goes a sheer, gold, pleated gown. A detail seen frequently on Egyptian representations and particularly suitable for this sheer over-dress is a fairly narrow, tapered belt, the middle of which is placed middle front below the bust. It crosses over middle back and ties in front with the ends hanging down to about mid-calf. In this instance the belt could be highly ornamented and bejeweled to match collar, bracelets, and armbands. An ornamental cape of some substance is also called for here. It could carry out the typical hawk's-wing motive in several shades of gold.

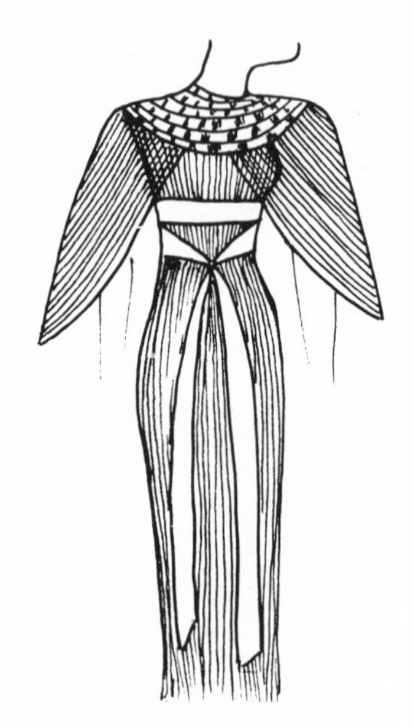

For Amneris's negligee, a tapered belt.

Capes are both practical and ornamental costume adjuncts, which can be dramatically helpful to the singing actor while being flattering in a purely decorative way. Their position on top of the costume has to be secured without impeding the singer's vocalism. A band sewn inside the cape at the shoulder seam near the neck opening, passing

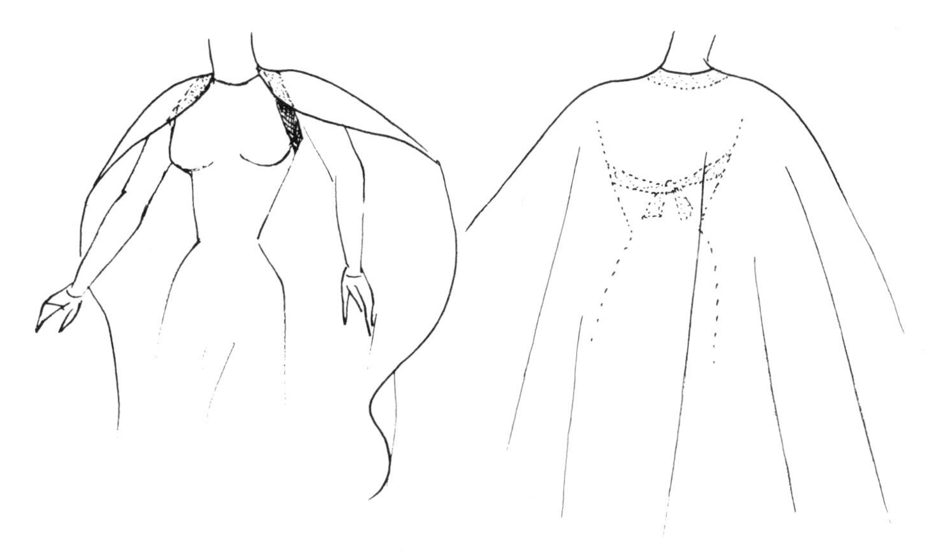

A way of securing a cape without impeding the singer's vocalism.

over the shoulders and under the armpits, and closing center back not only is absolutely surefire in this respect but also has the additional advantage of relieving any backward pull caused by a heavy cape with a train. Furthermore, if the cape does not close middle front but goes down on either side of the neck, showing the costume underneath merely as a panel, it will have a slenderizing effect, because it manages to conceal the contours of the figure. Opera costumers would be in a bad way without capes.

Nothing in this world is foolproof. There are performers who can use a cape to good advantage—touch it neither too much nor too little—while others will merely let it drag behind them. A performance of *Lohengrin* comes to mind, wherein Elsa and Ortrud, both lusty performers, were decked out with enormous capes, which they swung around with such energy that huge clouds of dust were raised at every turn, enhancing neither the music nor the drama.

But let us return to the imperious princess Amneris and concern ourselves with her wigs and headgear. The headdress of the famous queen Nefertiti seems to many the logical headdress for Amneris in the Triumphal Scene, but it has some decided disadvantages. Its use implies that the wig Amneris wore with the negligee has to be removed onstage, in view of the audience, always a hazardous undertaking. The Nefertiti headdress does not permit the showing of any hair and demands an impeccable fit. It is also not the sort of headdress that is flattering to a face deficient in the perfect symmetry of Queen Nefertiti's. If the slaves remove from Amneris's wig the wreath of lotus blossoms she may have worn with the negligee and replace it with an ornamental crownlike tiara, a much more felicitous effect will be achieved.

How important it is to attach headdresses securely must be evident to anyone who ever watched on television the crowning of Miss America and the ludicrous effect created by a precariously balanced or crooked tiara. It is unsettling to performer and audience alike. Bands or loops of horsehair, attached to the wig with small hat pins, or sometimes even Velcro and snaps, can render such an operation absolutely safe.

Amneris's Nile Scene costume should suggest a bridal gown, Egyptian style. A "Nile-green," pleated, chiffon gown with a silver collar and other accessories, under a pleated, sheer silver cape and a headband of silver lotus blossoms with a veil should create that illusion.

For the last two scenes Amneris is dressed in navy blue, the Egyptian mourning color. A navy-blue sheath under a sheer, pleated navy gown is trimmed in a dark jeweled collar. She now wears a long black wig of real hair, which is supposed to be her own (a mourning custom), a simple circlet with the asp's head to match the collar, and a blue veil.

RADAMES

Assyrian influence made itself felt in Egyptian military costumes (they can hardly be called uniforms) when the use of metal scales or coats of mail was adopted for the top parts, which existed in many varieties: a wraparound cuirass with short sleeves, a corselet with shoulder straps, or a calf-length hauberk. The often pleated wraparound kilt, the decorative collar, and the pendant apron were worn by all high-ranking military personnel, as were wristlets and anklets. It is up to the costumer to decide which type of military costume he assigns to whom, and in the case of Radames the deciding factor must be what looks best on him—what will do most to make him look like the handsome, virile, young general for whose favor two beautiful princesses vie.

Radames's first costume can be a cuirass made of silver scales with a pleated wraparound kilt in white or silver. His collar, belt, apron, wristlets, and anklets should be of the same design and have a military air about them. Egyptian soldiers never wore greaves. If Radames's legs look better covered up, a new Egyptian greave fashion

For soldiers and officers, various types of military uniforms.

will have to be created. A high-domed military helmet of the type seen on Pharaohs in military dress is suitable for Radames. He carries a sword and wears a three-quarter-length oval cape. Capes, whose dignity-supplying and figure-flattering virtues have already been extolled, were a frequent costume accessory for Egyptians of both sexes and unquestionably belong on a dashing young general.

In the Consecration Scene the libretto reads, "Radames is led in unarmed." Some have interpreted this to mean "without armor," and some stage directions even indicate that Ramfis puts armor on Radames after the consecration. Egyptians did not wear armor as we think of it, and luckily the text makes no mention of it (although the historical accuracy of librettos is not always reliable). Without a sword, helmet, or cape, Radames will appear sufficiently "unarmed." In lieu of his helmet, he will require a headcovering in the form of a simple Egyptian wig or a black skullcap with a silver headband. The libretto states that during the ceremony his head will be covered with a silver veil.

Radames's costume for the Triumphal Scene can be an elaborate gold version of his previous one. The use of the hawk's-wing motive on his chest, possibly spreading onto his now full-length cape, is an attractive idea.

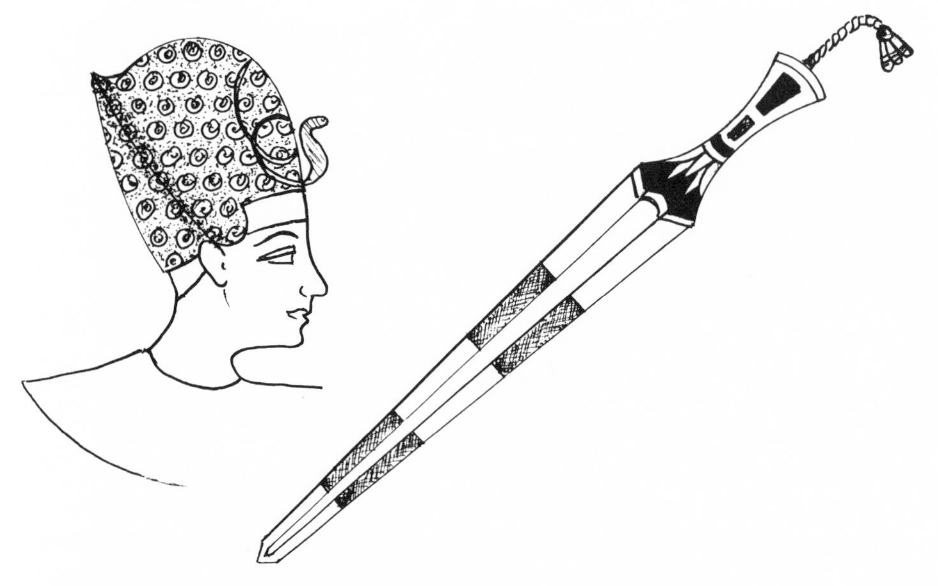

For Radames, a high-domed helmet and a sword . . .

For the Nile Scene, Radames's first-act costume is most suitable—without helmet, but with cape and sword. "Without helmet" because it looks silly to make love wearing a helmet. "With cape" because it is more romantic. "With sword" because he must surrender it upon being arrested.

In the first scene of act 4 he should wear what he had on in the previous scene, but only the cuirass and the kilt, none of the accessories. He must give the impression that he was stripped of all his insignias.

Radames's costume in the Tomb Scene should be a simple three-quarter-length, off-white robe. Of any Egyptian characteristics only the wig (without a headband) and perhaps a very simple collar remain. He is a man already beyond time and place.

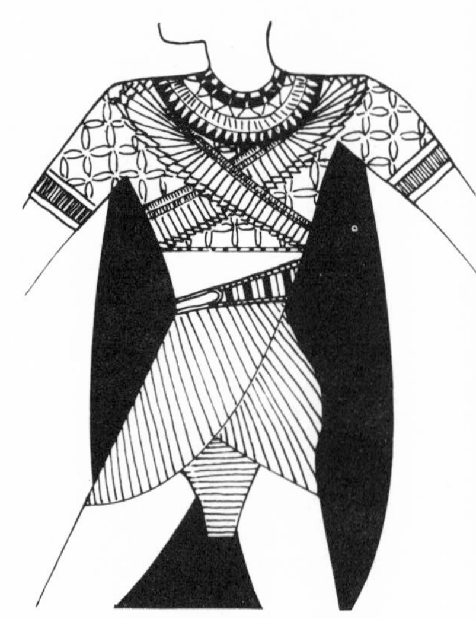

. . . as well as the hawk's-wing decorated uniform and oval cape.

AMONASRO

Among the very few references to costume in the *Aïda* libretto is the mention of Amonasro "dressed as an officer." If the Egyptian culture always conveyed a sense of great refinement, the Ethiopians must by contrast be portrayed as much rougher, even somewhat barbaric. Yet Amonasro must be of noble bearing. He is, after all, a king, even if he is in disguise. A belted tunic of rough-hewn fabric, decorated in the shoulder region with two vertical bands of coarsely woven strips of fur and leather, a collar belt, wristlets, and anklets (or high sandals) of leather, decorated with pieces of rough iron and ivory, will establish him as such. For some reason, Amonasro is always seen with what is referred to today as an "Afro" hairdo. It is not likely that an officer would be without some kind of military headgear, designed to harmonize naturally with the rest of his costume. A draped cape of matching fabric is also proper for Amonasro. In lieu of the usual necklaces of shells and tiger fangs, a pectoral of carved ivory will seem more dignified. In the Nile Scene he carries a sword.

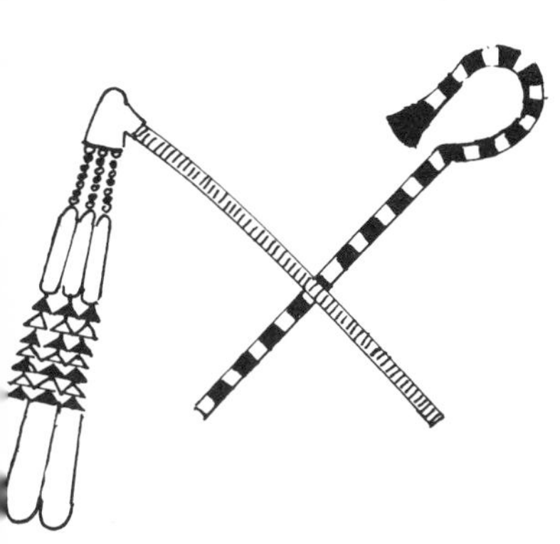

In the Triumphal Scene the Pharaoh wears the combined crowns of the Upper and Lower Nile and carries as scepters the flail and the crook.

THE PHARAOH

Ramses' function in the opera is largely ceremonial, and his costumes must be representative of his royal status—less formally so in the first act, but in all their regal spendor in the Triumphal Scene.

A light-colored, long gown with dolman sleeves and a deep border at the hem, embroidered in gold and colors, is suggested for the the first act. The necessary accessories with such a costume are a large collar, wristlets, an apron, and a pectoral, all jeweled. A pleated middle-front panel descending from the waist underneath the apron can be matched with a loose pleated panel with a train, attached to the collar in back. It will add to the king's regal bearing. He wears the white crown of Upper Egypt with the hawk's head in front.

The king's gown in the Triumphal Scene is like the previous one, but entirely in gold fabric. The accessories can be the same, or can now be a second set that is even more sumptuous. Instead of the loose back panel, he now wears a substantial gold cape with a train and he carries the royal emblems, a scepter and a flail.

Anyone who wishes to do so can experiment with securing the stylized braided beard. In reality it was held in place with a strap fastened to the headgear. This solution would not be conducive to sonorous vocalism. Also, the ornamental beard, while impressive when stationary, looks a little silly when the jaw starts moving in song or speech and the appendage with it. Maybe it would not be missed too much if it were eliminated. To the white crown of Upper Egypt the red one of Lower Egypt has now been added, carrying in front both the asp and the hawk's head.

On a jaw in motion, the stylized, tied-on beard may look silly.

Although Ramses' and Amneris's costumes are not identical, they should be conceived as a unit.

RAMFIS

A stylized leopard skin is the trademark of the high priest Ramfis.

The sole allusion to costume in the opera's text refers to the color of the priests' costumes, which is white. On a brightly lighted stage, a large mass of white costumes may have a blinding effect, while off-white will read as white without damaging the viewers' vision. Ramfis should wear a pleated, white robe with dolman sleeves. Its fabric is supposed to be cotton, but today something more wrinkleproof may be used. The yellow-and-blue-striped Khat headdress and a matching collar, apron, and wristlets can be its accessories. A leopard skin (or a stylized version thereof) draped around one shoulder is the Egyptian priest's trademark. It is suggested that only Ramfis should wear one to distinguish him from the other priests.

THE MESSENGER

The messenger is just another soldier and should be costumed as they are. He may have had a hard time getting through the enemy lines and could, accordingly, look somewhat the worse for wear. Some may argue that if he were dressed as a soldier he would have been an easy target for the enemy; they may prefer, therefore, to dress him in civilian disguise. That should be a bit beaten up too.

CHORUS, BALLET, AND SUPERS

The libretto of *Aïda* states that besides the principals, the stage is at different times populated by guards, ministers, priests, captains, palace officials, priestesses (dancers), female slaves, Moorish fan-bearers, Moorish dancers, male and female Egyptians, soldiers, trumpeters, fan-bearers, standard-bearers, twelve officers, captive Ethiopians and, in the Nile Scene, veiled attendants to Amneris.

The dancers in the Triumphal Scene are described in the libretto as "a group of dancing girls, carrying the treasures of the conquered," but this gathering is usually extended to a full-fledged ballet involving dancers of both sexes.

Each category—chorus, ballet, and supers—will be dealt with separately.

Female Egyptian civilians

The female civilians may wear an assortment of sheathlike garments in a variety of colors from the Egyptian palette. The garments start below the breast and have one or two halter straps. Nude fabric will take care of whatever should appear nude but must be covered. Fabrics with small, geometrical all-over prints can be used as well as solid colors with decorative borders. Collars, bracelets, and hip drapes are prevalent. Black, Egyptian-style wigs with a headband are worn by all. Everyone in the opera wears sandals.

Male Egyptian civilians

It is a good idea to divide the male civilians according to age and girth. The young and slim ones can wear the short wraparound kilt with its triangular over- or under-piece, a collar, and a skullcap, and remain bare-chested. The others can be in robes ranging from calf length to full length, with collars, aprons, and sometimes hip drapes. They can wear short wigs, skullcaps, or Khat headdresses.

Female Egyptian slaves

The female slaves attend Amneris and are costumed like Aïda, but in colors that are paler or at least different from hers.

Priests

The priests are costumed exactly like Ramfis, but without the leopard skin. Their accessories must be less prepossessing than his.

Priestesses

Since the priestesses are dancers, they may be in sheer, white, pleated gowns over nude body stockings. If their dance involves a lot of kneeling, it is a good idea to control the volume of skirt fabric with the typically Egyptian hip drape. On their wigs is a simple headband or a wreath of small lotus blossoms.

Moorish dancers and fan-bearers

The term "Moorish" should be taken with a grain of salt. Most likely these characters are Nubians and their skin is black. The group may comprise one or both sexes. Their costumes are scant and may have touches of color provided by bits of feather, which can also be used in the "Afro" hairdos.

The Ethiopian captives

The captives must be dressed in costumes that are in starkest contrast to the Egyptians, if not in the cut of their clothes then at least in the choice of the fabrics, which should be rough, and in the colors, which should be somber. They are a defeated people and they must look it. Yet it must also be evident that this is a people with its own culture, its own organized army, and manifestly plenty of possessions so valuable that the Egyptians covet them as spoils of war.

The weaving through of leather and fur strips, already mentioned in connection with Amonasro's costume, can apply to all Ethiopian dress, as well as the use of raffia for the same purpose. Animal horns and teeth, feathers, beads, and shells are suitable for decoration. With all that, the Ethiopian costumes must have a ragged, broken-down look and be of a simple wraparound cut in every variety of length and style: over one shoulder, under the armpits, or around the waist, secured by beltlike strips of fabric, leather, or rope. Headclothes, rough collars and wristlets, and leg wrappings can be added touches.

Ministers and palace officials

The ministers and officials constitute two groups of uniformed civilians who wear light-colored robes with geometric all-over patterns in gold or with deep decorative gold borders. Their accessories of collars, aprons, wristlets, and imposing headdresses are all in gold.

Captains, officers, soldiers, guards, trumpeters, fan- and standard-bearers

The uniforms of these characters should be variations and modifications of the different military costumes mentioned in the discussion of Radames's costumes: the captains are in gold, the officers in silver, the soldiers in bronze. It is entirely appropriate for the latter group to be bare-chested, so long as the supply of body makeup holds out. The rest of them have the wraparound kilts with aprons, collars, wristlets, anklets, armbands, and helmets. Swords, shields, and bows and arrows are the correct weapons.

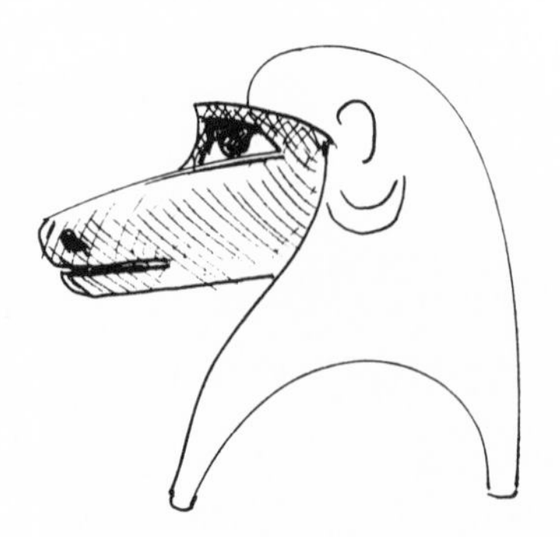

The Triumphal Scene ballet

This ballet has been choreographed in so many different ways that one is hard put to give specific guidelines for the costumes. The use of animal heads, specifically scarabs, ibises, and foxes, can be suggested, as well as the applicability of wigs and body makeup in bright colors, as seen on Egyptian wall paintings. No Egyptian representations show women in short garments. Not infrequently they are entirely nude or covered only with a hip girdle, but if they wear any clothes at all, they are long. Luckily, dancers no longer insist that they can perform in brief costumes only. In that respect, at least, it is now possible to be authentic. To use only wigs, or headdresses, and accessories on bodies that are otherwise nude or in body stockings is a conception that is entirely fitting for the re-creation of this Egyptian opera in our day.

The use of animal heads is suggested for the ballet.

CHAPTER 2

BRITTEN'S *Albert Herring*

A "billowy" Lady Billows.

IT IS A WELL-KNOWN fact that opera librettos are commonly condensations of existing plays, poems, or stories. A perusal of the original sources, which may uncover details that got lost in the adaptation, frequently yields new insights that prove helpful to stage directors, designers, and performers alike. In the case of *Albert Herring* the situation is rather reversed, for the meager story on which it is based, "Le Rosier de Mme. Husson," by Guy de Maupassant, served merely as a skeleton, which the librettist and composer fleshed out. There is much more to the adaptation than there is to the original, and here the value of a comparison lies in that it illuminates the adaptors' intentions.

Like many comedies, *Albert Herring* has a serious undercurrent, dealing as it does with the emancipation of a henpecked young man who unwittingly succeeds in "cutting the umbilical cord." He is abetted in this by his friends Nancy and Sid, two characters who are wholly the invention of the librettist and the composer. They are the opera's catalysts, not to say the "shock therapists." The three neighborhood children, Emmie, Cis, and Harry, are also the fruit of the librettist's fertile mind. They function like the choruses in Bach's oratorios. Sometimes they participate in the action and sometimes they comment on it.

If any fault is to be found in Eric Crozier's brilliant libretto, it is in the ages allotted to some of the characters. A man of twenty-two, which is Albert's given age, will not be threatened with corporal punishment by his mother and sent to his room, no matter how henpecked he is or how domineering she is. Albert is not all that meek, anyway; he protests plenty. To conform to the picture his words and his music convey, he can be no more than eighteen years old.

The libretto states that Nancy is "a young girl of twenty-six worried about reaching thirty unmarried." Neither her words nor her music bears out this contention. She sounds and acts like a seventeen-year-old, while Sid is probably nineteen, exactly the ages of two youngsters who would spike their friend's punch "for fun." They hope that their action will propel Albert into "breaking the apron strings," as Sid has urged him to do. What they do not foresee and do "bitterly regret" afterwards is the allegedly dire consequences of their undertaking.

The children's ages can safely be reduced by two to three years. To conform with their music and their behavior, they are kids of twelve, ten, and nine years at the most.

Since Eric Crozier is, happily, still among us (the sole living librettist mentioned in this book), it seemed logical to communicate with him about this chapter. He approves of its contents, including the more youthful ages of Albert, Nancy, Sid, and the children. *He* was guided by the limitations set by the actual ages of the performers at the world premiere of the opera.

Albert Herring is set in the year 1900, slightly updated from the 1880 of "Le Rosier." Since the date seems to be an arbitrary choice, one may want to settle for the 1890s as a happy medium. The fashions of that time make it possible for Lady Billows to look as billowy as her name implies. Surely the choice of that name was no accident.

The events in the opera occur on April 10, May 1, and May 2. Although the weather can still be rather beastly in Loxford around that time of the year, reference is made in the libretto to the unusually balmy temperature that prevailed that particular spring. The atmosphere and the music of the Party Scene frankly demand that everybody appear in spring finery anyway. The prevailing weather conditions would only have affected the clothes worn in the grocery-shop scenes, and, for the sake of variety alone, it would seem desirable to give the first scene in the grocery shop a slightly more wintery look.

Without ignoring European fashions, provincial English folk had a look all their own. The costumer of *Albert Herring* should try to catch that flavor, for, although the theme and the music transcend its locale, *Albert Herring* is surely a very English opera.

It is unlikely that Harry, Cis, and Emmie would be playing near the strolling Lady Billows, the Mayor, and Florence, although everybody is properly attired for the occasion.

By the time the 1890s rolled around, black had become the standard clothing "color" for males of all ages and standings. A cast of male characters all dressed in black can be quite effective and appropriate under certain circumstances, but in *Albert Herring* this approach would produce a funereal look that is not called for. It would rob Vicar Gedge of his distinction as a cleric, who traditionally dresses in black, and it would spoil Mrs. Herring's chance to dramatize her belief that Albert is dead by appearing in mourning.

Dressing all the male characters in suits is equally to be avoided, although this practice has been observed in some productions of the opera. To create as much diversity in attire, whenever relevant, should always be the costumer's aim. It aids the performers in their characterizations and prevents visual ennui. In act 2 this principle would put Harry in the sailor suit the libretto calls for, the vicar in his clerical frock coat, Mr. Budd in a uniform, the mayor in a Prince Albert coat, Sid in a knicker suit, and only Albert in an absolute suit.

As is true of most comedies, the humor in *Albert Herring* comes across best when it is played straight. Stage directors and designers often lack the confidence that the piece with which they are dealing has merit and is truly funny. In the theater, as in life, laughter is often mistaken for approval, and producing teams, desperate for a laugh

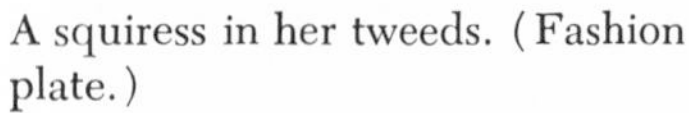

A squiress in her tweeds. (Fashion plate.)

Lady Billows and guests.

from the audience, tend to want to "whoop it up." A comedy is then turned into a farce and characters become caricatures. This warning applies especially to the roles of Mrs. Herring and Lady Billows, veritable character studies of two domineering mothers. Mum is a poor, ignorant, narrow-minded, self-pitying woman, who has nobody but her son to push around. Lady Billows is rich, but equally narrow-minded, and she is a crusader. Of her marital status nothing is known, but the entire village of Loxford is her domain and all its citizens are her children, whose blind obedience she demands.

There have been some productions of this opera where these characters as well as some of the others were so farcically costumed as to do serious harm to their individual roles and ultimately to the entire opera. "Leaving well enough alone" often seems a most difficult course to follow, although it is without a doubt the wisest.

LADY BILLOWS

There is nothing so formidable as an English squiress in her "tweeds." For Lady Billows's initial descent into her living room, a tweed skirt, a cummerbund, and a dark plaid blouse with leg-o-'mutton sleeves are suggested. She has, no doubt, a fob watch pinned

Lady Billows fancies herself the real Queen of the May.

near her shoulder and a pince-nez or lorgnettes on a thin chain around her neck.

When she enters the Herrings' shop she will have added a matching three-quarter-length tweed cape with a shoulder cape, lined in plaid. A small, mannish hat with a feather stick-up on the side, gloves, a pocketbook, and an umbrella complete her ensemble.

Lady Billows basically considers herself the only person truly worthy of being Queen of the May. Consequently, she would like nothing better than to dress for that great occasion in virginal white. But she realizes that in doing so she would steal Albert's thunder. As a compromise she may settle for white trimmed in black: a white taffeta skirt with black lace inserts. A matching white bolero with elbow-length leg-o-'mutton sleeves tops a long-sleeved bodice of tucked black tulle or black lace entre deux. A black velvet cummerbund with a jet buckle joins skirt and bodice. Her large-brimmed white hat is partly veiled in black tulle and is trimmed with black egrets and a jet ornament. She carries a white parasol and reticule, both trimmed with black lace, and lacy black gloves. A black ostrich boa rests lightly on her shoulders, while a jet choker and earrings provide the final touch.

Lady Billows will give grave consideration to appearing in the proper attire for her attendance to the sad events in the last act. She will probably decide that "light mourning" is appropriate here. At the same time she must convey an "I brook no nonsense" impression. A medium-grey faille dress with a black shoulder cape, a black toque trimmed with ostrich tips, and a black parasol, reticule, and gloves will fulfill this double assignment.

Lady Billows in light mourning, the morning after.

FLORENCE PIKE

Miss Pike is the village spy, the CIA, and the Gestapo all wrapped in one. Because she is a housekeeper and not a maid she can be included in the coronation party. Just the same, in the house she wears some kind of uniform. It is of medium blue, starched cotton, with a stand-up white collar and cuffs and a shiny black cotton bib apron, which has a pocket to hold her notebook. She wears a small black headdress, the housekeeper's equivalent of a maid's cap.

For her visit to the Herring establishment she removes cap and apron, donning instead a tailored peacoat-like jacket and an ill-assorted sailor hat.

At the party she wears a severely mannish tailor-made (she is always more or less in uniform). It is a suit of navy-blue serge with a vest. Her blouse has a man's stand-up or turnover collar and a four-

Florence Pike and Miss Wordsworth at the party.

Miss Wordsworth's tasteful improvisations.

in-hand necktie. A navy-blue straw boater with a quill, grey gloves and spats, and a dark pocketbook will all add to the character of this spiteful spinster.

MISS WORDSWORTH

Miss Wordsworth is a somewhat fluttery lady and apt to be all over the place even if she tries to be unobtrusive about it. She is, after all, only a schoolteacher and knows what is proper. She considers a visit to Lady Billows an "occasion" that warrants the wearing of her "good" walking suit, consisting of a wool skirt and a short peplumed jacket. When she unbuttons said jacket indoors, a high-necked frilly blouse with a jabot will be revealed. Her hat is small and somewhat dressy for such a suit. Hats are Miss Wordsworth's weakness and she tends to go overboard a little in that respect. She also wears gloves and carries a pocketbook.

Hats are Miss Wordsworth's weakness.

If a visit to Lady Billows constitutes an occasion, her attendance at the coronation party is an "event" to which Miss Wordsworth will attempt to do justice within her modest means. She assembles a patterned silk skirt and an elaborate silk and lace blouse with leg-o-'mutton sleeves. It boasts all the tucks and frills that used to adorn such a

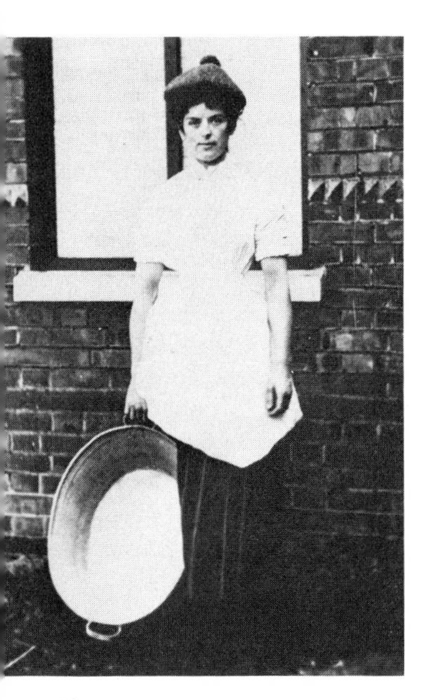
An old Nancy or a young Mrs. Herring—take your pick!

confection. Naturally, she sports an extravagant flower-laden hat. To avoid having all these disparate items look like a hodgepodge, the choice of her colors should be a monochromatic pastel. Miss Wordsworth has good taste; she joins blouse and skirt with a matching draped cummerbund and coordinates her gloves and pocketbook with care.

She will attune her appearance to the grave circumstances of the last act by wearing a more subdued hat with her first-act suit. She should have worn that hat in the first place.

MRS. HERRING

Besides being an unpleasant woman, Mrs. Herring is also a drudge. When Florence Pike descends upon her, she is apparently in the midst of doing the laundry, a chore to which she attends dressed in a dark cloth skirt, a slightly lighter cotton shirtwaist, of which the sleeves are pushed up, and a large blue-grey cotton work apron. The libretto reads, "Mum bustles in, drying her arms on a towel." She probably dried her arms offstage and is in the process of rolling down her sleeves when she makes her entrance. When Lady Billows enters, Mum hastily removes her apron and sticks it under the counter.

Mrs. Herring will not lose much sleep about what to wear to the party. It will be her "good" dress, the only one she owns. It is probably navy blue, the poor man's dress-up color, but since Florence is already in blue, Mum can be suitably dressed in maroon. The dress is definitely not made of silk and is considerably out of fashion. This is evident from the greatly reduced fullness of the sleeves and a skirt that still shows a hint of a bustle drape. Her hat is of the same vintage and of the capote type. It is small, worn off the face, and ties under the chin.

Poor though she is, Mrs. Herring wears cotton gloves and carries a modest pocketbook.

In the last act, realizing that Albert is "dead and gone," Mum rises to the occasion by dressing in a black skirt, a black shirtwaist, and a black shawl.

NANCY

Décolletages for daytime wear, which had exposed less and less skin since the Empire period, disappeared entirely after 1830. If it is deemed desirable to present a woman as seductive, it is not possible to get that point across by resorting to the device of baring her cleavage. Stage directors have occasionally intimated that Nancy falls into

A garden party in Suffolk at the turn of the century, not unlike the one Lady Billows gave for Albert.

the "seductress" category, although, judging from the libretto and her music, she is really a "nice" girl. Even if she contributes to the delinquency of a minor by spiking Albert's punch, her clothes have to remain décolletage-less.

As the bakery-shop girl, Nancy wears a light-colored or pinstriped cotton blouse with leg-o-'mutton sleeves, a blue-grey cotton skirt, which is short enough to show her high-laced or buttoned shoes and black hose, and a white pinafore apron with shoulder ruffles. She may wear a flat bow on top of her hair and a knitted shawl around her shoulders.

Nancy's "dressy" costume does not have to be a silk one but may be a linen jumper or pinafore-like dress over a perkily starched cotton blouse with elbow-length leg-o-'mutton sleeves. Again she wears a bow in her hair or a small sailor hat.

To protect her dress while she is serving the refreshments Nancy will put a dressy white bib apron over it.

In the last act she may repeat her first-act blouse and skirt. This time she omits the apron, whereby a V-pointed belt that joins blouse and skirt becomes visible.

If, besides Harry, Emmie, and Cis, all the children of Loxford had been invited to Albert's "King of the May" party, they might have done a Maypole dance.

Emmie or Cis, with flowers for Albert.

EMMIE AND CIS

The social status of the three children is not given, but one may assume that they are of the shopkeepers' class. Mr. Crozier points out that the children should be rather poor and not too well fed. He recalls the problem he had finding a suitable boy for the role of the apprentice when he staged the American premiere of *Peter Grimes* in Tanglewood in 1946. All the applicants looked far too robust and healthy. "All American children seem to eat steak for breakfast," he observes.

The girls may wear fairly dark, simple calf-length dresses. One might be a jumper with a blouse, the other a dress with a pinafore over it. Both dresses have puffed sleeves. One girl may wear a beret, the other a stocking cap. The one with the beret may have a muffler as well. Their shoes and stockings are black.

The libretto ordains "starched white frocks" for Emmie and Cis in act 2, scene 1. Eyelet-embroidered white cotton is very suitable for such dresses. They have high necks, full, elbow-length sleeves, and wide, pastel-colored sashes with a big bow at the back. Their large-brimmed hats, made of the same eyelet fabric, have large puffed crowns with bands and streamers that match the waist sashes. The

"Albert, hail! All hail we sing!" rejoice the participants in Albert's "King of the May" party. Had there been a church service as well, it would no doubt have looked like this.

girls' shoes and hose can remain black, or they can change to white stockings and black Mary Janes.

Long-sleeved, starched cover-all aprons were popular at-home wear for boys and girls at the turn of the century. They are suggested here for Emmie and Cis in the last act of the opera.

Albert delivering milk.

ALBERT

It is easy to visualize Albert in the first act dressed in grey Manchester (= corduroy) trousers on braces, a collarless striped neckband shirt with rolled-up sleeves, a work apron, and a tweed visor cap.

His King of the May costume is a white three-piece suit. With his white neckband shirt he wears a stand-up or turnover collar and cuffs, and a bow tie.

His straw boater is supposed to have a wreath of orange blossoms around the crown. Orange blossoms have little theatrical carrying power across the footlights. A wreath of daisies or another larger white flower will read better.

Upon his return from the "orgy," Albert wears a beat-up replica of his white suit, as well as his old "mac," the macintosh raincoat he put on just before leaving the shop.

Sid in front of the shop.

The Mayor in the Mayday procession.

SID

The color of Sid's clothes can be a little more positive than that of Albert's, in keeping with his more assertive character. With a pair of tweed pants on braces, he wears a colored neckband shirt without a collar, a somewhat soiled butcher's apron, and a straw boater or a brown derby.

Knickers were mostly a sportswear item. Since Sid arrives on a bicycle, they will be just right for his party attire, combined with a matching Norfolk jacket and vest. With this Sunday-best suit he wears a spanking-new visor cap, a white shirt, turnover collar, and four-in-hand tie.

Sid will remove jacket and cap and put on a white half-apron when he helps Nancy serve the food.

In the last act Sid repeats his first-act costume, substituting a vest for the butcher's apron.

MR. UPFOLD

The desirability of dressing only the vicar in black prompts the choice of another dark color for the mayor's first-act costume. Acknowledging the existence of outdoor frock coats as well as indoor ones, we would expect Mr. Upfold to wear one on top of the other when he enters the Herring shop. Accessories include a top hat, gloves, and a cane.

A four-in-hand necktie goes with a stand-up collar. The mayor may be a fastidious dresser.

For the coronation ceremonies, his frock coat *must* be a black one, but the pants are grey-and-black striped and his double-breasted vest is grey, as are his ascot tie, gloves, and spats. He wears a black silk topper.

Mr. Upfold may repeat his first-act costume in act 3, omitting the topcoat.

Vicar Gedge and his confreres.

MR. GEDGE

The vicar wears a black clerical frock coat buttoned to the neck with cloth buttons. Its stand-up collar reveals the clerical neckband underneath. Matching black ankle tights are tucked into black cloth leggings. At Mrs. Herring's he wears in addition a black topcoat, a shallow-crowned padre hat, and gloves.

SUPERINTENDENT BUDD

Particularly for American consumption, Mr. Budd should look like a London bobby. There is mention in the libretto of his "helmet," which doubly justifies his wearing of the navy-blue bobby helmet so strongly identified with British police forces. This hat was accepted military headgear in the late nineteenth and early twentieth century and was by no means exclusively English. Even the Vatican's Swiss Guards wore them at one time.

Because Mr. Budd is superintendent, his helmet sports a gold spike and his single-breasted, navy-blue uniform has gold buttons and insignia. He may have some stripes of rank on his sleeve and may add gold aiguilettes to his uniform at the party in order to promote a "full-dress" atmosphere.

Mr. Crozier confesses that he got carried away in promoting Mr. Budd to the rank of superintendent. The character is actually supposed to be merely a constable. That would, of course, eliminate the stripes of rank, the gold buttons, the aiguillettes and the gold spike. More's the pity. Whether he is a superintendent or not, Mr. Budd must under no circumstances appear in civilian clothes, as has been observed in some productions.

Superintendent Budd and his underlings.

Harry and his pals.

HARRY

Because the weather is nice Harry can wear sailor suits on all occasions; his suit for every day is a navy-blue one with short pants, accompanied with a navy-blue sailor's beret, and black hose and shoes.

At the party his sailor suit is white and his natural straw-brimmed hat has black streamers.

In act 3 he too may wear a cover-all apron.

CHAPTER 3

STRAUSS'S

Ariadne auf Naxos

RICHARD STRAUSS AND Hugo von Hofmannsthal, the spiritual parents of *Ariadne auf Naxos,* called their offspring a "child of sorrow." What they conceived was not unlike Siamese triplets. After delicate surgery only the babe Ariadne has grown into healthy adulthood, while the two others merely linger on. The parents may have been deluded into believing that this triple conception was viable because they were emotionally involved. That an old pro like Max Reinhardt fell for it is more surprising. Still, one can observe almost daily how talented, experienced people of the theater, musical and otherwise, put their reputation (and their investors' money) on the line to produce a property that with hindsight was doomed from the start.

The consideration that prompted Herr Jordan, via his Majordomo, to order a "simulcast" of the opera and the comedy is exactly what defeated the *Bourgeois Gentilhomme* project: the adherents of one aspect of the production got bored waiting for their innings, while those who had already had theirs could not bear to sit through the rest of it.

Examples of the Greek-Baroque style. (Costume designs by Inigo Jones.)

In Molière's play, the Music Master lectures his employer at one point about the necessity for "a man of quality, good taste, and refinement" to have a concert at his house every Wednesday or Thurs-

Theatrical court presentations in which royalty participated: Louis XIV costumed as "Le roi soleil."

day. That remark may have given von Hofmannsthal the idea of replacing the play's final ballet with an opera, but the resemblance between the works ends there. Of the play's cast, only four characters appear in the opera, all of them totally transformed: the Music Master, the Dancing Master, the Lackey, and the Composer. The latter's sole utterance in the play is "yes," while in the Prologue of the opera he is the most important character—if not an idealized reincarnation of Richard Strauss himself.

The locale of the opera has been moved from Paris to Vienna for reasons that have not been explained. There is no mention of a location in the opera text. It could take place almost anywhere in civilized Europe of that time. That the period was changed from the late seventeenth century of the play to the eighteenth century must be attributed to Mr. von Hofmannsthal's lack of expertise in such matters. He was not alone in lumping together all the Louis, whether Quatorze, Quinze, or Seize, and calling the whole group rococo. Van Hofmannsthal's reference to this matter in his letter to Strauss of March 20, 1911—"figures in eighteenth-century costume, hooped skirts and ostrich feathers"—attests to this tendency. Richard Strauss's early twentieth-century music surely does not suggest such a time change. This may seem like quibbling over a minor detail, but it is not. The subject matter of the Opera part of Ariadne is in the Greek-Baroque style, a genre that culminated in the late seventeenth century, gradually went into decline thereafter, and eventually disappeared.

The term Greek-Baroque warrants some explanation. The Greek revival originated in the Renaissance with a renewed interest in the classical Greek culture and Greek mythology. On festive occasions, allegorical figures would be presented in Renaissance adaptations of Greek dress. In time this custom evolved into theatrical court presentations in which nobility and even royalty participated. The practice culminated under Louis XIV at the court of Versailles, under Emperor Leopold I in Vienna, and under the Elector August II in Dresden.

As the fashions changed from those of the Renaissance, via Tudor, Elizabethan, and Cavalier styles, toward those of Louis XIV, stage costumes changed right along with them, always hewing closely to the prevailing fashion silhouette, while indulging in flights of theatrical fancy on the one hand and retaining some of the classical Greek features on the other. In time, with changing emphasis, additional interests were favored. A preoccupation with the Orient produced Turkish elements, particularly turbans, while the emergence of an American continent occasioned a predilection for "wild Indians" in assorted feathered attire.

For productions of classical operas by Gluck, Handel, Lully,

A predilection for "wild Indians."

Monteverdi, Mozart, and Rameau, to mention but a few, reinterpretations of Greek-Baroque styles are especially suitable, while comic elements can be derived from the commedia dell'arte theater that flourished during the same period.

Most stage presentations feature major and minor characters, but in *Ariadne* some figures stand out in bold relief while others seem merely sketched in. The opera thus produces a tapestry effect that is intriguing and unique.

All the Dramatis Personae who appear in the Opera have been seen, if not necessarily heard, in the Prologue as well. Zerbinetta's character is the only one equally well developed in both. She may change from civilian dress into theater costume, but her personality remains the same. She does not even have a civilian name—she is "Zerbinetta" onstage as well as off. Her fellow comedians have lost in the Opera those qualities with which their names are identified in the commedia dell'arte theater, while they are merely "passing through" in the Prologue. Much the same is true of the three Nymphs, although at least Echo's character is more clearly defined in the Opera. Ariadne and Bacchus are caricatures of opera singers in the Prologue. As sometimes happens in reality, it takes a theatrical character and music to elevate them to the ranks of full-fledged personalities.

Among the characters who appear only in the Prologue there are some other caricatures: the Majordomo, who does not even sing; the Officer, who sings only one sentence; the angry Wigmaker; and the insolent Lackey. The remaining characters of the Prologue have been allotted increasingly more music and personality, from the Dancing Master, who has a little more depth, to the Music Master, a person one could identify with, to the Composer, with whom the real composer may have identified and whose emotions are expressed with considerable penetration.

How thoroughly the librettist and the composer choose to develop a given character does not necessarily affect the costume he wears. A very unimportant character may, by virtue of his social standing, wear a very important costume. What does affect the treatment of the different characters is the overall color and flavor of a given scene.

Except the Officer, the entire cast of the Prologue belongs in a sense to the "serving classes," for it must be remembered that all performers were considered as such. A prominent actor, singer, or musician might at one moment be treated on an equal basis by those who enjoyed his performances, only to be reminded of his servant status the next. In reading Mozart's letters one is made quite aware of that. While popularity or amorous liaisons might improve a performer's

Strolling Actresses: somewhere between rabble and gypsies. (William Hogarth.)

situation, by and large they were treated in the manner in which the Majordomo deals with the Music Master. Actors of the Italian comedy, who enjoyed enormous popularity and were favored by crowned heads, were yet looked down upon and considered somewhere between gypsies and rabble. Hogarth's well-known engraving of travelling actresses dressing in a barn conveys that feeling quite well.

So much for the vagaries of being a performer at the end of the seventeenth century. In the meantime, backstage in the house of "the richest man in Vienna," the atmosphere of the Prologue can be greatly enhanced if the "performers" in the Opera can be seen changing gradually from their civilian dress into stage clothes. Although the libretto implies that they are already in their respective dressing rooms when the curtain rises on the Prologue, it would be helpful if they could be seen arriving instead. An inventive regisseur should have no trouble finding the proper occasions for their entrances without interfering with anyone else's business or their music.

It must be noted that Molière's play was first performed in 1670 during the reign of Louis XIV, and that Ernst Stern, the designer of the 1912 production of *Ariadne*, chose to costume the opera in that period, no doubt with the composer's and librettist's approval, and despite von Hofmannsthal's talk about the eighteenth century. Only

The Majordomo in a costume of the period, but Bacchus and Ariadne in classical Greek styles. (Costume designs by Ernst Stern.)

in the cases of Ariadne and Bacchus did the designer abandon this approach and opt for a more classical Greek style. This move must be considered ill conceived, although his reason for doing so may have been sound. True Greek-Baroque styles tend to have a rigidity about them that may seem out of tune with Strauss's music for these characters. It is up to the designer to adapt these styles to suit the music, and there is no doubt that that can be accomplished. Throwing in the towel is not the answer.

Mr. Jordan's guests, for whom the Opera is being performed, would be seated in boxes erected on either side of the proscenium arch. Aside possibly from the Officer, who appeared briefly in the Prologue, this should be entirely an anonymous crowd. Even the temptation to include Mr. Jordan should be resisted. He is represented in absentia by the Majordomo.

THE MUSIC MASTER

This somewhat downtrodden, yet dignified, old gentleman has few illusions left. Were it not for the sake of his young pupil, the Composer, he would probably not protest against all the indignities that are being visited upon himself and his profession. He wears a worn, dark velvet justaucorps over a complementary cloth vest and breeches. Vests frequently had long sleeves, which protruded beyond the three-quarter-length cuffed coat sleeves. The vest's sleeves were in turn open at the wrist to reveal the unadorned shirt's sleeve ruffle. The cravat was also simple, tied around the neck once, with the plain ends hanging down. His hose are dark and his slightly high-heeled shoes are black. His balding head has shoulder-length grey hair, and he wears spectacles. It would be appropriate for him to wear a black felt tricorn in the shape of that period. Men wore hats inside the house frequently, even at the dinner table, whether for utilitarian reasons—because the houses were drafty—or simply because it was the custom. When the wearing of wigs made hats superfluous, and maybe even destructive to the shape of the wig, men started to carry the hats under the arm and called them "chapeaux bras."

Vest sleeves protruding beyond the cuffs of the coat. (William Hogarth, *Thomas Smith, Jonathan Tyer's Book-keeper at Vauxhall.*)

THE MAJORDOMO

Monsieur Jourdain, the Bourgeois Gentilhomme of Molière's play, has been replaced in the opera by a representative, the Majordomo, a rigid authority figure who carries out his master's every whim without question. Making his a speaking part in an opera where otherwise every word is sung gives him an almost robotlike quality that is theatrically most effective.

The Prologue should have an air of backstage chaos about it, with performers running around half-costumed, workmen soundlessly (one hopes) hammering away at the scenery, some people tearing out their hair in despair. The Majordomo is oblivious to all this commotion. He probably has ulcers, but on the surface he is serene, a man of haughty composure. Such a man cannot afford to show himself in any way but fully dressed. Yet it would be nice if upon his first appearance he too were not quite ready for the "assemblée" that is to follow. The existence at that time of long-sleeved vests provides the opportunity to indulge in this theatrical nicety. The heavily galooned vest of his majordomo's livery is, like all vests of that period, so long that only a narrow strip of the breeches underneath is visible. Here the vest should be buttoned from the neck almost down to the bottom, showing only the elaborate cravat (and they could be quite elaborate) and the shirt's wrist ruffle. With an imposing red full-bottomed wig, white hose, and black shoes with high red heels, he will look for all the world fully clothed. Only when he appears again to upset the applecart for a second time will he have added the equally heavily braided justaucorps with its wide-cuffed, three-quarter-length sleeves, a baldric over his shoulder, a fringed sash low around the waist, and in his hand the tall majordomo's staff. That should make it evident that his costume was not quite complete the first time he was seen.

Composer with a boyish air. (Bonnart.)

Foppish Dancing Master, but not with a fiddle. (Bonnart.)

THE COMPOSER

The Composer is a complex, multifaceted character. His moods change from despair to rapture, from earthiness to unworldliness. Chameleonlike characteristics are not easily translated into a period costume. Some apparel has to be devised that suits all these alternating moods and is of the period as well. It is important at the same time that the costume disguise the singer's female attributes as much as possible. Luckily, men's clothes of that time are quite helpful in that respect, so long as the temptation is avoided of emphasizing his poetic youthfulness by dressing him in shirt sleeves and vest, with an open-neck collar. No woman will ever look like a man dressed in that manner. A light-colored beige or grey cloth justaucorps with matching breeches and a suede vest are suggested for the Composer. If the vest remains unbuttoned from the waist up, the loose shirt underneath and the tucked-in ends of the cravat will do much to camouflage the performer's bust. Very feminine knees and legs can be concealed in tall boots if need be, although they are not really in character for the Composer. The men's long, curly hairstyles of that time are far too feminine when framing a woman's face. It is necessary instead to catch the hair with a bow at the nape of the neck, giving the Composer the boyish air he requires. This male hairstyle just came into fashion at that time and would remain in vogue throughout the eighteenth century.

THE DANCING MASTER

A practical, down-to-earth man, adaptable, a bit frivolous and foppish, the Dancing Master is part of Zerbinetta's realm. His pastel-colored vest with elbow-length, turned-up sleeves is profusely festooned with ribbon loops. The very full sleeves of his shirt have a puff below the elbow, and his cravat is substantial but airy. He has a blond, curly wig with love locks. His hose are of a pastel shade to match his breeches. His light-colored shoes have high red heels, and he carries a fiddle.

THE LACKEY

That the Lackey considers himself the Composer's equal is clear from the way he addresses him. He is an uncouth fellow who wears an expensive lackey's livery, a modified version of the Majordomo's. Only his hairstyle betrays his ordinary status: it is shorter than shoulder length and straight.

If any supers serve as lackeys, their costumes should be identical to his.

THE WIGMAKER

Merchants, craftsmen, and artisans who slaved to supply their wealthy patrons with goods were usually too poor and too worn-out to attend to their own needs: the shoemaker would have holes in his shoes, the tailor would wear patched clothes, the milliner would go bare-headed, and the Wigmaker would be bald. He is a nonentity, although an angry one. He wears a coat, vest, and breeches, made of faded, unsubstantial fabric, each item of a slightly different color. His shirt and hose are a tattletale grey. He wears slippers.

A servile, angry Wigmaker, a little young and hence not yet bald. (Hippolyte Lecomte.)

THE OFFICER

Military uniforms were essentially the same as civilian clothes except in color and trim. Blue justaucorps with red trim or red ones with blue trim were frequent color combinations, but in this instance any color that fits with the color scheme could be used except pastels. Justaucorps and breeches are usually of the same color; the coat's lapels, which go down the full length of the coat, the cuffs, and the vest are of the complementary color and are braided horizontally. The Officer wears boots, carries a sword on a baldric, and has a waist sash and a large plumed tricorn to complete his costume. He has a curly, brown full-bottomed wig.

He and the Lackey are good examples of unimportant characters in important-looking costumes.

An unimportant character in an important costume. (Bonnart.)

THE WORKMEN

The workmen involved in readying the stage wear breeches in a variety of sturdy fabrics in subdued colors, homespun shirts with rolled-up sleeves, some vests, and some work aprons. Their hair is straight and relatively short. Their hose are grey or beige, their shoes black.

THE FOUR CLOWNS

The civilian clothes of the actors who interpret the parts of Arlecchino, Brighella, Scaramuccio, and Truffaldino can be quite disreputable but with a theatrical dash to them. The application of unexpected touches of color in a vest, a hat, or hosiery, or the dramatically draped but shabby cape can achieve this effect. Gradually the actors exchange part of their civilian clothing for items of their theatrical wardrobe, but they should not be seen fully "in costume" until their appearance in the Opera.

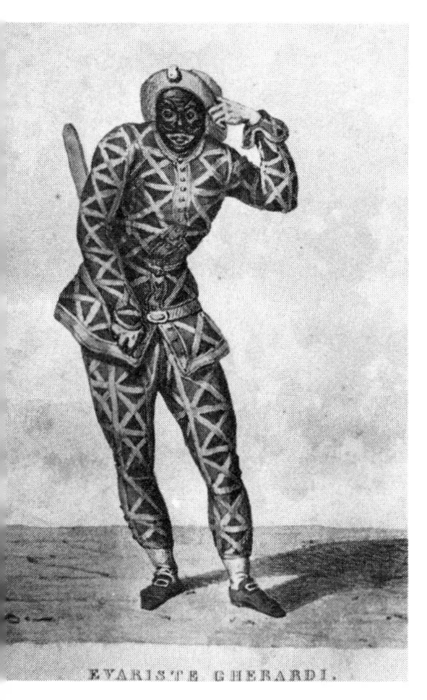

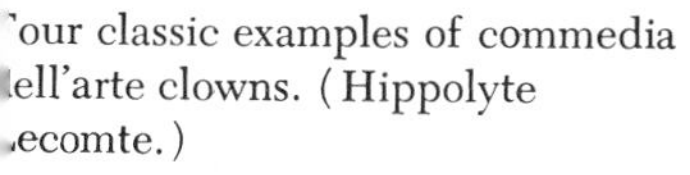
'our classic examples of commedia
lell'arte clowns. (Hippolyte
.ecomte.)

From the large population of the commedia dell'arte world, von Hofmannsthal picked some familiar names for his clowns. In the theater each has his own identity, but in this opera they are just four young scoundrels, all in love with Zerbinetta, who decides to throw in her lot with Arlecchino, the only one attractive enough to win her favor and also the only one who has any substantial solo lines. The other clowns should look comical. One might be short and fat, the next one tall and skinny, while the third one may be characterized by some other oddity. They must all be agile.

A student of commedia dell'arte costuming becomes quickly aware that a great deal of variation and leeway in the attire was possible. The costumes described here are the most characteristic, but a designer should feel free to use his imagination and create an integrated unit that sets the comedians apart from the mythological characters of the Opera without clashing with them.

Arlecchino wears his traditional hip-length jacket and long pants covered with diamond shapes in three colors. He has a black mask and frequently wears a soft ruff around his neck. He has a variety of headgear, sometimes a black scullcap under a bicorn of the same fabric as his costume. In his belt is a wooden dagger.

Brighella is costumed in a two-piece outfit like Arlecchino's, but instead of the diamond shapes, his has a row of horizontal green stripes down the jacket front, down the side of his pants and sleeves, and at the edges of his shoulder cape. His mask is olive green. At his belt is a pouch, and he too carries a dagger. On his head is a fluffy beret, worn off the face.

Instead of long pants, Scaramuccio wears knee breeches with his hip-length jacket. He too has a shoulder cape and a ruff. Sometimes he wears a scullcap, sometimes a beret. His costume was usually black, but need not be so in this instance. His hose match his costume.

The character of Truffaldino was a variation of Arlecchino and their costumes were very similar. It is suggested that the jacket, breeches, and beret, striped vertically in the green, pink, and white associated with Mezzetino, would be suitable for him.

The Tenor in the Prologue, in one of those lavish dressing gowns. (Bonnart.)

THE TENOR AND BACCHUS

According to the libretto, the Tenor is wearing his Bacchus costume in the Prologue but without the Bacchus wig. That is rushing things. It is better if at the initial encounter the Tenor is dressed in his civilian shirt and breeches underneath one of those lavish dressing gowns in which gentlemen spent so much of their time. Unless the singer is naturally bald, it is advisable to forego the effect of a shaven head through the use of a bald wig, which offers such a fitting problem. Instead, he can wear a smoking cap, which was the customary adjunct to a dressing gown anyway.

When the Tenor emerges for the second time he can wear part of his Bacchus costume, still underneath the dressing gown.

If the Tenor was seen arriving on the scene from outdoors, he should be bundled up in a huge cape, to protect his throat, wear a full-bottomed wig, a sizable tricorn, and a large muff.

Richard Strauss was a master of composing "anticipation music," and he succeeded in stirring up quite a bit of excitement with it. He did so in *Der Rosenkavalier*, before Rofrano makes his entrance with the silver rose, and again in *Ariadne*, when the Nymphs herald Bacchus's arrival long before he is seen. In *Der Rosenkavalier* what finally emerges is a small figure, clad all in white and silver in a Louis Quinze costume that flatters even a less well-proportioned figure. Bacchus is envisioned by the Composer as "a blessed youth, a god, a child." Judging from what has been seen of the Tenor in the Prologue, there may be some trouble ahead concerning his youth. In the Opera in the meantime, the Nymphs go right on singing about an "enchanted youth, a young god." If, after all this buildup, a middle-aged, paunchy gentleman arrives on the scene, the letdown can be

The Tenor arrives on the scene, protecting his vocal cords. (Engraving after J. D. de St. Jean.)

Three Greek-Baroque possibilities for Bacchus. (Hippolyte Lecomte.)

considerable. Alas, few young tenors can tackle the kind of music Strauss wrote for Bacchus. In order to live up to the Nymphs' introduction, Bacchus will need all the help he can get from the costumer. A clever adaptation of a Greek-Baroque costume is the right solution to this problem. For some reason people tend to shy away from this sort of costume for men, possibly because it has some kind of skirt effect that may appear comical or even sissy. It need not be so. A designer worth his salt will be able to adapt the baroque style for Bacchus in a manner that is both flattering and masculine, incorporating some classical Greek elements through the use of togalike draperies. Bacchus should wear gold or silver calf-length sandals and a blond or light brown curly wig with a wreath of grape leaves and tendrils.

For a role as relatively short as Bacchus's, it may seem wasteful to accord him a second costume, and yet it makes eminently good sense to dress him in great splendor for the apotheosis. In that event his first costume, which must be spectacular anyway because of the buildup, may be more in harmony with Ariadne's, more like a baroque travelling costume. The second costume must be quite resplendent, including the feather headdress von Hofmannsthal talks about, as well as a sky-blue, star-studded trailing cape.

Zerbinetta "en négligée" studies the score with the Composer. (Bernard Picart, *The Music Lesson*, 1708.)

ZERBINETTA

As can be expected, the Prima Donna and the Soubrette look down on each other, particularly since one considers herself part of the lofty realm of the opera singer, while the other is only a lowly member of a troupe of Italian comedians. Their status is actually not so different, but their characters are. Since they tend to play their parts in real life also and to dress accordingly, one like a prima donna, the other like a soubrette, it is in their costumes that the difference shows.

It is entirely plausible that Zerbinetta was seen arriving dressed in a ruffled, hooded taffeta cape, the hood resting lightly on a frilly Fontange. She will come out of her dressing room in one of those frilly negligees that were so well depicted by the contemporary artist Leclerc.

Because women were first permitted to appear on the stage long after the commedia dell'arte came into favor as a form of entertainment, the female roles (with the possible exceptions of Columbine and Pierrette) never obtained the universal identification of their male counterparts like Harlequin, Pantaloon, or Pulcinello. By the same token, their costumes lacked individual characteristics but borrowed

Zerbinetta could adopt some of Arlecchino's trademarks in her costume. (Porcelaine de Nymphenburg, ca. 1760.)

instead some elements from the male characters they complemented. Zerbinetta, a soubrette who has no special alignment with a male character, could here adopt some of Arlecchino's trademarks by incorporating his colored diamond motives in the bodice and/or skirt of her costume, which is otherwise entirely late seventeenth century in silhouette, but with a hemline that stops several inches above the ankle. Her headdress may be a theatricalized Fontange or the somewhat later miniature tricorn.

ıe arrival of the Prima Donna. onnart.)

Prima Donna in Fontange and ssing gown. (Engraving after). de St. Jean.)

THE PRIMA DONNA AND ARIADNE

If it is possible to recognize a prima donna in real life by her demeanor and the way she dresses, as indeed it frequently is, how much more so will this be true when she is portrayed on the stage in her civilian state. This lady, who constantly protests that she "must see the Count at once" (which count?), should come sweeping in, attired in a dramatic, hooded cape, which is possibly edged in fur. Her hood is draped over an elaborate Fontange, and she carries a muff. Her dressing gown is no less dramatic and can reveal part of the Ariadne costume underneath.

It seems logical that in dressing for the part she would first put on the Ariadne skirt, so that when she emerges from the dressing room the first time, she wears that skirt to a corset bodice, the Fontange, and her dressing gown. The second time around she wears the entire Ariadne costume under the dressing gown and has removed the Fontange but not yet put on her Ariadne hairdo. As has been suggested for all the performers, she too must not be seen completely in her Opera costume in the Prologue. As long as the audience has seen enough of the Opera costume in the Prologue to enable them to identify the performer as the same person, it does not matter how much of the Opera costume they have seen.

One practical note: bodices and skirts are usually swing-tacked together. If they are first worn separately, as happens here, a provision has to be made to hook them together later, lest a separation occur when the performer raises her arms.

Ariadne is a very sad lady, and her costume must convey that state of mind. A silver foundation veiled in shades of grey sheers may produce the desired effect. A Greek-inspired Baroque wig and tiara, veil attached, belong with her costume.

It is important to remember that Ariadne spends a good deal of time in a reclining position, and her costume must look equally good standing up or lying down. The performer should rehearse such scenes in costume and learn how to adjust her attire (unbeknownst to

Three Greek-Baroque variations of Ariadne-type characters. (Hippolyte Lecomte.)

the audience) so that it looks well in either position, so that she does not step on it while getting up, and so that the sheer draperies do not lie in an unsightly heap when she is lying down.

For the apotheosis Ariadne also requires a spectacular and happy costume in all its Greek-Baroque opulence, with a feather headdress and a sky-blue, star-studded cape like the one that adorns Bacchus.

Ariadne in a reclining position. (Bonnart.)

THE THREE NYMPHS

It is not absolutely necessary that the three Nymphs appear in the Prologue, but it is very desirable that they do. As civilians they are the opera-singing equivalents of Pousette, Javotte, and Rosette of *Manon*. They make their entrance in hooded cloaks which are not so frilly as Zerbinetta's but not so grandiose as the Prima Donna's. They must strike a happy medium between the two. The choice of fabric and the color of these garments may anticipate the characters they portray in the Opera.

Their negligees are also not so frivolous as Zerbinetta's, but it must be equally clear that they do not reach the prima-donna class by a long shot.

The Nymphs' Opera costumes are soft interpretations of Greek-

Greek-Baroque interpretations for the Nymphs' Opera costumes. (Hippolyte Lecomte.)

Baroque styles, in colors appropriate for their characters: greens and browns for Dryad, the wood nymph; aquas and turquoises for Naiad, the water nymph; and possibly grey sheers over blue for Echo, depending on how the designer translates something as abstract as an echo into a costume. These ladies also wear Greek-inspired wigs and headdresses.

Compared with Ariadne's subdued opulence, the Nymphs may seem a little joyous, but that is as it should be. She is sad and they are not. Once it comes to the apotheosis, Ariadne will overshadow them with equal justification.

THE AUDIENCE

If it has been determined that a stage audience should watch the Opera from boxes on the stage, they must be dressed as "Personnages de Qualité": elegant Louis XIV gowns with the inevitable assortment of Fontange headdresses for the ladies and justaucorps with full-bottomed wigs for the men. Their costumes must be in a very restricted color range, so as not to divert the real audience's eye from the opera in progress. For once they must almost disappear into the scenery. If the Prologue's Officer is among the guests, the color of his uniform will have been determined by his being one of them.

CHAPTER 4

ROSSINI'S
Il Barbiere di Siviglia

It is not surprising that there is a considerable dissimilarity between Mozart's *Le Nozze di Figaro* and Rossini's *Il Barbiere di Siviglia*; after all, the two composers wrote in different styles, were of different nationalities, and lived in different times. They did not even set the same play to music, but rather two plays by the same author, one a sequel to the other.

It is far more amazing that a marked difference exists between Beaumarchais's *Le Barbier de Seville* and *Le Marriage de Figaro*, since five of the leading characters appear in both plays. True, there is a time lapse of three years between the events in the two plays, and one may expect that the characters have matured accordingly, but Beaumarchais changes them so drastically that the resemblance becomes almost coincidental. In fact, the Figaros of librettists da Ponte and Sterbini resemble each other more closely than Beaumarchais's Figaros, primarily because of da Ponte's modification of the *Nozze* Figaro figure. The producer of the *The Barber* (as the opera shall henceforth be referred to) will wisely acknowledge its indisputable merits and ignore the existence of the play's sequel.

The Barber has not escaped the proclivity of stage directors and designers to update opera plots. By some stretch of the imagination, the opera's proceedings could occur in a later period, were it not for

Attractive women's costumes appropriate for Rosina, from Goya's tapestry cartoons. (Goya, *El Pelele*

the character of Don Basilio. The device of using the lay brother or "abbé" figure for impoverished music teachers, confidants, and intriguers disappears after the eighteenth century. The circumstance that Basilio is a man of the cloth gives his character a special significance. Beaumarchais meant, no doubt, to expose the corruptibility of the French clergy of his day through Don Basilio. In the opera Basilio is no less venal. Moved to a later period he becomes merely another civilian and thereby loses much of his character. In that event, Almaviva's disguise as Don Alonzo also becomes meaningless, for his opening lines as well as his music clearly parody a man of ecclesiastical bent. He who converts Alonzo to a civilian misses the point and robs the Lesson Scene of much of its humor.

Visually, the music of *The Barber* conjures up Goya, particularly the Goya of the tapestry cartoons, but some of his other works as well. Goya was an artist with a wide range of interests, and many of his etchings and later paintings are social documents beyond the scope of *The Barber.* His late eighteenth-century oeuvre, however, captures in color, humor, and sentiment much of what Rossini's music expresses in the opera.

The character of Marcellina, Dr. Bartolo's housekeeper and former mistress, who is talked about in the play but never seen, has been entirely omitted in the opera. When the need for another female voice was felt, one of Bartolo's two male servants was changed to a woman. Thus the old La Jeunesse of the play, to whom Figaro gave a sneezing powder, became the similarly afflicted Berta in the opera, while the play's other servant, l'Eveille, to whom Figaro administered a sleeping potion, became the opera's mute but yawning Ambrogio. Yet, a "Marcellina" is mentioned in the opera: she is Figaro's alleged sick daughter, to whom Rosina has sent candy. Bartolo does not quite believe this fabrication, although it is only in another reference later on that he remarks that Figaro has no relatives.

In the score Fiorello, a character of the librettist's invention, is called Almaviva's servant. He strikes one as more of a "contractor," a man who for a fee will perform certain services, be it providing musicians for a serenade or weepers for a wake, and he must be dressed accordingly.

A police force as we know it today did not exist in the eighteenth century, nor quite yet in Rossini's own time. "Keepers of the peace" have been around since time immemorial. In the play the fellows who come to arrest Almaviva are alguazils. They were city officials who, among other things, preceded the parade of bullfighters. They wore black sixteenth-century costumes. In the opera something more conspicuous seems to be called for, as will be discussed further on.

ROSINA

There is no logical reason why Rosina should wear more than one costume in this opera, but absolute logic is not warranted in this instance. Theater has a logic of its own and the argument that it is visually not satisfying to behold a leading character like Rosina in the same costume throughout the entire performance makes perfect theatrical sense.

In keeping with the eighteenth-century custom that people spent a good deal of time "en négligée," such a garment is suggested for Rosina's first appearance. She can change into a dress, preferably before Almaviva's scene as a drunken soldier. Rosina's negligee must look very "jeune fille": simple, sheer, and crisp. As her music and text indicate, she is no clinging vine, and her other costumes must be in the same vein. With the negligee she might wear only a ribbon in her hair, tied into a small flat bow on top to make it look "Spanish."

A choice of negligees for Rosina.

The young women's costumes that Goya paints in his tapestry cartoons are attractive and particularly appropriate for Rosina. A cutaway velvet bodice ends in tabs just below the waist. It has long, tight sleeves and a sheer little shoulder puff. The sheer fabric also serves for the bodice's stomacher and for the full, ballerina-length skirt, which is often trimmed with ruffles of narrow ribbon. There is an elegant lace apron in the color of the bodice. An interesting effect can be achieved if the sheer fabric is backed in a lighter shade of the bodice's color, so long as the backing and the overlay do not match.

It is sometimes difficult to persuade singers to wear the headgear that logically belongs with a costume, in this instance the typically Spanish long snood that was worn by majas and majos alike. It would be a welcome variation to the fall of sausage curls stuck to the back of the head, which female singers seem to regard as the ultimate solution to all their coiffure problems, regardless of its appropriateness as to period and style.

The typically long snood, worn by majos and majas alike. (Detail from Goya's *Las Floreras.*)

Would it not be nice if Rosina could crown the happy outcome of events by appearing in the finale in a bridal gown? Unfortunately, theatrical logic or not, there is no way that this can make any sense; the original plan was that she would elope in the dead of night, something one does not ordinarily accomplish in wedding apparel.

After Almaviva's alleged betrayal, she consents to marry Bartolo, but she would not get herself all decked out with something old, something new, etc. for that. It is going to be a very small-scale ceremony in the first place, with possibly only Basilio and Ambrogio as witnesses, and it is much against her inclination in the second place.

A more formal gown for the wedding ceremony. (Goya, *Doña Tadea Arias de Enríquez.*)

A Spanish headdress of ribbon loops for Rosina. (Goya, *Donna Isabel de Porcel.*)

erta: a sloppy, careless dresser.

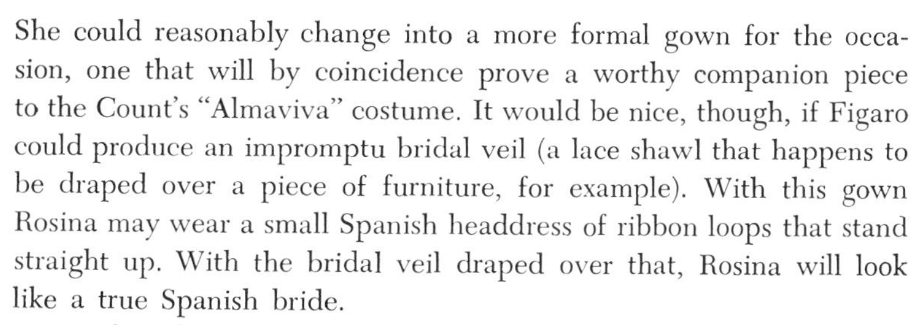

She could reasonably change into a more formal gown for the occasion, one that will by coincidence prove a worthy companion piece to the Count's "Almaviva" costume. It would be nice, though, if Figaro could produce an impromptu bridal veil (a lace shawl that happens to be draped over a piece of furniture, for example). With this gown Rosina may wear a small Spanish headdress of ribbon loops that stand straight up. With the bridal veil draped over that, Rosina will look like a true Spanish bride.

Before the on-again, off-again escape plan was foiled by Bartolo's removal of the ladder, Rosina had given up the idea of eloping. She can therefore not enter the room with a cape and a hat as if she were ready to depart. Neither would she go out of the window without some kind of wrap though. The problem can be solved by dispatching Figaro to Rosina's room in order to fetch one.

BERTA

As one listens to the music of Berta's aria it is not difficult to visualize her walk: she obviously shuffles. This condition is only partly due to her natural gait. She happens to wear a pair of worn-out mules without heels. The only way she can keep them on is by shuffling.

Berta is a slovenly, comic figure of uncertain age. She may be the type who wipes her nose on her sleeve after she sneezes. Her clothes should not be ragged, for she works in a respectable household, but she is a sloppy, careless dresser: her hemline is uneven, her petticoat shows, one of her stockings is falling down, and her bandana is carelessly twisted around her head, allowing some strands of hair to fall in her face. She wears a laced bodice with a peplum, and long, rolled-up sleeves, a full, tucked-up skirt over a petticoat, a sizable work apron, a fichu, and a bandana. The humorous effects one tries to achieve in Berta's costume must be very subtle. She is a minor character and must not steal the show.

A romantic costume for the impecunious Lindoro. (Goya, *Count Fernan Nunez.*)

ALMAVIVA

When a performer changes his identity as many times as Almaviva does, it is helpful if he can retain one article of clothing throughout all his costume changes. Symbolically this device conveys: "Although outwardly I seem to be different, underneath I remain the same." In Almaviva's case the symbol of unity is a pair of boots, which he can wear with every costume, even his Alonzo disguise. (They will barely show there.)

The costume of the impecunious student Lindoro, although simple, must be attractive and even romantic. The romantic aspect can be supplied by an immense cape, one end of which will be thrown over his shoulder toga-style. Only a clod will fail to look romantic in such a garment. For the rest he wears a bolero jacket, a vest, ankle tights, a jabot, and a cummerbund. It is nice if he wears a bicorn atop a bandana with this outfit. If a bicorn does not flatter his features, there are plenty of other Spanish men's hats to choose from.

The "Almaviva" revelation. (Goya, *Portrait of Floridablanca.*)

Berta's comic appearance should not rouse the audience to more than a snicker, but Almaviva's soldier's disguise should be hilarious. It is a bad mistake to make him look elegant in his uniform, as is sometimes done. The entire drunken scene is high comedy and Almaviva should look funny. Since he is wearing boots, it is clear that he is a cavalry officer. That he is a "horse doctor" requires no further identification, as long as he does not look too respectable. An incongruous bright red Cossack coat, a few sizes too big, might serve the purpose. The white tye-bag wig he wears is somewhat askew underneath an outsized tricorn hat with enormous plumes. He brandishes a very large cavalry sword on a bandoleer. If it drags behind him a little, he can trip over it ever once in a while. He should not have a big moustache, though, for Rosina must be able to recognize her Lindoro.

Almaviva does much strenuous singing in this opera and changes his costume three times. It is sensible to contrive to ease his burden a little in the costume department by letting him change his pants only once. When he removes his Lindoro costume he will put on his ultimate Almaviva breeches. This will work only if his boots are thigh high and the soldier's coat as well as the Alonzo costume is long skirted. Hence the choice of a Cossack coat for one and a cassock for the other.

As Basilio's pupil Don Alonzo, Almaviva should emulate his teacher's appearance as much as possible. Only Basilio is a slob and Alonzo is neat. With his cassock he wears clerical tabs, a clerical sash, and a padre shovel-hat, a slightly smaller version of Basilio's. A page-boy wig and steel-rimmed glasses (the Benjamin Franklin type) will add to his characterization.

The Count Almaviva costume is a very elegant three-piece cut-away suit of velvet and/or brocade, with all the trimmings: embroidery, lace jabot and cuff ruffles, order sash, and dress sword. So that he may be able to identify himself to the police sergeant, he wears a jeweled decoration around his neck, which, half concealed in the lace of his jabot, is not too evident until he presents it. A voluminous cape and a tricorn trimmed around the edge with curled ostrich feathers complete his costume. It is important that his cape conceal the suit underneath entirely until the moment of the Almaviva revelation.

'he majo costume for Figaro (here 'ithout the usual small shoulder-uff). (Goya, detail of the tapestry artoon *La Vendimia.*)

FIGARO

The majo costume as Goya paints it is perfect for Figaro. It consists of a hip-length, slightly cutaway jacket and matching knee breeches. The fabric of the contrasting vest is often used as well for a small puff at the shoulders, the facing of the jacket's lapels, and vertical strips at the wrist and knee closings. In addition he wears the traditional Spanish cummerbund, a jabot, white hose, and buckled shoes. On his head is the no less traditional long snood with its small bow in the middle front. For the elopement scene he brings a big wrap-in cape.

r. Bartolo in an old-fashioned it and full-bottomed wig. (John ingleton Copley, *Portrait of hn Hancock.*)

DR. BARTOLO

Dr. Bartolo is a physician and by rights ought to be dressed in black. In an opera with a small cast of principals, like *The Barber*, one would not want to costume more than one of them in black. In this case that one has to be Don Basilio. Bartolo can wear another dark color. To emphasize his age he is dressed in an old-fashioned square-cut suit, the predecessor of Almaviva's more fashionable cutaway suit.

With his jabot, Bartolo wears a cravat tied into a bow, Steinkirk fashion. Together with a grey full-bottomed wig this will make him look like an old fuddy-duddy. Like other men of the eighteenth century, Bartolo's head is shaven bald underneath his wig. When, therefore, his grey wig is removed for the shaving scene, he will require a bald wig underneath it.

To create the impression of a totally shaven head requires a superb wig and a great deal of labor to put it on, without any guarantee of success. It is better to use an "almost bald" wig with a fringe of hair at the edges, except at the forehead region, of course. Although it is not absolutely correct, it will look much more convincing.

In the shaving scene a dressing grown and a day cap on top of his bald pate are indicated for Bartolo. He must under no circumstances appear in his shirt sleeves in the presence of company.

When Bartolo leaves the house he puts on a three-quarter-length cape, wears a tricorn, and carries a cane. With his high-heeled, buckled shoes he wears dark hose.

In the Shaving Scene, a dressing gown and day cap for Bartolo. (Giuseppe Bottani, *Autoritratto.*)

DON BASILIO

In the eighteenth century lay brothers wore cassocks or soutanelles, the same as ordained priests did. The word "cassock," the English term for a priest's habit, is derived from the French word "casaque," which originally meant Cossack. (Eventually it would also mean a number of three-quarter-length women's overblouses.) In France as well as in several other countries a priest's frock is called "soutane." A soutanelle is therefore a small or short soutane. In time a soutanelle became a three-piece, black cloth suit, worn with a short shoulder cape in the back, clerical tabs, and a black skullcap. There is no clearer way to differentiate between the Don Basilios of Mozart's *Figaro* and Rossini's *Barber* than by stating that the former should wear a soutanelle and the latter a cassock.

Clothes were very costly in the eighteenth century. Many young noblemen who had not yet come into their inheritance became lay brothers. That way they needed only one black suit, in which they could move with impunity among the most fashionable crowds or in the most exalted circles. Other poor men with pretensions followed the same course. Joining the army was another way out of this predicament.

Dr. Bartolo feeling the pulse of one of his patients. (Tadeo Kuntze, *La visita del medico.*)

Basilio's moral untidiness shows in his costume through a generally disreputable appearance: his cassock fits badly; its sleeves and skirt are too short. The fabric is faded and has dirt spots. His elbows are worn through and mended. His large padre shovel-hat, his clerical

Mozart's Don Basilio in a soutanelle.

Rossini's Don Basilio and Alonzo in cassocks. (Goya, *The Devil's Lamp*, detail.)

tabs, and his sash are all equally tawdry and in disrepair. On occasion he is seen wearing red or horizontally striped red and white hose, which is not a bad idea, for along with everything else he is a bit of a clown. Owing no doubt to his remark in the play that it is raining cats and dogs, he sometimes enters carrying an umbrella. It too has seen better days. His one time pageboy coiffure is now mostly bald. What little hair he has left is straggly.

The musicians, a bunch of poor yokels. (Goya, *Il cieco con la chitarra.*)

FIORELLO AND THE MUSICIANS

From their groveling behavior and the condescending way in which Almaviva throws money at them, it is evident that the musicians are a bunch of poor yokels, who accordingly are dressed in shabby Spanish clothes in earth tones, with a few of the blankets referred to in this country as "serapes," skimpy capes, sashes, bandanas, leggings, boleros, breeches, espadrilles, some tricorns, some snoods, and some stocking caps.

Fiorello, the entrepreneur who engaged them, wears a similar type of civilian suit, but his is in much better estate. He can also afford a cape of more substance.

THE POLICEMEN AND THE POLICE SERGEANT

For *The Barber* as well as for *Figaro* Beaumarchais advocated the use of costumes in the "old Spanish style," a concept of the eighteenth-century French theater that holds only historical interest for us. The uniforms of the alguazils who constitute Beaumarchais's police force were actually in the old Spanish style as it was understood then, but they were black and lacked the air of idiotic ferocity that is needed here and that no eighteenth-century uniform can provide. Something like the uniforms of the Vatican's Swiss Guards, who at that time wore hats with ferocious plumes, not to mention their ruffs and halberts, seems more appropriate. The sergeant could in addition have a sword and an armor breast plate.

Policemen of idiotic ferocity. (Jean le Grott de Lucerne, *Soldat de la Garde du Pape.*)

AMBROGIO

Ambrogio, whether he is young or old, is a grey little man. His shirt, vest, breeches, hose, slippers, and stocking cap are all in various shades of grey.

THE NOTARY

The notary wears the traditional academic gown with the judicial tabs and a white lapel wig. (See p. 158 for a discussion of the notary's profession.) In the eighteenth and early nineteenth centuries, clerical persons could not be represented on the stage. In theatrical productions, therefore, notaries performed the civil ceremonies that would normally be performed by the clergy.

An academic gown for the notary. (Thomas Rowlandson, *A Counsiller.*)

CHAPTER 5

PUCCINI'S *La Bohème*

The modified 1840 silhouette. (Fashion plate.)

MURGER'S *Scènes de la Vie de Bohème*, from which the libretto for Puccini's *La Bohème* was culled, was written between 1845 and 1848. In the text there are two references that set the action accordingly in the "184 . . .s." The printed score of the opera gives the time as "about 1830," a discrepancy that may seem insignificant to the casual observer. "Give or take ten years, what's the difference?" A comparison of the fashions of the 1830s with those of the 1840s, however, shows that there is a considerable difference. The fashions of the 1830s dictated for women an hourglass silhouette requiring great shoulder width, which was achieved through the use of large shoulder collars and, from a dropped shoulder, huge leg-o'-mutton sleeves. This effect was offset by a tiny waist and balanced by a bell-shaped skirt. In the forties all this had been modified considerably. The waist remained slim and the skirt bell-shaped, but the shoulders were normal and the hairdo, which in the thirties had been bouffant and curly, with a peculiar loop of hair on top of the head, was now invariably drawn flat around the ears, in the manner familiar to us from the portraits of the young Queen Victoria. Why the 1830 silhouette should have been preferable to those performers involved with the original production of *La Bohème* becomes apparent the moment we look at the styles of 1896, the year of the *Bohème* premiere:

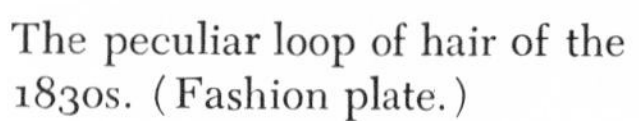

The peculiar loop of hair of the 1830s. (Fashion plate.)

The similarity between the 1830 and 1896 silhouettes. (François Courbon.)

again the hourglass silhouette, again the leg-o'-mutton sleeves, the tiny waist, the bell-shaped skirt, and even hairdos with a topknot. Although the resemblance was a superficial one, for the corsetting of the 1890s gave the female body a stance totally different from the early Victorian one, it managed to make the singers feel comfortable and elegant in terms they understood: those of the fashions of the day. Opera singers ever strive for this ideal. With the passing of time, the modes of the nineties also changed, and what has happened to the 1830 costuming of *La Bohème* in ensuing productions is a matter of record. The styles have been continually distorted and modified to conform more to prevailing taste. Such changes are unnecessary. The clothes of the 1830s have great charm, and within a given period it is always possible to find suitable and becoming variations for each individual and every kind of figure.

Corsetting of the period determines the stance.

The male silhouette of the 1830s paralleled that of the women in a modified way. Here too the accent was on width, produced by the use of dropped shoulders, high, wide, sloping coat collars, wide lapels, and sleeves that were so full at the top that they had to be shirred or pleated into the armhole. A small waist was emphasized and fullness at the hip was accomplished through the cut of the skirt part of the coat as well as through the shape of the pantlegs, which started very

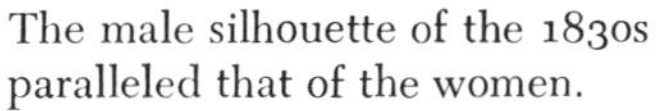

The male silhouette of the 1830s paralleled that of the women.

Men wore tailcoats or frockcoats.

narrow at the ankle but gained in fullness upward, until they were gathered into a tight waistband.

Daumier, Deveria, Gavarni, and Ingres are only a few of the artists of that era who gave us abundant depictions of Parisians of all walks of life going about their daily pursuits. Studying their works one is not hard put to visualize the various scenes of *La Bohème*.

The four Bohemians are a desperately poor lot. They are not beggars dressed in rags, but they run them a close second. Opera singers, for reasons of their own, always want to look beautiful, and it requires some persuasion to convince them that it is possible to be dressed shabbily and be sympathetic and even attractive just the same. Most Bohemians one sees on the opera stage look much too prosperous.

With the girls the situation is somewhat different. Midinettes like Mimi and Musetta sewed every stitch of their own clothing, and when they did not have rich lovers to provide them with the finery they otherwise could not afford, they nevertheless managed to look attractive and dressed in the latest fashion.

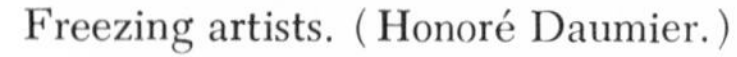

Freezing artists. (Honoré Daumier.)

A boyish Rodolfo in a shorter coat.

ACT I

Until Schaunard's arrival with a supply of food and fuel, the conversation between Rodolfo and Marcello centers on how cold it is. The wearing of an occasional muffler and some halfhearted arm swinging will not convince the audience of their plight. In addition to wearing all the clothing they own—in multiple layers—the two must wrap themselves in blankets or whatever else they can lay their hands on. As the temperature in the room rises, they can gradually divest themselves of these items.

Men's indoor clothes of the thirties consisted primarily of frock or tailcoats, lighter hued vests, and pants that ranged in color from beige to grey and were frequently made of plaid or checked fabrics. In Daumier's drawings in particular one notices a shorter coat, somewhat the forerunner of our sack coat. This style is good for Rodolfo because it gives him a boyish look. If Rodolfo is not a tall man, his pants should not contrast too widely with his coat as to fabric or color, lest he look cut in half. It is also wise to be wary of plaids that are too bold, for on a short man the 1830 style can easily look like baggy clown pants.

Top hats in many subtle varieties. (Grandville, *Chapellerie.*)

Since it is conceivable that in the course of the opera the Bohemians are seen in some state of undress, it is worth mentioning that shirts were made of white linen with collars attached. Those collars had points that touched the cheeks (if they were not turned down) but left the chin bare. Ruffled shirt fronts had come back into fashion, but cuffs were plain. Cravats and stocks of every variety were worn around the neck, often concealing the shirt front entirely. Undershirts and drawers were of cotton in summer, flannel in winter. Some drawers came with feet attached. Vests, whether plain or patterned, never matched the coat, were mostly single-breasted, and always had lapels. Sometimes they were straight at the bottom, sometimes pointed. The wide-brimmed artist's hat usually associated with Rodolfo was rarely worn then. Somehow it looks more Italian than French. Stovepipe hats were the standard headcovering for men virtually throughout the nineteenth century. Luckily they came in many subtle varieties, so that Rodolfo will have no trouble finding one to suit his personality as well as his features.

The Bohemians' clothes should have an improvised air about them. None of these fellows are fashion plates. It is important also to differentiate as much as possible between them, so that each one has a personality of his own.

Rich children in smocks. (Waldmüller, *Die Familie Eltz.*)

Marcello wears a smock and an artist's black velvet beret. Smocks were not exclusively a painter's attribute. A typically French folk garment, they were worn by peasants and workmen alike, as well as by children of both sexes.

To go to Momus, Marcello exchanges his smock for a frock coat and puts a big topcoat over it but keeps his beret and a muffler or two.

Colline, the philosopher, is evidently the least fashion-conscious of the four. He is urged by his friends to go get a shave and a haircut. He must therefore appear rather unkempt in that department in act 1 but be noticeably more trim in the next act. His topcoat—the one with the many pockets—which he buys or has mended in act 2 (the stage directions are not very clear on that point), sells in act 4, and favors with a farewell aria, must have been a so-called greatcoat, although a delapidated version of the species. It was not common then for coats to have a great many pockets. Colline must have had them sewn on specially to accommodate his many books. Possibly the "mending" the vendor does actually consists of the sewing on of additional pockets, which would make a nice piece of "business" (the sewing can all be faked with Velcro). If in addition the pockets are made out of different fabrics, all contrasting with that of the coat, the garment would acquire a colorful, patched look entirely in keeping

The vendor who patches Colline's coat and sells Schaunard a horn. (Ravenel, 1875).

Schaunard's enormous topcoat.

A ragamuffin. (Honoré Daumier, "Types Parisiens," *Charivari*.)

Benoit in a dressing gown, smoking cap, and slippers.

with the character of Colline. A battered top hat and a supply of ragged mufflers are also in order for this amiable, dignified slob.

Schaunard, presumably the youngest, the most frivolous, and the best dressed of the boys, makes his entrance in one of those enormous topcoats that were then so much in vogue. It reaches almost to the floor and sports a somewhat moth-eaten collar and cuffs. His top hat has a conical crown and a narrow brim. Since he does not have as much singing to do as the others, he might be induced to don a "waist-cincher" to give him that fashionable look. Underneath his topcoat he wears a well-cut but worn tailcoat.

With Schaunard enter two little boys variously referred to as "street Arabs," "street urchins," or "ragamuffins." Every crossword puzzle devotee knows this means that they are poor little beggars. They are dressed in ragged coats or smocks, three-quarter-length pants, visor caps, and ragged mufflers.

And now Benoit, the landlord, arrives on the scene. One wonders what kind of landlord it is who comes to collect the rent on Christmas Eve. But his dubious timing is occasioned purely by the condensation of various incidents from the original stories, which included this scene, but not on Christmas Eve. All rationalizations that Benoit is very likely a wealthy man who dresses accordingly and does not live in the building should be overridden. The only thing that makes any sense dramatically and visually, particularly in view of the ensuing action, is that he is a poor schnook who lives in the building and dresses in an old bathrobe or dressing gown with carpet slippers, baggy pants, and a smoking cap. If that demotes him to the station of "concierge" rather than "landlord," so be it.

Despite the apparent ease with which Mimi and Musetta change bedmates, Mimi in particular comes across as essentially virtuous. We think of her as a demure young woman, and for that reason alone the choice of 1830 costumes is a happy one. They epitomize demureness, a characteristic so greatly strived for in the Victorian age. The fabric of Mimi's dress may be a small flower print or a subdued plaid, in colors that are not too bright. Bright colors were reserved mainly for spring and summer. Midinettes often wore black aprons, and Mimi should have one too. In her condition she would not venture out into the drafty hallway without a shawl. Hers is made of a simple piece of fabric, which she embroidered with "lilies and roses," as she sings in her aria, thereby turning it into an attractive accessory. That is what Mimis are all about.

A very demure Mimi, with her embroidered shawl. (Achille Devéria.)

ACT II

After all the discussion concerning the low temperature on this Xmas Eve, Mimi and Rodolfo will march straight from Rodolfo's room to Momus, there to sit outside in their indoor clothes and freeze to death. In a verismo opera that is too much to swallow, although it never seems to bother anyone in the audience. After the first-act curtain came down, Mimi most likely rushed upstairs to get a wrap while Rodolfo grabbed his topcoat and a hat. Sidewalk cafés were very popular in Paris, summer and winter. A hundred years later the little coal stoves, which made the customers burn on one side and freeze on the other, were still abundantly in use. No more in 1930 than in 1830 could one sit in a sidewalk café in Paris in the middle of the winter without a hat and coat. It is the voice of experience that speaketh! No second act of *Bohème* should be without those little coal stoves.

In France, Christmas is very much a family feast, and one sees little evidence in the street that this is the season to be jolly. What should be evident in the second act of *La Bohème* is that everybody is going to attend midnight mass later on and is dressed for it. In the surging crowd of strollers, shoppers, and vendors, one wants to see as much diversity of character as possible: people of all walks of life, of all ages. A few picturesque types, some clergy, some military, some exotic merchants, and some beggars. Some rich and some poor children, some boys and some girls. If one is dealing with a conductor who wants SOUND! let some of the adults sing along with the children. No one will be any the wiser. But for heaven's sake, no grown-ups dressed as children, and, particularly, no women dressed as boys. That is the sort of thing that gives opera a bad name.

Indoor bonnets or "cuffiettas." (Fashion plate.)

In the meantime it has become even colder than it was in act 1, for now we are outdoors and the sun has set. Therefore, as was mentioned before, Rodolfo has added his somewhat worn topcoat, possibly with a shoulder cape attached, and a low-crowned, broad-brimmed top hat, while Mimi has removed her apron and has donned a bonnet and a modest but substantial wrap—modest in keeping with her modest circumstances, but substantial enough to protect her from the elements. Most Mimis appear in act 2 hatless, which is a very serious mistake. Women of Mimi's station never ventured outside without a head covering of some sort, and they frequently wore one indoors as well. Throughout the Victorian age women wore "bonnets": the soft, brimless type indoors, on top of which was put the stiff-brimmed outdoor type, the "poke bonnet." The popularity of the latter rivaled that of men's top hats. The bonnet Rodolfo buys for Mimi is the soft indoor variety; otherwise, he could not keep it underneath his pillow after Mimi leaves him. Only in the English language is confusion possible between the indoor and outdoor types, since both are called "bonnets." In Italian the former is called "cuffietta," the latter "cappello." Mimi clearly talks about her "cuffietta"; she describes it furthermore as being pink, embroidered, and with ribbons. The reasons advanced for a hatless Mimi in this act are mostly rationalizations, none of them valid. It is said that Mimi has to be bareheaded in order to model Rodolfo's present. Since she has no mirror handy to put it on properly, she is far better off simply taking it out of the box and holding it up for everyone to admire. The real reason is probably that both stage director and singer are afraid that the brim of the poke bonnet will cast a shadow, thus obscuring the performer's features. It need not be so. Circumventing this problem is a matter of millinery engineering, a bit tricky maybe, but entirely feasible. Another argument is that singers dislike anything tied under the chin. Ties can either be eliminated entirely or used for decorative purposes only. There are many other ways of securing a hat without resorting to ties. The truth of the matter is that singers dislike anything, real or imagined, that interferes with their freedom of vocalization, including hats. It is a great pity, for headgear is a very important part of costuming, can be a tremendous help in characterization, and never need be a hindrance.

Outdoor or poke bonnets. (Augustoni [Lithographer], *Les Amusements de l'Hiver.*)

The time has come to introduce Mlle. Musetta, that flamboyant lady of varying moods: a seductress with a fierce temper and a heart

A daring, large-brimmed pancake hat for Musetta.

of gold, or so she appears in each succeeding act. Her attire must reflect these different aspects of her character, but not in such a way as to suggest that she has a split personality. In this act she is clad not only flamboyantly and seductively but also expensively, for she is momentarily being kept by the rich, elderly, and foolish Alcindoro. To express the expense and the flamboyance of her costume poses no problem, but to indicate seductiveness in an outfit to be worn outdoors in the dead of winter offers some serious problems indeed, particularly in this country, where seductiveness is equated with exposed skin. In this respect we have learned nothing from Gypsy Rose Lee, who tried to show that the removal of a glove can constitute an act of seduction. How then are we to costume Musetta seductively without running the risk of her succumbing to an attack of mammary chilblain? One particular article of clothing fashionable at that time is especially helpful. It is the "pelisse," which is actually a coatdress. Medieval in origin and at one time fur lined, it had now developed into an outer garment, heavily lined for warmth but cut like a dress. A large fur stole, which in the course of the action can be lowered to reveal a daring décolletage, is also very useful. A poke bonnet is too demure for Musetta; the fashionable large-brimmed pancake hat, worn at a daring angle, is far more suitable for her. When the lady removes a shoe in

A seductive "pelisse" for Musetta.

Alcindoro in the uniform of a "Councilor of State."

The Drum Major.

full view of the audience, her hosiery and petticoat may also be revealed in the process and hence deserve some attention. Since it is winter, Musetta probably wears the fashionable ankle booties in fabric or leather. They have a little heel and are laced or buttoned. For the purpose of easy removal on stage, a fake Velcro closing may be in order. Hose were usually white and frequently had "clocks" or openwork at the ankle. For theatrical effect, Musetta's hose and shoes should complement her dress. Petticoats, always white, did not have a ruffle at the hem. Instead, there was a deep, quilted border, often embroidered, which helped give the skirt its bell shape. This device might be considered the forerunner of the crinoline. Short gloves or mittens are the accessories that complete Musetta's getup.

Alcindoro, Musetta's companion, is a "Councilor of State," and since he is supposed to look both rich and foolish, he should wear his state uniform, which is not unlike that of an ambassador. With a large triple-tiered cape and a plumed chapeau, he will look properly pompous and ridiculous.

If toyseller Parpignol's cart is gayly decked out, so should he be. A brightly colored top hat stuck with pinwheels, a brightly patched smock with an equally bright sash, several loud-colored mufflers, and pants in a large plaid will accomplish that feat.

According to the score, the military band that parades at the close of this act belongs to the army branch of the Sappers (military engineers). They wore blue tailcoats trimmed in red and tall black shakos with white stick-ups. It was not unusual to reverse the colors of a regiment's uniforms for the band, and, in this case especially, one should not hesitate to dress the band in red coats for the sake of a rousing finale and a bit of Christmas cheer. The Drum Major, who should look quite resplendent, wears tall white feathers on his shako, has gold epaulettes, a baton with a golden knob, a tasseled gold sash and cross-belt, plus some medals and gold braid.

Children's costumes varied widely, depending on the wealth of the parents. While rich children looked like miniature grownups, the poorer exponents of both sexes simply had to settle for the wearing of smocks. But whatever the garment, regardless of the wealth or sex of its wearer, it was certain to sport leg-o'-mutton sleeves. Leg-o'-mutton sleeves were a virtual mania in the thirties.

ACT III

If the sweepers, who open this act, did not inform us that it is cold, the listener would know it just the same from the music. But it is more than the cold of a snowy early February morning. The

Children with leg-o'-mutton sleeves.

music paints an atmosphere of utter bleakness and forlornness, which neither the drinking song emerging from the tavern nor the chatter of the milk vendors can dispel. It seems as if the entire scene has been overlaid with a grey wash. Such an all-pervasive mood will affect the costumes as well, but an entirely new set of them will not be needed here. The stage lighting will be able to create the desired effect.

Once again we are faced with the problem that three of the principal singers emerge from a hot interior into the bitter cold, with consequent danger to their health. One likes to think that as an opera *La Bohème* is realistic enough to motivate Musetta, Marcello, and Rodolfo to hastily grab a shawl, a cape, and a coat before venturing outside.

This is Mimi's most down-and-out moment in the entire opera, and she should wear a much more somber dress than in the previous act—one without the relief of a lace collar or cuffs, with limp leg-o'-mutton sleeves and an equally limp skirt. She is furthermore wrapped in a very large dark shawl.

Marcello claims that Musetta teaches music to the customers at the inn. She is probably more what we call today a singing waitress, or what the Germans call *ein animier Fraülein*, a pretty girl who flirts with the customers and spurs them on to eat and, especially, to drink.

A down-and-out Mimi. (Fendi, *Vor der Lotterie*, 1829.)

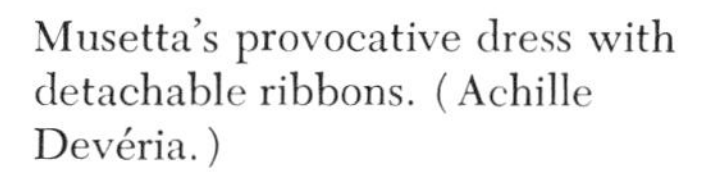

Musetta's provocative dress with detachable ribbons. (Achille Devéria.)

A fur boa for Musetta. (Achille Devéria.)

Her dress should accordingly be on the provocative side, but nothing so expensive as what Alcindoro provided for her. A lacy blouse, a plaid taffeta skirt, and a saucy bonnet are good choices for Musetta. A large, colorful paisley shawl is not to be forgotten. Musetta's mood is exactly the opposite of Mimi's. It is a good idea if the ribbon Marcello produces and moons over in the last act is part of Musetta's third-act costume, rather than coming from nowhere. It could somehow get detached in her altercation with Marcello, or he could actually tear it off. Since the advent of Velcro, such matters are no longer a problem, tearing sound and all. It is only suggested that an ample supply of those particular ribbons be laid in, for they have a tendency of disappearing backstage and in dressing rooms.

The street sweepers are a freezing, ragged, somberly colored bunch of chaps, dressed in layers of patched and ragged smocks, visor caps, work aprons, mufflers, and the like.

The custom officials wear long, greyish uniform topcoats with a little shoulder cape, not unlike our West Point cadets' winter coats. Small shakos with tapered crowns go with that and, as a variation on an old theme . . . mufflers.

For a fleeting touch of color, which matches their music, it is nice to costume the milk vendors in regional French dress. It was

Milk vendors in regional costume. (Collage by the author.)

customary for peasants to travel to the city to offer their wares for sale, and they would quite naturally wear their regional clothes—in this case, however, with additional heavy woolen shawls.

The other characters in this act, the customers who leave the inn and the sweeping woman who goes to fetch Marcello, can repeat their costumes from the second act.

ACT IV

How long Mimi stayed with the Viscount is not known. According to Rodolfo, Mimi was a dying woman in February. They stayed together until spring, as they had agreed, and then she moved in with the Viscount. Since her condition grew increasingly worse, it is safe to assume that it is now early summer in Paris.

With the arrival of clement weather, the Bohemians have peeled off several layers of their winter wear. Rodolfo is in his shirt sleeves, vest, and pants. Marcello has unbuttoned his smock, revealing a cotton undershirt, while Schaunard, always the best dressed of the four, appears in a plaid, single-breasted frock coat. Only Colline does not look noticeably different from before. Being a distracted philosopher,

more subdued, sympathetic
ısetta. (Achille Devéria.)

ıightgown for a dying Mimi.
'oilette négligée.")

he does not know what time of the year it is. No doubt he has shed some mufflers, but that is about it.

A much subdued and very sympathetic Musetta wears a light but vivacious summer dress, with a shoulder cape, a flower-trimmed bonnet and . . . earrings.

Traditionally, Mimi shows up in the last act in a very rich costume, fur trimmed even, despite the balmy weather. It was supposedly bought for her by her latest lover, the Viscount. How this tradition was established we will probably never know, but it is a fair guess that the original Mimi decided that, after playing Cinderella for three acts, costume-wise, she was damn well going out in a blaze of glory. It matters not that it makes no dramatic sense; it makes perfectly good prima-donna sense, particularly since the only other female principal had a chance to display her finery in the second act. As a result, we usually see a dying Mimi dressed to the nines. Forthwith she will be put under the covers with all her petticoats, there to expire in bulky discomfort, but pretty as a picture. How much more credible it is to think that this deathly sick woman, who roused herself from her bed with her last ounce of strength, would have thrown a cape over her nightgown to undertake her last journey in order to die near the man she loves. Her appearance in a floor-length hooded cape over a nightgown not only has a strong dramatic effect, but also is very practical since the cape can be removed when she is put to bed. The muff, purchased through the sale of Musetta's earrings, is usually small and white, which is just as it should be. It is like a child's and denotes innocence and purity. One would not want to see Mimi die clutching a large brown or grey muff.

CHAPTER 6

BIZET'S
Carmen

In the adaptation of Mérimée's *Carmen*, Bizet's librettists, Meilhac and Halévy, made drastic changes in the story. Guiraud, who prepared the Opéra-Comique version for use at l'Opéra, also made modifications. It is important to scrutinize these changes. Producers, stage directors and designers cherish the idea of "going back to the original," ignoring in the process that it was not the original that the composer set to music. Only a few years ago a famous conductor stated in a newspaper interview: "José is a killer. He has killed before and he will kill again." Mérimée's Don José had indeed killed two people before he got around to Carmen: a superior officer (roughly the equivalent of Zuniga in the opera) and García, Carmen's husband. In the opera, however, Carmen is José's only victim. Following the libretto rather than the original, Bizet's music depicts José more as a good boy who comes to a bad end at the hands of a femme fatale. Mérimée's José had become a notorious bandit with a price on his head. If the title of the opera were *Don José* instead of *Carmen*, a suitable subtitle would be: "The Deterioration of a Character." Through four acts we watch José disintegrate. Ultimately he kills in desperation.

The Empire costume silhouette do[es] not suit the *Carmen* music.

The character of Carmen too has undergone some drastic modifications en route from novella to grand opera. Gone are her girlishness, with its frequent outbursts of laughter, her sense of loyalty toward her Rom, and her almost businesslike running of the smugglers' affairs. What remains is a self-destructive, sultry seductress with an inexhaustible audience appeal. Her total dedication to love and liberty, her seductiveness, her flaunting of conventions, and her defiance in the face of death are evidently qualities many would emulate.

One allusion to Carmen's girlishness remained in the Opéra-Comique version: in act 2 Don José says, "You crunch those bonbons like a six year old child." Guiraud excised that line.

The librettists took José's remarks about "pretty girls with blue skirts and hair falling in braids" and created out of it the character Micaela. In fact, she is but the visible extension of a far more dominant force in José's life—one who was barely hinted at in the story—*his mother*. She and Carmen are the only women who have a hold on Don José.

Mérimée's *Carmen* deals basically with the clash between the exponents of two different cultures, each with its own mores and code of honor. Carmen is well aware of this and warns José of the dire consequences of a liaison with her: "Dog and wolf cannot keep house together long," she says. The libretto offers no such insights but lets the tale run its fatalistic course unimpeded.

The action of *Carmen* is usually said to take place in 1820. How that date was arrived at is not known. Don José told his story to the "author" in 1830, a few days before his execution. The date 1820 implies therefore that l'affaire Carmen-José lasted almost ten years. Reading the story, one does not get that impression. As Escamillo said, "Carmen's love affairs don't last six months." Even if the year 1820 were the correct one, it would not be a propitious period for costuming *Carmen*. Its rigid late Empire silhouette suits the music no better than it would become the character of the heroine. The year 1830, in which the story is set, is not very appealing either. Somehow it is difficult to imagine Carmen with leg-o'-mutton sleeves. The year 1875, in which the opera had its premiere, would put all the women in bustles, which is not our idea of *Carmen* either, although the first Carmens inevitably leaned in that direction. It is best to set *Carmen* in a mid-nineteenth-century silhouette, when women's clothes of all classes required solely one or two ruffles at the bottom of the skirt, long tight sleeves, a Spanish shawl, a Spanish comb, and a scattering of mantillas to produce the pseudo-Spanish flavor Bizet also created in his music.

t is difficult to imagine Carmen
/ith leg-o'-mutton sleeves.

George Borrow, an Englishman who, in the middle of the nineteenth century, made it his life's work to study Gypsy life everywhere, and especially in Spain, remarks that it was almost impossible to distinguish in dress between lower-class Spaniards and Gypsies, except

An elegant Carmen, with plenty of jewelry, and a sultry Don José. (Viviane Romance and Jean Marais in the 1947 *Carmen* film by Christian-Jacque.)

that the former were neat and clean, while the latter tended to be slovenly and dirty. The difference was to be found in the Gypsies' skin and hair color, the eyes, the teeth, and particularly the gait, which was so distinctive that one could recognize them from afar even from the rear. Borrow also observed that Gypsies never wore mantillas, something that Mérimée, who supposedly studied Borrow, ignores. He has Carmen play peek-a-boo coquettishly with her mantilla all the time.

In 1947 a French *Carmen* film was produced, based on Mérimée with Bizet's music as background. Viviane Romance was Carmen, Jean Marais, Don José. Mlle. Romance was the most perfect Carmen ever: like Bizet's music, very French, yet sufficiently Spanish. She was very elegant, but in rags, as Carmen should be. As Don José, M. Marais merely attempted to out-sultry Carmen.

One item that is worth retaining from the 1820 period is the Spanish dragoon uniform. At that time it had a tailcoat. With changing fashion it was replaced by a frock coat. To the average Morales and Zuniga, but above all to Don José, a tailcoat is by far the more flattering garment.

Theatrical performances are not exercises in costume history. It takes a bit of good judgment on the part of the designer to know where to be a stickler for authenticity and where to practice leniency. Toreador costumes are a case in point. They developed gradually from the eighteenth-century majo costume we have admired so many times on assorted Figaros. Modern audiences have some idea of what to expect when they are going to see bullfighters, and it is wiser in this instance to present them with a parade of modern-day toreros than to startle them with a lineup of what they could mistake for Figaros.

n old-time toreador in a majo
it, looking like Figaro.

ACT I

Carmen calls José a "canary" because of his yellow uniform coat, and so, yellow uniform coats it shall be for all the dragoons of the "regiment of Alcalá" and its officers. With the yellow coats went red collars, cuffs, and ankle tights, all of them trimmed with black braid. The dragoons had white crossbelts and black leggings and carried lances. Officers wore boots and carried sabers. Everybody wore a black, crested helmet topped with a red brush, its visor covered with leopard skin. Corporals Morales and José have corporal's stripes, which in José's case must be detachable in preparation for his forthcoming demotion. Tiny hooks on the stripes and tiny thread loops on the sleeves will make this backstage operation easy and the result invisible. Lieutenant Zuniga deserves epaulettes, a military sash, and an additional horsehair tail on his helmet.

The company of dragoons we see onstage when the curtain rises is "at ease": they may have their coats unbuttoned and are free not to wear their helmets. Once the relief company comes with José, everyone must button up and the helmets must be worn. There is a special reason for mentioning this. As we know, singers are not fond of wearing hats. Male singers more so than female singers, tenors more so than basses, and Don Josés more so than anyone else in the world. They detest helmets and love to go on stage bareheaded. To do so is, unfortunately, a severe breach of military etiquette that cannot be condoned.

odern toreros.

To judge from the dragoons' comments, the square's milling crowd is a motley one; young and old people, rich and poor, vendors, beggars, a bit of everything or, to use a favorite phrase, people of all walks of life. Here is an opportunity to create a colorful scene to match the music.

Mérimée remarks about the Spaniards' fondness for wearing black, but unless one wants to make a special point, one cannot costume singers in black when the music is colorful. In acts 1, 2, and 4 of *Carmen* such a point would be ill chosen.

While lower- and middle-class citizens of Spain retained a considerable number of regional Spanish elements in their clothes, the well-to-do dressed entirely "à la Française." It is a good idea, however, to introduce a few Spanish elements into the clothes of the affluent as well, in order to produce a more homogeneous stage picture. This objective is easy to accomplish. As was mentioned before: a mantilla here, a Spanish shawl there, a few tiered skirts, some long, tight sleeves with a little puff on top, and the Spanish look has been achieved. For the men a smattering of 1850-style boleros, which are basically tailcoats without tails, will help. A few added cummerbunds, voluminous capes with shoulder capes, a little braid here and there, some fancy buttons and the stiff-brimmed, low-crowned sombrero, and there stand the elegant, rich Spaniards.

The stiff-brimmed, low-crowned sombrero for well-to-do Spaniards.

Peasants usually own two kind of clothes: their workaday togs and their Sunday best. A girl like Micaela would not travel to Seville but dressed to the nines. As her appearance must strike a contrast with Carmen's, it is fitting that there be some rigidity to it, or, if one wishes, prudishness. That quality happens to be typical of Spanish peasant wear and also suits Micaela's character. Her stiff blue skirt has plenty of petticoats; her dark bodice with its long, tight sleeves may show a little of the chemise underneath to fill in the décolletage. She wears a sheer apron with some ribbon or lace trim, tied in the back with a lot of ribbon loops. She can have colored hose and black pumps with a little heel and silver buckles. Her hair, dressed in two long braids, is caught in a draped bandana, which is topped by a rather elaborate straw bonnet. To denote her innocence and to contrast her with the black-haired Carmen, she is sometimes presented as a blond, an unlikely hair color for a Spanish peasant. Chestnut or henna are more suitable for her hair. A *Carmen* performance is recalled that boasted a henna-haired Carmen and a Micaela with exactly the same shade of hair. It is wondrous what a little lack of communication will do.

Micaela in a rigid "Sunday-best" costume with an elaborate straw bonnet.

The music of the little boys who follow and mimic the soldiers is cheerful and happy. There is no reason for them to look drab, although they are poor and ragged. Colorful rags are prescribed for them. Short wooden swords, folded paper bicorns, bright sashes, and bandanas are part of their getup. There is no reason why there cannot be a few colorfully ragged little girls marching along too.

The tenors who whisper words of love to the gradually returning cigarette girls were probably seen earlier as part of the milling crowd. They can be a mixed assortment as far as their social status and even their ages are concerned. Old roués have been known to whisper words of love too. For middle-class males, boleros and ankle tights

'he little boys following the sol-
'iers are poor, but they need not
e drab.

Happy little boys, and maybe a few little girls, to follow the soldiers.

Very wide sashes.

with cloth or leather leggings, wide waist sashes, and hats atop bandanas are the most characteristic wardrobe items.

The word has spread that a cigarette factory is a hot place to work and that the workers are prone to shed a layer or two of their clothing in order to be more comfortable. No wonder the audience sits there with bated breath, waiting to see what female pulchritude is about to be displayed. Alas, the first time we see these ladies, they are returning from lunch and are on their way back into the factory, fully clothed. The scene has been staged the other way around, possibly because the Schirmer piano-vocal score disseminates this erroneous information.

Mérimée's Don José talks about Carmen's red skirt, and no Carmen should be without one, as long as hers is the only one. It does not even have to be the brightest red in order to stand out. The shortness of that skirt was another point of observation. Everything is relative, and we who are used to miniskirts have a different idea of the meaning of "short" than Don José. Luckily Mérimée made a drawing of Carmen and José, which shows Carmen's "short" skirt down to her ankles. We will settle on a ballerina-length skirt as a good compromise for all but the richly dressed ladies. In act 3, however, long skirts are in order for everyone.

Singers are always scared to death that a full skirt gathered into a waistband will make them look hippy. This generalization does not uniformly apply. Sometimes such a skirt can even disguise the hips and point up by contrast a small waist. A skirt that is gored or cut circular and then gathered will reduce the bulk of fabric over the hips. The same holds true for petticoats. In a recent *Carmen* production where all the women naturally wore skirts of this genre, the Carmen had evidently decided that this was not for her. She came out in a little number pulled tightly over the hips and noticeably shorter than anyone else's. The skirt made her look like a freak and damaged an otherwise fine interpretation.

Carmen's "short skirt," down to her ankles. (Carmen and Don José, after Merimée's sketch.)

The skirt fabric for Carmen and her coworkers should be lightweight and have a nice swing to it. Wool challis is a good choice. The fabrics can be plain or have a small pattern. Most of them will have one or more ruffles at the bottom. The petticoat fabric must have a smooth surface lest the top skirt cling to it. Petticoats, also with a ruffle at the bottom, require carefully controlled fullness, for they establish the silhouette.

Peasant blouses with drawstring necklines and sleeves of various lengths are the right thing for Carmen and her colleagues. Peasant blouses can become messy looking when the fullness shifts to the wrong location. A fitted lining underneath the blouse, to which all this fabric can be anchored, will avoid such embarrassments. Laced bodices with or without armholes are suitable additions to the above, as are shawls, which can be worn around the shoulders or tied sideways around the waist. They should not be the long-fringed, richly embroidered Spanish shawls our grandmother used to drape over the grand piano, but far more modest examples of the species.

Bandanas were a favorite head covering for both sexes. The women's, folded into a triangle, were large enough so that the ends could cross over at the nape of the neck underneath the free-hanging square corner and be brought back to the top of the head, where they were tied into a knot or twisted around each other.

When discussing the proper hairstyle for a role, a singer will often say, "I have always worn my hair this way," referring to her latest coiffure. At times old photographs have to be produced to prove otherwise. This situation is indicative of how strongly hairstyles settle into the wearer's mind as being *right*. Not only right for this moment but unequivocally right. Accordingly, there is great resistance to changing a hairstyle for performance purposes. Lip service will be paid to the demands of historical periods and only token accommodations made. Even period wigs will be styled to conform to the present fashions. Only to a slightly lesser degree does this apply to men as well as women. In this case, beards and moustaches are the culprits. An entire book could be produced with examples that would prove the point. It is small wonder then that we see Carmen these days in a long bob of curly hair. It may be all wrong historically, but it feels *right* at the moment. It will probably always remain thus.

Carmen shares the Gypsy love for lots of jewelry, which is fine and dandy so long as it is noiseless, which is more easily said than done. It will already be a great help if it is at least nonmetallic.

Flushed with excitement at the idea of being able to display a chorus of scantily clad women on the opera stage, some regisseurs conceive of the idea of presenting them in camisoles and pantalettes. Alas, the working classes did not go in for such refinements. Their underwear consisted of shifts and petticoats, nothing more. The top part of a shift did not differ much from a scanty blouse. It is suggested, therefore, that the women who run out of the factory after the Carmen-Manuelita melee wear their blouses and petticoats, with a few shawls thrown in to cover some chubby arms. The scene will be visually effective as well as a little more correct historically.

ACT II

Lillas Pastia's establishment was in Triana, a notorious section of Seville where smugglers, bandits, and other unsavory characters hung out. Accordingly, his tavern is no palace but rather a dive, and it is unlikely that anyone would put on his best bib and tucker to pass the time there. One wonders what Escamillo and his pals are doing in this section of town. Just slumming, maybe.

In the Gypsy Song, Carmen describes what the Zingaras are wearing: "orange with red and zebra stripes, with rings of copper and silver." The combination is a good idea for Carmen herself: a dress (or blouse and skirt) of orange with red and a shawl of black with white (not necessarily zebra stripes).

Mercedes and Frasquita, whom we encounter here for the first time, are dressed no differently than the other women, except that their flightiness should be emphasized and the colors must set them apart.

'he double-twisted bandana.

Larger and somewhat more elaborate shawls and additional jewelry will sufficiently dress up the first-act women's chorus costumes. Elegant ladies would be out of place in these surroundings, but a rich man might pick himself up a girl here.

The other men in the tavern are soldiers, a few guitarists, some waiters, and smugglers, including eventually Remendado and Dancairo. The soldiers are relaxing, as is evidenced by a few unbuttoned

Gypsies of Triana, where Lillas Pastia's was located. (Dessin de Rouargue, *Gitanas de Triana, faubourg de Seville.*)

coats with shirts underneath (but not today's T-shirts). The civilians wear bolero jackets, vests, ankle tights with leggings or long, bell-bottom pants, sashes that are at least a foot wide, and a variety of felt hats, often on top of bandanas. Bandanas could be in a patterned fabric, but sashes were always plain. Fabrics were rough; there were some leather elements and much braid decoration. Shirts were mostly white, full sleeved, often slightly double-breasted, with filigree buttons and some embroidery along the collar's edge. Colored, striped, and smocklike shirts were worn in other regions of Spain, and the costumer should not hesitate to avail himself of these styles, particularly for the rougher characters.

Felt hats on top of bandanas.

Unless one reads the 1875 *Carmen* libretto or listens to the Opéra-Comique version, it is difficult to differentiate between El Dancairo and El Remendado. Originally these fellows had distinct characters; Dancairo was the blustering boss-smuggler and Remendado his fumbling, always contradictory sidekick. With each succeeding version they lost some more lines and some more character, "but the memory lingers on." While interpreters of the parts may find it useful to explore the originals, the costumer may give Dancairo some kind of a fur jerkin, because he is the boss, and keep Remendado in vest and shirt sleeves.

Smocklike shirts.

A fur jerkin for Dancairo.

. one-eyed Lillas Pastia type. (1947 *'armen* film by Christian-Jacque.)

Lillas Pastia and his helpers do not differ in looks from the other toughs, but for some additional colored half-aprons.

One must envisage Escamillo and his entourage as a group of city fellows, dressed in the various town suits that were seen in act 1. Escamillo wears a very light beige or very light grey bolero jacket with a velvet collar, lapels, and vest. If he is tall, three-quarter-length flared pants over boots; if he is not, full-length pants. Also a sash, a cape with shoulder cape, and a sombrero.

There is a good deal of dancing in act 2, notably during the Gypsy Song. Professional dancers may be mixed in among the patrons of the inn, but the audience should never know who are the dancers and who the singers. Opera companies have a long way to go in their attempts to achieve this lofty aim. In real life, some people happen to dance better than others, and others still may choose not to dance at all but just to clap their hands to egg the others on. That is how it should be at Lillas Pastia's.

ACT III

The locale, the atmosphere, and above all the music of this act demand a very different look from the preceding and succeeding acts.

Topskirts used as shawls.

Heavy woolen shawls.

Micaela's third-act headdress.

It must be realized also that the smugglers' female companions are not the same women who work in the cigarette factory. Only Carmen manages to make cigarettes during the day and smuggle at night. But then, she is a very extraordinary girl. Ideally, an entirely different look is called for—darker in hue, heavier in texture, longer in skirt—because the action takes place in the mountains, because it is cold there at night, and . . . because of the music. A quaint regional habit among some Spanish women can be exploited here: they raised the backs of their skirts and used them in lieu of shawls. Needless to say, the petticoat revealed in this manner was no less substantial than the skirt itself. One may not want to see an entire chorus of women with skirts over their heads. The use of heavy woolen shawls is an entirely acceptable alternative. Bolero jackets with or without sleeves are suitable complements to such skirts.

Most *Carmen* producers no longer cling to the once-popular idea of costuming the leading lady in this act in a mannish-looking outfit (e.g., culottes and boots), an absurdity that almost threatened to become a tradition. A combination of a dark wool, maybe paisley, skirt and a solid plush or leather jacket or bolero is more the sort of thing to suit a fatalistic card trio. Mercedes and Frasquita, the other participants in said trio, are in a much more lighthearted frame of mind,

Don José: the disintegration of a character.

and, although their general style of dress is no different from that of the others, their evident frivolity must show in the colors of their costumes and in a possible additional ruffle or flirtatious shawl.

In this act Micaela's first-act costume is traditionally supplemented with a hooded cape that matches her skirt. The idea of a cape is a good one, but it should only harmonize with the costume, not match it. Micaela is not wearing an "ensemble." Also, for reasons hard to fathom, Spanish women just did not wear hoods. They did not lack in a variety of head coverings, but hoods were not among them. One of the formalized shawl-like headdresses is suggested here for Micaela. Her stockings and apron are much darker now.

In order to demonstrate the gradual deterioration of José's character, someone came up with the idea of letting him retain his army coat throughout the opera, while changing the rest of his costume to increasingly broken-down smuggler's wear. The army coat would also become the worse for wear act by act. While the idea has merit, it also has a drawback, namely that it makes him easily recognizable as a soldier. Since he did not exactly receive an honorable discharge from the army it is not a status he may want to flaunt. The stage director must decide. In civilian clothes, José looks good in maroon corduroy or something subdued like that, with all the accessories. He must have a serape available to wrap around the wrist of his stabbing hand in his fight with Escamillo.

Escamillo is in the mountains for a dual purpose: he is looking for Carmen and he is rounding up bulls, or vice versa. For such jobs he dresses casually, but appropriately, in a suede bolero and vest, ankle tights, leggings, sash, bandana, and hat. He too needs a serape to wrap around his wrist, and both fellows need knives.

The other smugglers will add serapes, ponchos, and blankets to their previous outfits to protect them from the mountain chill.

Vendors peddling their wares.

ACT IV

Tradition can be a tyrant. The tradition that operas performed at "l'Opéra" in Paris *must* have a ballet forced composers to write ballet music where none was warranted. In the case of *Carmen*, some of Bizet's other music was adapted for the purpose. In our day most producers are happy to omit the ballet altogether. But if there must be a ballet, its content will depend entirely on what the choreographer and stage director wish to create. The inclination would be toward a folk ballet, which is suggested both by the nature of the music (the *L'Arlésienne Suite* usually) and by the rich heritage of Spanish regional costumes that lend themselves so well to ballet. Only the bata-type dress, with its princess-line torso, ruffled skirt, and long train, should be avoided here, because it belongs to a later period.

The vendors who peddle their wares are identified as female sellers of oranges and fans, while their male counterparts offer programs, wine, cigarettes, and water. No distinctive costumes for those trades existed per se. It may be assumed that the vendors were poor people who dressed up a little more colorfully for the occasion in order to attract customers. A bright sash and a colorful shawl can do wonders in this respect.

Bullfights are events attended by all classes, and those who can afford it show off their best finery. For the women, that means pointed bodices with long, tight sleeves, or long-sleeved boleros, tiered or ruffled skirts that are heavily petticoated and lace mantillas over Spanish combs. The extravagantly embroidered and fringed Spanish shawls may be used now too. The less affluent can dress up their costumes from previous acts with colorful shawls, combs, flowers, and mantillas.

The gentlemen who accompany the rich ladies may be either entirely 1850 European in dress or, as was advocated earlier, may add some Spanish attributes like cummerbunds, boleros, and sombreros.

The procession of bullfighters is preceded by the alguazils, town officials in black sixteenth-century costumes. Chulos, the toreador's

assistants, wear a modified version of the toreador's costume. The bandarillero's costume is identical to the toreador's but more subdued in color. In the bullring the picadors are on horseback, but in the parade they are on foot. Their bolero jackets and vests are like the toreador's but of a dark color. They wear beige leather ankle tights and leggings that sometimes reveal armorlike knee protectors. They have wide-brimmed beige felt hats with a strap under the chin and a red pompom at the right side of the crown.

The alcalde (mayor) wears a black, ambassador-type uniform with a plumed chapeau, a cape, and a sword.

From Mérimée we know that every time Carmen latches onto a rich lover, he begins by providing her with an expensive wardrobe. It is not surprising then to see her appropriately decked out in a rich gown Escamillo supplied. Although it is popular to costume Carmen in white in this act, one costumer at least prefers her in black or red. To present Carmen as the virgin bride at this stage of the game is hypocritical, and unless the Carmen in question is a svelte one, it will make her look as big as a house.

Black lace or black point d'esprit over three shades of red (from light red at the top to dark red at the bottom) is this costumer's choice The gown has a matching bolero of black sheer over red sheer, trimmed with black spangles and jet beading. There are toreador-type shoulder epaulettes of spangles, jet beads, and beaded fringe. The mantilla over a Spanish comb can be black lace or red lace, whatever looks best. The height of the performer has much to do with that. The entire process can be reversed when the gown is of red lace over black.

When Mercedes and Frasquita arrive with Zuniga they are also dressed to kill. Their smuggling connections may have provided the wherewithal for such stylish appearances. It might be a nice touch if in the third act Dancairo and Remendado could display some smuggled merchandise, among which the gowns. Maybe also they had just stolen them from some innocent travellers whom they recently waylaid.

What was said about Carmen's white gown pertains as well to a white toreador's suit for Escamillo. White is totally out of character for both. Their love duet is musically enough out of character. There is no need to rub it in.

Escamillo's "suit of mirrors" could be in gold with a red sash and tie, pink hose, and a strong pink toreador's cape, lavishly embroidered and lined in red. Accessories include black pumps and the little black astrakhan toreador's hat, worn level with the eyebrows.

Bullfighters' breeches are made out of a heavy jersey fabric, on which the embroidered panels are superimposed. This particular quality of jersey is impossible to obtain here. Stretch fabrics, which are readily available, are a very successful substitute for it.

Just because José carries a knife does not imply that he intended to kill Carmen at the outset. He had a knife in the third act also. It is one of the smugglers' tools. All the same, he is a desperate man and he should look like one: ragged and unkempt, he wears a torn shirt showing as much of his bare chest as his figure will allow, an unbuttoned vest or bolero, muddy and torn ankle tights with leggings, and a sash. If he still wears the uniform coat, that too should be a sleeveless and torn version of the original. It is the sad ending of a once so promising career.

A last-act Carmen, not in white.

CHAPTER 7

MOZART'S

Così fan tutte

Don Alfonso, elegantly and fastidiously dressed. (Labille Guillard, *Portrait of Robespierre.*)

THE THEATRICAL CONVENTION of unity of time persisted through the eighteenth century. It compressed a play's action into a twenty-four hour period and in so doing rendered many otherwise perfectly credible stories unbelievable from our point of view. We have only to imagine that the events in *Così fan tutte* occurred in the course of a three-month period to find them perfectly plausible, the wedding included.

What remains a little odd is Don Alfonso's behavior. Even a cynical bachelor does not play that kind of game with his best friends. There are a number of operas in which a middle-aged bachelor plays tricks on, or puts obstacles in the way of, young lovers. One eventually reaches the conclusion that what prompts the old man's action is his coming to grips with a painful fact of life: as a love object he is no longer in the running. He may be the young ladies' best friend and confidant, but the relationship will never amount to more than that. Because he himself was for a long time the "young man about town" whom no one could resist, this realization is for him a particularly bitter pill to swallow. The process of coming to terms with this situation arouses anger and creates an urge for revenge. This is exactly what motivates Don Alfonso. In that context the opera's subtitle, "A School for Lovers," applies to him as well.

Don Alfonso negotiating the rental of two Albanian costumes. (Arif Pasa, *Official Costumes of the Ottoman Empire*, ca. 1825.)

Of the other characters in the opera, the one most taken in by Don Alfonso's machinations is, oddly enough, the maid Despina, for she imagines herelf to be a co-conspirator, while in reality she is as much in the dark about the Albanians' true identity as the sisters are.

Così fan tutte is considered by many to be Lorenzo da Ponte's finest libretto, but it is not easy to share their enthusiasm. Dramatically, the second act is a letdown. All the spectacular events occur in the first act: the officers' sudden departure, the arrival of the Albanian disguises, the mock suicides, Despina's appearance as a doctor—it is one incident after another. Even with its abundance of gorgeous music, act 2 cannot hope to match the excitement of act 1, let alone surpass it. As a result the second act is usually drastically cut.

It is important to be aware of a piece's weaknesses as well as its strengths, for only then can an attempt be made to offset the libretto's failings and bolster the sagging tensions. Via the costumes, it is possible to create some visual excitement in the second act, and that in itself will prove dramatically stimulating.

The costumer of *Così* for once does not have to worry about the period in which the action takes place as opposed to the time when the opera was composed. Both are of the years 1789–90. Stylistically one is inclined to lump the entire eighteenth century together and call

Costumes worn by Mozart and his contemporaries. (*Wolfgang Amadeus Mozart*. Lithograph by Jab after Hamman.)

The high- and long-waisted fashions worn simultaneously. (Marie Victoire Lemoine, *Mme. Vigée-Lebrun and her pupil Mlle. Lemoine.*)

it all "rococo," whence to leap straight to the Directoire period, perhaps with an amused glance at the Incroyables and Merveilleuses. Fashions actually changed only gradually, and in 1790 people wore clothes that were a charming transition from the late Louis XVI fashions toward those of the early Directoire. They were worn by Mozart and his contemporaries, and they are ideal for *Così fan tutte*. The fashions of this period, logical though they be for this opera, are not universally used to costume it. One tends to go back to a slightly earlier time, and it is not difficult to understand why, although it must be considered a cop-out. The 1790 women's fashions are not the most readily flattering to the average Fiordiligi and Dorabella. The combination of a waistline already raised in Directoire style with a still somewhat bouffant skirt can create a dumpy look in unskilled hands. It takes a bit of doing to make it look right, but then, it takes a bit of doing to make anything look right. In this case it is well worth the effort, for the fashions of that time are unique and suit the subject matter and the music of the opera especially well. Leafing through actual fashion plates of those years, one notices that both the high waist and the natural one are featured at the same time, so that one has the choice of using the one that becomes the singers most. It would not be very wise to mix the two styles, though.

A move to the actual Directoire period could be justified by a very practical consideration: the omission of wigs for the men. It must also be said that in practice Directoire costumes work very well for this opera. What makes the idea of omitting wigs so attractive, particularly for Guglielmo and Ferrando, is the very quick costume change these two characters have to undertake in the second act, from their Albanian disguises back into their uniforms. It has to be accomplished in a matter of seconds. In a tight squeeze like that, having to adjust wigs in addition to everything else may be just the straw that breaks the camel's back. One wig askew and all is lost. Nothing looks more amateurish. (It *is* possible to use wigs, though.)

The story of *Così* is supposed to be based on an incident that actually had taken place in Vienna at that time and was "the talk of the town." Listening to the overture one can well believe that it was indeed that. It is such a gossipy piece of music, it almost begs to be staged. . . .

ACT I

Through the windows of the café we can *see* Don Alfonso arguing with Guglielmo and Ferrando. The moment they open the door to

Two suggestions for Guglielmo and Ferrando's uniforms. (*Right*, Tallandier, *Général Kléber*.)

enter, we can *hear* them as well. That at least is what the opening music suggests.

That two officers each have a personality of their own is evident from their music, their looks, their behavior, and their bearing, but it does not manifest itself in their clothes. A uniform is exactly what the word implies, and Guglielmo and Ferrando wear identical costumes. One might argue that they do not necessarily belong to the same regiment and differentiate between them in that way. This approach has been tried and must be considered a mistake. Their uniforms must be bright and snappy, while at the same time harmonizing with the decor and the other costumes of scenes 1 and 2. The Napoleonic-type uniform, with its light plastron, vest, and ankle tights, is particularly flattering, even on the less than svelte, because it creates a light middle section on what may be otherwise a fairly dark uniform coat. Essential accessories to those uniforms are tye-bag wigs, sashes, epaulettes, boots, full-length capes, swords, and bicorns or shakos.

As behooves a Don Alfonso–type middle-aged bachelor, the third party to the argument is soberly, but elegantly and fastidiously dressed. He is obviously wealthy, for he can afford to bribe half the town of Naples and bet 200 zecchini to boot. His costume should reflect this detail in an understated way. Dark green, maroon, or grey

Neapolitan peasants. ("Costumes de l'ancién 'Principato Ultra.' ")

Lounging clothes for the opening duet. (N. Heidelhoff's "Gallery of Fashion.")

are good colors for him. He is not in mourning as far as we know and should therefore not wear black. There is some embroidery at the edge of his coat, collar, cuffs, and pocket flaps, as well as on his contrasting but harmonizing vest. He too has a voluminous cape and a tri- or bicorn. One of those fuzzy grey wigs that were so popular then would look right on him.

The inn where the opening scene takes place is not a very formal establishment, and the waiters, waitresses, and the innkeeper are of the rustic sort, the girls in laced bodices, peasant blouses, tucked-up overskirts over cotton underskirts, aprons, and headdresses, all with a slight Neapolitan-peasant touch. The same goes for the men, in their cloth breeches, shirts, vests, and aprons.

One never ceases to marvel at the sensuousness of Mozart's music, particularly that which he composed for female voices. The sisters' opening duet is a good example: it is typical "lounging" music. Although this is an outdoor scene, there is no doubt that these girls are lying down in hammocks or on lounging chairs; they are not strolling around with hats and parasols. If, God forbid, this opera had to be costumed in modern dress, the sisters could be put in baby-doll nighties, in bunk beds, drooling over Polaroid shots of their boyfriends. In 1790 they should be dressed in flowing, pastel-colored negligees,

Fiordiligi more serious, Dorabella more frilly. (N. Heidelhoff's "Gallery of Fashion.")

Two possibilities for Despina. (Emma Calderini, *Populana della Brianza* and *Donna di Dignano d'Istria.*)

Fiordiligi's a little more serious, Dorabella's a little more frilly and flighty, in keeping with their characters. It should not seem odd that they receive gentlemen callers in such attire. Negligees and dressing gowns were still considered acceptable morning dress for members of the leisure classes.

Whether "brazen hussy" or "saucy wanton" is the term most applicable to Despina is a toss-up. She is a young, sexy, impertinent woman, elegant and full of fun. Although of lowly origin, she has worked herself up by her wits to be a "ladies' maid," quite a few steps above the sisters' other servants, whom we shall meet in act 2. There have been reports of Despina being played as an old hag. Anyone who is not tone deaf knows that she is young. She might be costumed in an elegant Neapolitan regional dress with headdress and apron.

Don Alfonso's remark that the officers have missed the boat and have to follow the regiment in a smaller conveyance makes a lot of sense, for it is certainly more plausible that he could bribe a few people with a launch to pretend to leave than bribe an entire regiment, which obviously never did leave.

There is already so much activity in the first act that one might be inclined to reduce the "soldiers' chorus" and the "march of the

The Neapolitans engaged by Don Alfonso for the day to do his bidding.

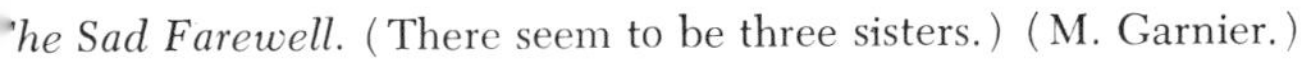

The Sad Farewell. (There seem to be three sisters.) (M. Garnier.)

The inn's hired hands.

The sisters decide that it is time to get dressed. (N. Heidelhoff's 'Gallery of Fashion.")

Neapolitans" to the barest minimum and save the mob scenes for the second act, where they are sorely needed. The officers' orderlies must be there, of course, in uniforms that are modified versions of their superiors': no capes, no epaulettes, sashes, or swords. Instead of boots they wear cloth leggings.

For the accompanying populace, it would be nice if the inn's hired hands had been bribed into service. The fact that the audience already saw them in the previous scene makes it even more obvious that the whole thing is a sham. They will need a few additions to their costumes though: shawls and hats for the women, coats and hats for the men.

After Despina has given the sisters some sound advice, they apparently decide that it is time to get dressed, and they consequently confront Sempronio and Tizio (the officers' Albanian aliases) in two lovely, young ladies' daytime dresses. Again, Fiordiligi's more serious, Dorabella's more frilly. To demonstrate their feelings of bereavement, they also wear large mourning veils, which are attached to their coiffures and cover a great deal of their dresses.

When considering the officers' disguises, the term "Albanian" must not be taken too literally. It merely implies costumes that are exotic and pseudo-oriental. Although the Albanians must look amusing

The term "Albanian" must not be taken too literally. (Hippolyte Lecomte.)

enough to warrant Despina's reaction to them, they must also be handsome enough to justify the sisters' attraction to them.

In order to facilitate the crucial costume change in the next act, it is expedient to let the fellows remove only their uniform coats (to which the vest fronts are attached) and retain their uniforms' ankle tights and boots underneath the Albanian costumes. The latter consist of long, extravagant oriental coats, feather-laden turbans, and extreme moustaches. The coats must be rigged for easy removal. Velcro works well in this instance. Although a Velcro closing requires time and care when the costume is put on, it allows the costume to come off in one fell swoop. In this case, there is plenty of time to put the coat on properly backstage, and the fact that it is taken off backstage as well means that the audience will not hear the tearing sound the Velcro produces.

Ferrando's romantic and poetic nature finds expression in his Albanian costume, while Guglielmo's costume is only slightly more sober and realistic. At the same time, Sempronio must harmonize with Fiordiligi and Tizio with Dorabella.

Despina's doctor's disguise, while meant to be funny, should not stretch credulity too far: the sisters' music is endowed with too much human emotion for them to be made fools of. A very long, black,

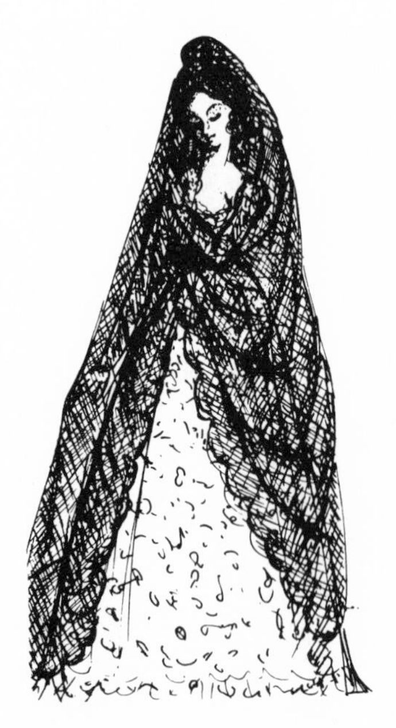

For the sisters, large mourning veils to express their bereavement.

Costumes for the Masquerade Scene.

square-cut coat, which covers Despina's dress completely, combined with the Puritan-type tall doctor's hat, so familiar from Molière's plays, is a simple, effective, and amusing disguise. The hat may have a red or grey wig sewn into it. A large doctor's bag contains the oversized magnet and maybe some other typically eighteenth-century doctor's paraphernalia.

It is interesting to observe that the theatrical convention of mistaken identities and disguises was at its highest when personal hygiene was at its lowest. There may be a connection: when everybody smelled to high heaven of dirt mixed with perfume, it became impossible to use one's olfactory sense as a means of recognition. That we use this sense for purposes of identification is borne out by one of my own experiences. As a child, sitting in Santa Claus's lap, I once identified him as my father in disguise because of their identical smell, a mixture of soap and tobacco.

ACT II

The sisters' mood of despondency and outrage does not change noticeably until after Despina's second-act aria. This scene is often played in front of dressing tables in the sisters' boudoir. At first they cling desperately to their mourning veils, but gradually they are coaxed into replacing them with large garden hats and matching shoulder capes, which complement their first-act dresses and get them in the mood for the ensuing masquerade. Two harmonizing parasols would fit in very nicely also.

The Masquerade Scene is frequently cut or reduced to a duet with an offstage chorus. While one can sympathize with the notion of saving money by eliminating another set of chorus costumes, in this case the economic benefits do not justify the sacrifice of a badly needed visual shot in the arm.

The participants in this pastoral scene are evidently once again the personnel from the inn, whom Don Alfonso engaged for the day to do his bidding. Here they have put on a set of commedia dell'arte costumes in order to echo the serenade the Albanian suitors perform for the sisters' entertainment. Among the choristers are some musicians, presumably the same ones who will perform at the wedding later on. Musicians of that genre are always in the servant category and should be dressed accordingly, in simple, unadorned, servant-type costumes, geared to the occasions for which they will perform, and preferably all alike. In this scene a flower wreath may be added to their costumes. There seem to be flower wreaths everywhere in this scene. The pastoral episode may not add anything to the opera's dramatic development, but it creates a welcome musical and visual diversion.

Unless the officers were such frequent overnight guests of the sisters that each kept a complete uniform at their house, it is more plausible to assume that they were billeted there. Fiordiligi's attempt to depart dressed in her fiancé's uniform in order to die in battle at his side never quite works. Even if she manages to get the uniform coat over her dress, there is neither the time nor the opportunity to get into the rest of the costume, and one just does not go to battle in a skirt. The most satisfactory solution is the use of one of the capes we saw the officers wearing in the opening scene. The garment will cover her dress completely while the military headgear and the sword will do the rest.

The wedding preparations and the marriage ceremony must not be brushed under the carpet as far as the chorus is concerned but should, on the contrary, be visually exploited to the full. In the preparation scene, everybody—the maids, the cooks, the lackeys, the musicians, the gardeners, and any other kind of servant one can think of—is in their work clothes. This does not imply that a complete costume change has to be undertaken for the bridal chorus. It is a matter of dressing *down* the same costumes for the preparation and dressing them *up* for the wedding. At first, coats can be omitted and dust caps and work aprons can be used as cover-ups. Skirts can be hiked up to show petticoats. For the wedding, coats, fichus, and mob caps are added. Bridal corsages may be provided for everyone so that the scene will look spiffy and festive.

If economy is an issue, Fiordiligi and Dorabella may have to be content with adding a bridal veil and a bridal bouquet to their previous costumes, but it is wonderful if they can come out in complete bridal gowns at this point, particularly since they had "matrimonio presto" on their minds anyway. The gowns need not be white; "white for brides" was not yet the accepted custom then. Although paniers were no longer fashionable then, one did still resort to them for gala occasions. This may be just the gala occasion to put this custom into practice.

For the Albanians, a change of costume is not warranted beyond the addition of some extravagantly draped capes, which must be secured to the costumes in such a way that they will not constitute an additional complication in the quick change to come. Bridal corsages, more substantial than the servants', will also enhance the bridegrooms' festive looks. Don Alfonso might also get into the swing of things by changing into something more festive, but it is by no means necessary.

For gala occasions one still resorted to hoops. (Fashion plate.)

Despina, however, would most likely put on at least her Sunday-best cap and apron.

Since Despina's doctor's costume was black, it is pleasant to make her lawyer's robe red. A white lapel wig belongs with that, and glasses with a false nose attached may add to her nasality.

When it comes to making very quick costume changes like the one the pseudo-bridegrooms now have to undertake, experience teaches that the most important thing is the avoidance of waste motion. The performers should be instructed not to do anything themselves but to just stand there like dummies while the wardrobe people do the work. Each of the latter must have an assigned task: one person removes the Albanian coat, a second one puts on the uniform coat and closes it. (A sturdy industrial breakaway zipper is much better here than Velcro.) A third person changes the hats and/or wigs, and so on down the line. It is very important to take the time to rehearse such a change carefully and repeatedly, to time it properly, and to iron out the problems. It may get a laugh from the audience if something remains unfinished, is awry, or comes apart, but this laughter is not the sort professionals should strive for: laughter does not necessarily indicate approval.

CHAPTER 8

MOZART'S

Don Giovanni

THE SCORE OF *Don Giovanni* sets the time and place of the opera's events as "Seville, seventeenth century," which must be narrowed down to "the second quarter of the seventeenth century," commonly referred to as "the Cavalier period." The opera has been mounted in various other times, notably the earlier Elizabethan age (or rather its Spanish equivalent), the Rococo era, and the Directoire period. As mentioned in the introduction to this book, there is a reason why *Don Giovanni* should not be set in a time that is later than that in which the music was composed. It is simply that at parties people dance only to contemporary music. The music Mozart composed for Don Giovanni's party is identified in the host's Champagne Aria as "minuet," "follia," and "allemande." However, a small amount of dance music does not have to dictate the period in which an opera is set. We do not flinch at the eighteenth-century minuet the nineteenth-century Verdi wrote as dance music for the guests of the sixteenth-century Duke of Mantua in *Rigoletto*, and only a few sticklers raise an eyebrow at the number of nineteenth-century waltzes the twentieth-century Richard Strauss composed for an eighteenth-century *Rosenkavalier*. On the other hand, a *Don Giovanni* set in our time would have the guests dancing to disco music. Evidently it is all right to go back in time but not forward.

Dutch patricians in jolly respectability. (Willem Buytewech, *Voorname Vrijages.*)

If there are overriding reasons for moving the scene of action to a time long after that in which the dance music was composed, the inventive stage director will find devices to make the musical anachronism acceptable—a masquerade party, for instance. But if it is at all possible to go back in time, the Cavalier period is ideal for this opera and particularly for the character of Don Giovanni himself. More than in any other period, the men's clothes of that time express the swashbuckling abandon his personality requires. Although women's clothes of this era are much less flamboyant, they suit the two leading female characters perfectly.

There is another, nonmusical reason why *Don Giovanni* should be set before the eighteenth century. *The Marriage of Figaro* reminds us that with the passing of time the master-servant relationship underwent a marked change until, in the late eighteenth century, it reached the point that the servant challenged some of the rights that the master had for centuries assumed to be his by virtue of his noble birth. In *Don Giovanni* the "Seigneur" certainly exercises all his "droits" totally unchallenged, unless one considers Masetto's idle threats and Leporello's vows to quit a challenge. There can be no doubt that in *Don Giovanni* the emancipation of the servant is still a long way off, and that the seventeenth century is an advantageous time for the opera's action.

The fashions of the seventeenth century varied somewhat from country to country. Paintings from Holland's "golden age" portrayed affluent patricians in their jolly respectability. Abraham Bosse was among those who depicted the refined Frenchmen of that time, clad flamboyantly before the Edict of 1633 and more soberly afterwards. Velásquez painted Spanish ladies in court costumes whose silhouette seems too rigid for this opera. Although the locale of *Don Giovanni* is Spain and the town of Burgos is mentioned once, this is a very Italian opera, and one would be inclined to research the costumes from the wealth of Italian paintings and engravings of the second quarter of the seventeenth century. Justus Sustermans and his school come to mind in that respect. They seem to have a close affinity with the mood and the atmosphere of the opera.

Men's Cavalier suits consisted of a doublet, breeches, and a cape. The doublet, which frequently had open seams to reveal the shirt underneath, was high waisted and had small epaulettes and a peplum consisting of overlapping tabs, which were laced to it at the waist. Sleeves varied greatly in shape, from straight to puffed, and shared the vogue for open seams. A unique feature of the seventeenth-century doublet and one that put its stamp on the entire Cavalier style was the prominence of the collars and cuffs, which were made of linen

Refined Frenchmen before the Edict of 1633. (Abraham Bosse, *The Ball.*)

for simpler folks and of lace for the more worldly and affluent. The cuffs were fairly standardized, but collars varied greatly in size and shape. For the costume designer they provide an opportunity for characterization as well as a means of seeming to widen or narrow the figure of the wearer. Regardless of their size or shape, the collars always descended directly from the jaw-line, sloping toward the shoulder. As might be expected, singers are not always happy with such enclosures around the throat. Special care is required to make the collar look attractive on someone with a short neck, but a few tricks of the trade can see to that. Under no circumstances must the collar lie flat on the shoulders, thereby producing the notorious "aging Lord Fauntleroy" look.

A man's Cavalier suit.

Breeches were quite full then. When they were worn with shoes, they ended below the knee, where they were tied with a decorative band with hanging ends. When worn with boots, they would descend to the top edge of the boot or even go inside it. The Cavalier boot, which was an exceedingly popular fashion item, had a shape all its own. Initially cut to be worn very high on the leg, spreading in funnel shape to accommodate the thigh, they were now pushed down in big folds toward the calf, with the top folded as a wide cuff. Inside the boots, "boothose" were worn. Cut like the bootleg, they were made of

Lace collar descending from the jawline. (Giovanni Bernini, *Thomas Baker, High Sheriff of Suffolk.*)

The "aging Lord Fauntleroy" look.

One boot up and one boot down. (J. Sustermans, *Portrait of a Nobleman of the Medici Court.*)

Shoulder capes tied diagonally across the back. (Abraham Bosse, *Le jardin de la Noblesse Française.*)

thin linen, with a lavish lace trim on the cuffs. An oblong piece of leather, scalloped at the corners, covered the instep of the boot to conceal the place where the spurs were tied on. These boots added to the look of careless elegance that is part and parcel of male Cavalier fashions. Their popularity was so great that they were worn indoors as well as out, and noblemen owned them by the dozen.

Although full-length and three-quarter-length capes were worn at that time, shoulder capes were seen more often. They had square collars and were tied diagonally across the back. Large-brimmed hats trimmed with ostrich plumes were worn at rakish angles atop shoulder-length natural hair, dressed longer and curlier as time went by. Doublets, capes, and breeches were lavishly trimmed with braid, buttons, lacings, and rosettes, the latter most frequently placed at the waist and on top of the shoes. Shoes and boots had "Cuban heels." Gauntlets were also part of these extravagant fashions, which were called "À la Mode."

The Edict of 1633, promulgated by Mazarin in order to put an end to the excesses in male clothing, was strictly a French undertaking. Yet its sobering effect was also felt in other countries, and costume designers can avail themselves of either end of the fashion spectrum for purposes of characterization. The simpler styles are more in harmony with the women's fashions of that time. They too had high-waisted bodices with tabbed, laced-on peplums. The sleeves, usually three-quarter length, were full, often puffed, and, like the men's, frequently open at the seams to show bits of lingerie. They ended in lace cuffs, while one or more sheer or lace collars framed the large décolletages. Skirts worn over hip rolls and petticoats were bouffant but fairly simple. Hair styles emphasized width through curls and ringlets over the ears. There was a fringe of small curls on the forehead, and the hair was twisted in the back into a flat bun on the crown of the head. Simple feather ornaments were worn horizontally on the head.

In the introduction I mentioned that in a time when the fashions of the day stress a slim silhouette, the bouffant styles of a past era may require some modification in order to make them acceptable to present-day wearers. Cavalier fashions are a case in point, and it is up to the costume designer to accomplish the adaptation without losing the intrinsic character of the style of the period. Lowering the waistline to its natural position will do much to reconcile opera singers to the otherwise most flattering costumes of the Cavalier period. In addition, the gentlemen may want to have the volume of the breeches reduced somewhat. This modification too can be adopted with impunity, as long as the breeches do not become skintight, which would indeed be a serious mistake.

DON GIOVANNI

Luigi Bassi, the first Don Giovanni, is supposed to have complained about the small amount of music allotted to him, and he deserves our sympathy. Compared with the other leading singers, particularly the women, Don Giovanni was given short shrift, and it is amazing that Mozart, who was always ready to oblige his performers—who gave the Vienna Donna Elvira an additional aria, substituted another one for Don Ottavio, and threw in a duet for Zerlina and Leporello—did not write one additional note for the leading character. Not only does Don Giovanni lack a great deal of music to sing, but also dramatically he is something of a paper tiger. Leporello might have produced five catalogues, but during the twenty-four hours in which the opera takes place, his master is not doing very well in the conquest department. Those who have heard about the Don by reputation but attend a performance of the opera for the first time often wonder what all the shouting is about.

An Italian Don Giovanni. (Giovanna Garzoni, *Amadeo I di Savoia.*)

Aside from a more profound philosophical interpretation, Don Giovanni's case history is a rather simple one: this young nobleman

.mboyant and flattering costumes,
oon to any Don Giovanni.
›raham Bosse, *Le jardin de la
blesse Française.*)

suffers from an obsessive neurosis, the fear of being unable to "score" with women. He sets out to prove himself wrong, but each time he succeeds he immediately doubts that he will be able to do it a next time; therefore, he has to prove it to himself again and again and again without ever being convinced. That pattern is supposed to be typical of obsessive neuroses. Hence the "1003" in Spain alone; hence the lack of discrimination as to the age, status, or attractiveness of his conquests. Although this preoccupation dominates the behavior of Don Giovanni, he is otherwise every inch a nobleman. He has his own code of honor, is obviously no coward, and has enough wit to extricate himself from many a scrape. That he manages to get away with his outrageous behavior is due to his irresistible charm. If I may be permitted a bad joke, he can evidently charm the pants off anyone. An abundance of this quality is absolutely essential to any interpreter of the part, and in this respect also, the choice of the flamboyant and flattering costumes of the Cavalier period should be a boon to any Don Giovanni.

The audience first observes the gentleman as he escapes from Donna Anna's apartments, with that lady in hot pursuit. It stands to reason that for an occasion of nighttime prowling he would choose attire of a dark and unobtrusive color. A dark green velvet doublet and breeches, full-length cape, and matching hat are very suitable for that purpose. He carries a sword on a baldric over his shoulder and wears black Cavalier boots. In a dark scene like this one, care must be taken that the prominent collar and cuffs of his doublet are not dead white, or they will glow disturbingly in the dark. Whether or not the Don should wear a mask is up to the stage director. The wearing of masks was quite prevalent then and not necessarily tied in with the period of Lent and its preceding masquerades. For women, masks were a fashion item, worn to protect and preserve a fair skin. If the Don does not wear a mask here it would more easily explain why so much time elapses in this scene before he manages to escape from Donna Anna: the darkness, his unfamiliarity with the surroundings, and his attempts to hide his identity by masking his face with his cloak.

In the chapter about *Così fan tutte* reference is made to the eighteenth-century theatrical convention of using a twenty-four-hour time unit for the action of a play, something that no longer needs to be adhered to today. Whether the following scene takes place the next morning or whether a few days have passed is not important. There is no doubt that Don Giovanni went home and changed clothes. It is daylight now, and the atmosphere of this scene is very different from the previous one, requiring a costume of much lighter hue. The color to be chosen depends naturally on the overall color scheme that has been decided upon, but the costume must be a most dashing one, consisting again of doublet and breeches, a shoulder cape this time, hat, gauntlets, boots, baldric, and sword.

No change of attire is needed in the next scene until after Don Ottavio's aria "Dalla sua pace," when Don Giovanni enters dressed for the forthcoming festivities. A stage director once developed a routine that works very well for this scene: Don Giovanni appears on a balcony of his palace, which faces the courtyard where the feast is to be held. He is dressed in an elegant shirt and the brocaded breeches of his "ball suit." The shape of his legs permitting, he now wears hose and shoes with fancy rosettes. If his calves cannot bear close scrutiny, he is better off in boots. (Alas, Cavalier boots must always harmonize with the costume, which can become a severe strain on the budget.) Down in the courtyard stands Leporello, who is holding the Don's doublet, a set of collar and cuffs, the sword, and the baldric. On the tip of the sword the servant hands his master these items one by one, giving him the sword itself last. All this is done in leisurely fashion, enabling the Don to get himself all decked out during an exchange with Leporello of secco recitatives, which precede the Champagne Aria. A shoulder cape and hat are also possible but not essential.

Don Giovanni in another dashing outfit, with a sceptical Donna Elvira. (Dutch Costumes by Knilling.)

In the first scene of the second act Don Giovanni is on the prowl again, and once again it is evening. A costume not unlike the one he wore in the opening scene of act 1 is suitable here, but it need not be quite such a dark color. Its most important features are the full-length cape and the hat, both of which he will subsequently exchange for Leporello's. In order to make this change of identity successful, it is absolutely essential that the exchanged items contrast greatly with each other and display traits that are very typical of the character to whom they originally belonged. Master and servant continue to wear each other's outer garments into the Graveyard Scene, where they may reverse the process at the discretion of the stage director. There is no indication in the score where the return exchange takes place. The statue does not seem to be confused about who is who, but then, he is no ordinary mortal. It does not seem logical, however, that Don Giovanni should order Leporello to read the inscription on the statue and subsequently address it disguised as someone else.

Don Giovanni serenading. (Abraham Bosse.)

In the final scene I like Don Giovanni to wear the breeches of the first act's opening scene, but this time with hose and shoes. If he has a good figure, he can wear an elegant open-necked shirt with it. If not, an additional sleeveless, vestlike doublet will be more flattering, while still maintaining the nonchalant "at-home" look that should be strived for here. It is entirely appropriate attire for a licentious young nobleman on his way to hell.

n Italian Don Ottavio. (Pietro
Iartire Neri, *Ritratto di un soldato*.)

Iale fashions after the Edict of
633 for Don Ottavio. (Abraham
osse.)

DON OTTAVIO

Don Ottavio is usually regarded as a nonentity if not a ninny. Aside from the Commandant, who is not on the scene long enough for us to assess his personality, Don Ottavio is the only one in the cast whose character would not provide an interesting case history. Saying that Don Ottavio is a dull man is tantamount to stating that normal people are dull. If he is portrayed as a man of great and quiet strength instead of as a spineless sap, he will gain considerably in stature and yet not be out of place among the "freaked-out" characters who surround him. The more sober Cavalier styles of "after the Edict of 1633" seem particularly suitable for him. Don Ottavio's whereabouts at the time of the Commandant's demise are a mystery, which does not have to bother anyone except the costume designer, who has to determine the clothes he will wear upon his entrance. The libretto states that servants "return with Don Ottavio and enter the palace in the background," whatever that means. In order to be able to get there so fast he must live across the street, or in a guest house on the estate, or something like that. On the other hand, Donna Anna's account that she mistook Giovanni for her fiancé indicates that she was not surprised by his visit to her, although "it was already quite late," which suggests that he is living in the palace. One can conjecture about this ad infinitum. I believe that the opening scene gains a great deal dramatically if only Don Giovanni and Leporello are clothed in daytime outdoor wear, while everybody else, including Don Ottavio, who has retired for the night, if not necessarily gone to bed, is roused unexpectedly and therefore appears in a state of partial undress that denotes hasty improvisation. In the case of Ottavio that would mean breeches, a shirt, a long cape or armhole cloak, and, naturally, a sword. This combination would serve whether he is first seen entering the place or emerging from it. In subsequent scenes Don Ottavio will naturally be fully clothed. He is not a blood relative of the Commandant and would not dress in mourning, but it would seem reasonable that out of sympathy and respect for Donna Anna's feelings he would don what might be described as "light mourning": a grey doublet, breeches, and shoulder cape, trimmed in black and accessorized in black. He can wear shoes or boots, whichever look better on him. Since most of his scenes are outdoors, boots are probably the better choice.

At Don Giovannni's party, Ottavio, Anna, and Elvira appear in dominoes, and they are masked. Dominoes are usually black, but in this instance a color is preferable so Donna Anna will be the only person entirely in black. A changeable fabric—moire, taffeta, or antique satin—is suggested for the dominoes; black and purple would be a good choice for Ottavio. Masks on sticks are favored over masks that tie around the head, because the former are much more easily removed at the moment of unmasking.

The Commandant. (Bernardo Strozzi, *Doge Pallavicino.*)

THE COMMANDANT AND THE STATUE

If the impression is given that everybody in the house of the Commandant is roused by Donna Anna's screams and comes running to her aid in whatever state of dress or undress they happened to be in, plus what they hastily threw on, the Commandant should be no exception. He wears a full-length, ample nightshirt, over which he hastily put a dark dressing gown–like garment, possibly trimmed with fur. He enters with drawn sword.

To produce a marble statue, equestrian or otherwise, is not so difficult as it might seem. If it is equestrian, the horse part is entirely the scene shop's responsibility, while the costume designer attends to the man. Depending on how much money is available for the project, the shop could construct a robotlike figure that does not even have a person inside it but is entirely mechanically controlled. On the other hand, a whitewashed suit of armor can produce a very convincing and striking effect. The use of a visor helmet is helpful because it conceals many of the wearer's features and produces a suitably hollow sound, which in turn can be amplified. A full-length, ample cape makes a striking impression and lightens the wearer's burden by eliminating the entire back part of the armor. The cape must be totally rigid, however, for marble does not move. The same holds true for feathers atop the visor helmet. The combined use of armor and chain mail for the arms and legs will further improve the statue's mobility at the Dinner Scene. The term "whitewash" should not be taken too literally, for real whitewash produces a completely dull surface, while marble has a certain sheen to it and is not dead white, particularly not in the moonlight. If the statue is not an equestrian one, its immobility in the Graveyard Scene will be greatly enhanced by letting its gauntlet-covered hands rest on the hilt of a tall upright sword.

The Statue. (Suit of armor designed by Étienne Delaune, ca. 1550.)

LEPORELLO

A wealthy nobleman like Don Giovanni can undoubtedly afford to dress his servants in style, his personal valet included. Yet the music Mozart wrote for Leporello belies that notion. To this listener

. by the time you read . . . ." A very neat Leporello.

he comes across as an unkempt slob who drools, wipes his nose on his sleeves, and wears clothes that are full of grease spots because he is a messy eater. He is comical in his attempts to emulate his master's amorous tactics, but without the Don's nobility and charm he does not get very far. Just the same, he manages to make some conquests of his own, as is attested to by Don Giovanni, who relates how, wearing his servant's cape and hat, he won over a maiden who mistook him for Leporello. Leporello's clothes must be of good quality, since the Don paid for them, but they show signs of gross neglect. Cloth breeches of a subdued color with a sleeveless open doublet of a lighter shade are suitable for him. Underneath the doublet he wears a horizontally striped jerkin, of which only the sleeves and the middle-front part are visible. His collar and cuffs are in off-white linen. They are none too clean and are lacking in starch. The brim of his felt hat is somewhat wilted and is trimmed with some pheasant feathers that have seen better days. The cloth cape is three-quarter length and not as voluminous as the Don's. Yet it cannot be skimpy either, for when he exchanges hat and cape with his master, these items must cover Don Giovanni enough to make the disguise credible. That there must be a considerable difference in texture and color between the master's and servant's hat and cape was already mentioned in the discussion of Don Giovanni's costumes. The audience should never be in doubt as to who is supposed to be imitating whom.

It is hard to believe that Donna Elvira could be taken in for so long, a point that may have prompted some producers to cast the two roles with performers of very similar stature and to costume them very similarly as well. But nothing wreaks more havoc with the dramatic situation than if no one knows who is who. Furthermore, Mozart's music makes the two characters so different that it is much wiser to stretch the credulity a little as far as Donna Elvira is concerned. She is a lady who has a history of being very easily taken in anyway.

MASETTO

Peasant costumes as we know them today developed primarily in the eighteenth century and took great flights of fancy in the nineteenth. Before that time they were functional clothes of great simplicity, which echoed the prevailing fashions but faintly, were made of rough-hewn homespun fabrics, and frequently gave evidence of their wearer's great poverty. For the young bridegroom Masetto such a costume will not do. His must be neat and have a festive look, yet be simple as well: a peasant in his "Sunday-best" attire. Something on the order of homespun beige woolen breeches with a sleeveless leather

Masetto with a selection of the Don's conquests. (Georges de la Tour, *The Fortune Teller.*)

doublet of a deeper shade and sleeves to match the breeches would accomplish that feat. His collar and cuffs are white and may have a cotton-lace edging. He may have a waist sash and a conical hat with a medium-sized brim. A stocking cap is another possibility. He wears hose and shoes with a modest rosette or, better still, cloth or leather leggings. A flower bouquet with flowing ribbons, pinned to his shoulder, will designate this ill-tempered country bumpkin as the bridegroom.

THE MALE PEASANTS

Masetto's friends wear costumes similar to his but in soberer colors so that he will stand apart from them. To make it festive all around, they may have smaller versions of his nosegay, with considerably shorter ribbons, pinned to their shoulders. When they set out to beat up Leporello (or so they think), they may add a few ponchos, serapes, and short capes to give them a mock threatening air.

THE COMMANDANT'S SERVANTS

If the servants were fully clothed, they would wear dark, Puritan-type breeches and doublets with white linen collars and cuffs. To convey the idea that they were roused from their sleep, or at least from having retired for the night, some of them can be in breeches and shirts, with some shirts tucked in, some hanging out, and some in between. A few of them may have managed to put a doublet over the shirt or are in various stages of doing so and buttoning up. Their hose are dark and the shoes have small rosettes.

DON GIOVANNI'S SERVANTS

Unlike Leporello, Don Giovanni's other servants wear breeches and doublets of Puritan cut that are neat, bright colored, and moderately trimmed with braid. Collars and cuffs are of white linen. Their hose are light colored but not white; shoes are black. The shoe rosettes can be made of the braid that trims the costumes.

DON GIOVANNI'S MUSICIANS

Musicians were considered servants then and may be costumed like them, but possibly in a different color. A stage director may want to distinguish between the various orchestras by putting them in different colors. One of the orchestras may even be the village band, in which case the players should look more like the peasants and need not be dressed alike.

MALE GUESTS AT THE PARTY

Besides Ottavio, Anna, and Elvira, some couples of Don Giovanni's class may dance the minuet. The gentlemen should wear Cavalier suits that are not as fancy as the Don's but not as subdued as Ottavio's. Their costumes must be complete with shoulder capes and plumed Cavalier hats, whether this scene is played indoors or out. As has been mentioned elsewhere, men frequently wore hats indoors until wigs became fashionable, and even then the custom of baring the head indoors developed only gradually, as better heating throughout the house made it more tolerable.

DONNA ANNA

Wealthy people of past centuries who desired to have their images immortalized posed in their best bib and tucker for the fashionable painters of the day. The poorer folks, who could not afford such extravagances and could not have cared less, were only depicted by those artists who had an interest in studying and recording the characters and mores of the common people despite the lack of remuneration. As a result, it is much easier for the researcher to reconstruct the clothing of poor people in their various pursuits, and in different stages of dress and undress, than that of the affluent, who were only shown fully clothed, at least until the eighteenth century, when appearing "en négligée" became fashionable. We can only speculate as to what a young noblewoman like Donna Anna would wear after she retired for the day and prepared to go to bed. It is very likely that what she really wore corresponds little with our notion of such attire, once again because insufficient heating prompted people to wear much sturdier clothing at night than we do now. Pictures that present lying-in and sickroom scenes attest to this fact. We must also remember that in this case the lady was dressed properly enough to be able to receive her fiancé, who was evidently in the habit of dropping in for a nightcap. A beautiful nightgown, fashioned along the lines of gowns of that period, and a young but elegant negligee along the same lines would seem entirely in order, were it not for the fact that when the audience first beholds Donna Anna she is already in a state of great agitation, which will be followed by outbursts of uncontrollable grief and cries for vengeance. Donna Anna's behavior is dominated by these alternating emotional states throughout the opera, except during the few moments when, at Don Ottavio's urging, she tries to control herself. Much has been written about the question, Did she or didn't she (succumb to Don Giovanni's advances)? but "only her hairdresser knows for sure." This writer believes that Donna Anna's problem lies in the paradox that if she had submitted to the Don, her father would still be alive, but because she resisted and roused the entire neighborhood with her screams, her father is now dead. She suffers feeelings of guilt as a result of having been virtuous, which understandably causes a deep emotional conflict.

Donna Anna preparing to retire. (Thomas Watson, *Amelia, Countess of Ossory.*)

A portly Donna Anna. (Van Dyck, *Henrietta of Lorraine.*)

There is nothing small-scale about Donna Anna, and her clothes should be equally dramatic. The pale-colored nightgown of a soft and flowing fabric has full, long sleeves caught in several puffs. The negligee of a heavier, but still flowing, silk is of a darker color; it is open in front, has a slight train, and can have a Medici collar. The sleeves are wide and through open seams reveal those of the nightgown underneath. The so-called hanging sleeves of a slightly earlier period also produce a dramatic effect, which will underscore the emotional outpourings and might therefore be preferable for the negligee. Anna exhorts Don Ottavio several times to swear that he will avenge her father's death. If there is no stack of Bibles handy to swear on she might use a crucifix she wears around her neck, dramatically draw Don Ottavio's sword, or, best of all, use the sword of the fallen Commandant, which might easily have been left behind when he was carried off.

In order to break up the unrelieved blackness of Donna Anna's mourning gown, a combination of two contrasting black fabrics is suggested: velvet and brocade, or brocade and a dull satin or peau de soie. The puffed sleeves can be of a sheer black fabric inside the more dramatic oversleeves made out of the gown's fabric. A trailing overskirt can be split in the middle to show the brocaded underskirt. The Medici mourning cap with its point on the forehead and long mourning veil is a suitable accessory.

Donna Anna bringing flowers to the Commandant's grave.

Donna Anna's domino for the Party Scene would be intriguing in a changeable black and gold or black and silver fabric. In order to reduce a bulky silhouette, the petticoat could be omitted in this scene.

If, in order to denote the passing of time, or simply to break the visual monotony, it is deemed desirable that Donna Anna have a change of costume, the second one could be a lighter mourning. Black could be combined now with dark silver, and the mourning veil shortened or omitted altogether.

Donna Anna's aria "Non mi dir" is supposed to take place in her sitting room, thereby requiring a change of scenery for the sake of one aria, which always proves to be very awkward. One stage director had the brilliant idea of moving that scene to the graveyard, the place of action of the previous scene. Anna and Ottavio come here to put flowers on the Commandant's grave. In that case, Anna requires an additional sleeveless mantle over her gown, which she will wear again in the Epilogue.

Spanish Donna Elvira. (Velásquez, *Lady with a Fan.*)

DONNA ELVIRA

The character of Donna Elvira is also a study in hysteria, but sorrow and guilt feelings are not part of her emotional makeup. Although she seeks revenge for having been abandoned, she is at all times ready to forgive and forget. The obvious futility of her efforts makes her a truly pitiful figure. She is a noble lady, however, and always behaves like one.

The travelling costume of her first appearance consists of a Cavalier-type doublet with its lace collar and cuffs, a matching skirt and shoulder cape, a pair of gauntlets, and a female version of the plumed Cavalier hat. The brim of the hat is angled so that it conceals one side of her face entirely, which is the reason why Don Giovanni and Leporello do not recognize her. It is important, therefore, that these gentlemen are at that side of the stage where her brim is down. Olive-green velvet would be a suitable choice for this costume, which without cape and hat will serve very well for some of the ensuing scenes.

Donna Elvira's domino, like the others, is made out of a changeable fabric. A black and green combination is suggested for her. If Anna's petticoat is removed for that scene, so must Elvira's be.

In the second act Elvira is at her most vulnerable and requires a gown in a rich, warm color. An additional sleeveless mantle is suitable for the outdoor scenes. She will wear it again in the Epilogue, but not when she crashes Don Giovanni's dinner party.

A brimmed hat to mask Elvira's features. (Rubens, Portrait of the artist and his first wife, Isabella Brandt.)

ZERLINA

"I would and yet I wouldn't" is the theme song of this charming but vacillating creature. It almost comes as a surprise that when push comes to shove, she "wouldn't." If I were Don Giovanni, I would be terribly provoked, for she certainly indicated that a little roll in the hay with such a nobleman was well within the realm of possibility. To make that point, stage directors have ordered hay wagons to be constructed at enormous expense. The problem with this idea is that after the point has been made, there stands the damn hay wagon on the stage, getting in everybody's way.

Seventeenth-century peasant brides went to somewhat greater lengths to dress for the occasion than their prospective mates. Particularly among the Italian peasantry of that time, one finds examples of the heavily beribboned bodices we associate with fancy peasant wear. A light color to harmonize with that of Masetto's costume is the obvious choice here. Her skirt is a little shorter than ankle length and quite full. She wears a very fancy apron and a flowered headdress, which may also have a stand-up pleated ruffle if a Spanish touch is desired. It becomes a little tedious to see Zerlina in her bridal finery throughout the entire opera. She may either have a second costume, for which there is no very good motivation, or she may change her apron and headdress to simpler ones. That makes more sense. For "Vedrai carino" she may have an additional cape to put protectively over Masetto; she will wear it again in the Epilogue on her way home to have supper. When Anna and Elvira wear their mantles in that scene, and Zerlina her cape, it will establish a sense of finality: It's all over and everybody's goin' home.

A festive Zerlina. (Massimo Stanzioni, *Popolana con polle.*)

DONNA ANNA'S SERVANTS

It stands to reason that not only male servants responded to Donna Anna's cries in the opening scene, but a few of her maids also came rushing in. They too are in the process of getting into their

wedding costume for Zerlina.
mma Calderini, *Donna benestante Quarto Sant'Elena.*)

sober, Puritan-type costumes: dresses that, when complete, will have aprons, white collars and cuffs, and caps.

FEMALE PEASANTS

Modified versions of Zerlina's costume, including "Sunday-best" aprons and headdresses, should be worn by the female peasants.

FEMALE GUESTS AT THE PARTY

Variations of Elvira's second costume are right for the female partygoers. They may wear shoulder capes but no hats.

FEMALE GUESTS AT THE BANQUET

Some stage directors like to surround Don Giovanni on this occasion with a bevy of wenches, and some take this opportunity to bring the "catalogue" to life: a young one, an old one, a rich one, a poor one, a pretty one, an ugly one, a skinny one, and a fat one. I would be satisfied if they were all pretty, clad in casual but voluptuous dresses, with much exposed skin. Bare feet and loose hair will also attest to their equally loose morals. When Don Giovanni decided to go to hell with himself by inviting those girls over for the evening, he evidently did not realize that he was going to play with fire.

CHAPTER 9

DONIZETTI'S *Don Pasquale*

THE HISTORY OF *Don Pasquale* is not unknown. It bears repeating, however, for there is more to it than meets the eye. The plot is based on another opera that enjoyed popularity in its time: *Ser Marcantonio,* by the composer Stefano Pavesi to a libretto by Angelo Anneli. Donizetti assigned the writing of his text to a young man by the name of Giovanni Ruffini. He then proceeded to put so much pressure on his librettist to get the work done and subsequently changed so much of what the man had written, that the harassed young author refused to have his name connected with the final product. As a result the composer himself or other librettists were for a long time credited with the book of *Don Pasquale.*

In the earlier opera Tobia (Malatesta) has his own girlfriend, who is Medoro's (Ernesto's) sister. He also has a real sister, Bettina (Norina), with whom Medoro is in love and who becomes Ser Marcantonio's alleged bride.

By eliminating Malatesta's girlfriend and turning Ernesto's fiancée into Malatesta's "so-called" sister, Donizetti changed the complexion of the entire plot significantly and made Malatesta a much more complicated character. In spite of the enormous speed with which Donizetti composed the opera, one cannot escape the impression that the plot was very carefully thought out. What emerges is a study of the relationship between a young woman and three bachelors and their reactions to one another. It has much more serious undertones than a cursory examination might lead one to suspect. It is not enough to say that Malatesta has resolved to teach his longtime friend Don Pasquale a lesson because the old man has foolishly decided to get married, for in the process the good doctor manages to dupe his friends Norina and Ernesto as well. Somehow he never gets around to keeping his promise to Norina that he will let Ernesto in on the joke, which was her condition for participating in it in the first place. The whole situation makes a great deal more sense if one proceeds from the premise that Malatesta is also in love with Norina, which incidentally gives Malatesta's aria in praise of Sofronia a very different perspective as well. To Norina, however, Malatesta is just a good friend. She is in love with Ernesto, who is young and handsome; she might consider a man like Don Pasquale because he is rich, but she cannot think of Malatesta in any of those terms. The libretto, which states that Don Pasquale is in his seventies and that Norina and Ernesto are young, leaves us in the dark about Malatesta's age. All we learn about him is that he is "a man of experience, easygoing, enterprising, a physician, friend of Don Pasquale, and very good friend of Ernesto." Malatesta's music is never less than elegant. He was probably once the toast of Rome, the most eligible bachelor, adored by all women. But time takes its toll, and now he is no longer considered in that light. Like Don Alfonso in *Così fan tutte*, he is now coming to terms with this new situation and in the process takes, perhaps unwittingly, a little revenge. Malatesta is essentially a nice fellow who basically loves the friends he dupes. Once he has vented his spleen he leads the plot to a happy end.

Don Pasquale has been costumed in many different periods, from the eighteenth century to the flapper period, via everything in between. The music is best served by keeping the opera visually in the nineteenth century. One period that is particularly felicitous is late Empire, because it enables Don Pasquale and his household to remain ancien régime until Sofronia "does them over." That change, though spectacular, is fairly easily accomplished, even as far as the scenery is concerned. A drastic change from pre-Sofronial to post-Sofronial is essential to the plot of the opera.

If an opera has a small cast of principals and only one female part, it stands to reason that the choice of a suitable period for its setting will center on the question of what will be most becoming to the leading lady. If she happens not to look good in Empire gowns, the entire "ancien régime" idea may have to be scrapped in favor of a period whose styles are more flattering to, in this case, Norina.

There is no good reason to choose the eighteenth century for a setting, Charming though it always is, there are already enough operas that lay claim to that period with more justification. Besides the Empire style, the era of the 1840s, when the opera was written, seems a logical choice. It is an epoch that expresses the charm this work denotes, unlike the ensuing Second Empire fashions, which are too grandiose for *Don Pasquale.* The bustle period, which is next on the list, does not quite seem to have the right flavor for this opera, but should not be absolutely ruled out either. Turn-of-the-century fashions can be splendid for Norina, but they are quite dull for the men. The idea of the flapper era proves particularly jarring in the last scene, when the young lovers, looking for all the world as if they are going to dance the Charleston, sing instead the most romantic nineteenth-century Italian music of the entire opera.

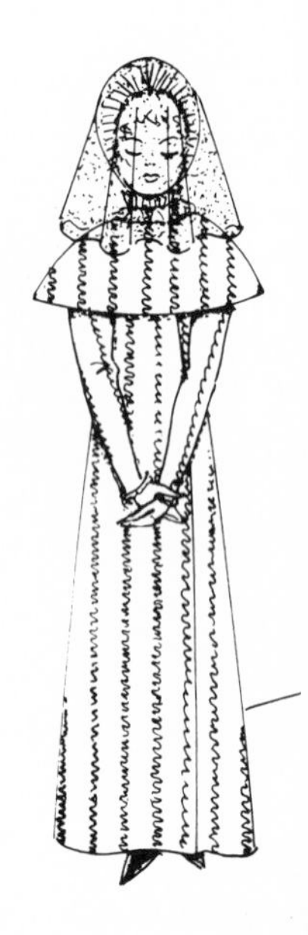

The preference from this quarter is the Empire period. A discourse on the costumes in that style should offer enough observations to suit those who favor a transfer to another period.

NORINA

Norina is a young widow, says the libretto, and although there may be no further significance to her status, it gives the costumer a chance to dress her in a "raffinée" negligee. It consists of a very low-cut black satin slip under a sheer black coat with long tight sleeves, which have the small Empire puff at the shoulder. The coat is made of black lace, point d'esprit, dotted organza, or another similar fabric. It is edged all around with a narrow box pleating, which is duplicated at the wrist. The coat closes right under the bust with a black velvet bow with long ends. Around her neck, Norina wears the Empire double box-pleated ruffle, also in black. She has a pair of elegant black mules or slippers.

The widow Norina in a "raffinée" mourning negligee.

Throughout the opera Norina's hair is dressed in typical Empire style, to which different hats or headdresses are added to suit the occasion.

The servant who hands her Ernesto's letter can just as easily be a maid. That will make it possible for Norina to summon her to carry in a selection of possible Sofronia outfits for Malatesta's approval. They must all be terribly wrong for the purpose, until at last he agrees to one of them. The situation is somewhat reminiscent of the Lisette-Prunier scene in Puccini's *La Rondine,* and it is one the audience will enjoy if the singers are having fun with it.

Norina should also have fun with her convent dress. Many operas are deadly serious, and there is a great deal of satisfaction to be de-

he transformation from Sofronia to Norina in four easy steps.

rived from producing and performing them, but *Don Pasquale* should be a joy for all those involved in it (which is no reason to take it less seriously, of course).

If one had the opportunity to see the other young women who receive their education at Sofronia's convent it would become evident that they are all dressed alike. Theirs is in fact a uniform, although not in the military sense. It should be the epitome of demureness, made of a medium-blue or light-grey fabric. In this case it is even better if it is a coat rather than a dress, for reasons that are nowhere stated in the libretto but that have proven to be a clever bit of staging. The coat has long sleeves, naturally, and a shoulder cape. Sofronia wears a demure bonnet with a face veil, which she consents to remove after much persuasion. But that is only the beginning, for the costume has been rigged so that she can remove separate elements from it one by one. Thereby she gradually unveils a daringly low-cut flaming red dress underneath. The "rigged" part of this operation is quite simple: the sleeves, instead of being set in the armhole, stop at the armpit, where they are held in place with elastic. The shoulder cape must be long enough to cover the missing part of the sleeve. After having lifted the face veil, Sofronia proceeds to remove the sleeves as if she were taking off a pair of long gloves. The shoulder cape is the next thing to go, disclosing the coat's sizable décolletage, which reveals a glimpse of the dress underneath and its short puffed sleeves. The coat itself, fastened only at one point under the bust, but with a sizable overlap to prevent premature exposure of the dress, comes off last, and there stands Sofronia, demure no longer but exceedingly desirable. The purpose of this little striptease is twofold. In the first place it will raise Don Pasquale's blood pressure a few units every time a little more bare skin becomes visible, but it also puts Sofronia in the appropriate attire right after the wedding ceremony, when her behavior no longer tolerates a demure convent dress. It is terribly important for the performer to practice how to remove these costume parts in a seductive manner, something that does not necessarily come naturally to everybody.

Norina's opera dress must be both striking and outrageous. It might be a gold-embroidered, sheer Empire gown under a jewel-toned, velvet, trailing court mantle, edged in fur. Accessories include long opera gloves with many diamond bracelets on top (the ultimate in vulgarity), a diamond necklace, chandelier earrings, and a tiara. The tiara must be trimmed with many plumes as well. According to the libretto, Norina also carries a fan.

When the court mantle, gloves, and all the other accoutrements are removed, the dress alone should be quite suitable for the last scene. Only a lace stole must be added, as protection against the evening breezes.

A "manteau de cour" for Sofronia's trip to the opera. (1814 fashion plate, d'après Horace Vernet.)

DON PASQUALE

It was noted earlier that Don Pasquale is in his seventies. Although he is a wealthy man, he has allowed his personal appearance, as well as that of his surroundings and his servants, to be neglected. Without any family there is no incentive, and people are apt to let things slide.

In the first act Don Pasquale wears a dressing gown and a smoking cap of ancien régime vintage. They were once of excellent quality but should have been replaced long ago. Underneath his smoking cap, his head is shaven bald. A bald wig with a little fringe of grey hair at the edge in back is more successful than a totally bald wig. With the dressing gown, he wears grey hose that are falling down, slippers, dark breeches, and an eighteenth-century shirt with a self fabric cravat tied loosely around his neck, its ends hanging.

To receive Sofronia, Don Pasquale gets all dressed up, and the difference from his previous costume must be spectacular. Yet he looks ridiculous, for several reasons: first of all, this outfit is no less ancien

A toque with plumes and an ermine-trimmed coat are nothing to sneeze at for the opera either.

All dressed up and nowhere to go: Don Pasquale in his wedding suit. (Alessandro Longhi, *Ritratto di Angelo Memmo.*)

régime, although it is very showy. Second, it no longer fits him. Don Pasquale has gained quite a bit of weight since he wore these clothes last, and he almost bursts out of them. Finally, the oddly assorted elements with which this outfit is put together do not match too well. He wears white hose now and his black, buckled shoes have red heels. His powdered wig sports a high pompadour. Judging from the way he struts around, he considers himself quite a peacock.

In the first scene of act 3, Don Pasquale wears the breeches he wore in act 1 under his dressing gown, but this time with a matching cutaway coat and a harmonizing vest. His grey hose are not falling down now, and his buckled shoes have no red heels. He wears a modest queue wig, and his jabot and cuff ruffles are subdued. His appearance must be in strong contrast with Norina's and that of his entire entourage. Toward the end of this scene, he is a pathetic and thoroughly humiliated man. In the final garden scene, a harmonizing cape and possibly a tricorn can be added to this costume.

ERNESTO

It is difficult not to accuse young Ernesto of wishy-washiness. A victim of his uncle's displeasure and subsequently of Dr. Malatesta's scheme, he immediately throws in the towel and is ready to give up without a struggle what he holds most dear. The thought of getting a job and earning his own living evidently never occurs to him. In that respect he is a true exponent of the romantic age, when suffering was considered a prerequisite of true living. If this were not a comic opera, he would surely have committed suicide.

A romantic, but wishy-washy, Ernesto.

Ernesto's behavior must then be accepted at face value, and he should be made to look as romantic and attractive as possible. It must show in his appearance that such mundane considerations as earning a living never enter his head. There should also be no doubt in the audience's mind that he and Norina are the only possible romantic combination.

The generation gap between uncle and nephew can be emphasized in the first act if Ernesto also appears in a dressing gown. His is a most romantic, latest Empire-style model, accented with a fashionably tasseled smoking cap atop his up-to-date hairdo. (As a means of achieving this hairstyle, the use of a pageboy wig put on backwards has proven most successful.) Under the dressing gown, Ernesto wears long pants or ankle tights. In the case of the latter, he also needs white socks and pumps. His neckwear must be equally stylish.

Ernesto's second-act costume can be nothing other than an equally romantic travelling suit, consisting of a light-colored, woolen tailor cutaway coat, with its large lapels and turnover stand-up collar, a long, lapelled vest, ankle tights, and boots. When he bursts in for the second time for "les Adieux," he carries in addition a voluminous triple-tiered travelling cape and the fashionable large-brimmed top hat with a conical crown.

For his rendezvous with Norina in the garden, he dons another romantic tailsuit to harmonize with her gown and a different voluminous cape, more romantic and less functional than the first one.

A more dashing Ernesto. (Ingres, *Portrait of Count Antoine Apponyi.*)

DR. MALATESTA

A good way to describe Dr. Malatesta might be to call him an "aging bon vivant." He is elegant, clever, and witty, but he must not compete visually with Ernesto.

In a recent production of *Don Pasquale* the part of Dr. Malatesta not only was performed by a young singer but also was acted as if he were a young man. The stage director attempted to solve the problem this created vis-à-vis the looks and desirability of Ernesto, who was played by a considerably older man, by giving Malatesta in his last-act costume a green carnation to wear in his lapel. In Edwardian England this was the insignia of some men who were amorously inclined toward members of their own sex. Oscar Wilde wore such a boutonniere, and Noel Coward wrote a song about it. So few people are familiar with this custom that it must be considered an inside joke without any theatrical validity. More important, however, there is nothing in Malatesta's lines, music, or stage directions that alludes to such inclinations. Whereas it is entirely within the realm of possibility that Dr. Malatesta (or Don Alfonso in *Così fan tutte*) is homosexual, it takes more than a stage director's guess to determine it and more than a green carnation to get the point across to the audience.

Since the last scene of *Don Pasquale* takes place in a garden, one may assume that the time of action is summer. Ergo, Dr. Malatesta does not require a topcoat upon arriving at Norina's or Don Pasquale's house. He should wear an elegant frock coat of a medium color, with lighter pants, a fancy lapelled vest, a fashionable stock, a top hat, and a cane. Although, strictly speaking, Malatesta could wear the same suit throughout the opera, it is visually more satisfying to give him a change of costume for the last scene: this time an elegant but subdued tailsuit with a matching top hat and large evening cape.

Dr. Malatesta, an aging bon vivant. (Ingres, *Portrait of M. Leblanc.*)

CARLO

Because Malatesta's cousin Carlo had to obtain a costume in order to disguise himself as a notary, it is theatrically most logical to

A long coat for Malatesta. (J. D. Court.)

see him appear in legal robes with a full-bottomed wig. Barring that, he should be in a late eighteenth-century black suit with a tye-bag wig and legal tabs.

NORINA'S MAID

Norina's maid, who would most likely be young and pert, in contrast to Don Pasquale's old servants, is dressed in a young and pert Empire maid's costume with apron and cap. The dress can be of a light, striped cotton with white accessories. Like her mistress, she wears a double box-pleated ruffle around her neck.

DON PASQUALE'S SERVANTS

To Norina's dismay, Don Pasquale has only three servants, one of whom she identifies as the majordomo. They are the only people in the opera for whom a "before-and-after" contrast is demonstrable. Their first- and second-act costumes must be thoroughly ancien régime. For theatrical purposes, they can look a little more down-in-the-mouth than Don Pasquale's financial situation would lead one to expect. Their costumes were at one time identical, but some haphazard replacements of breeches or vests, made as these items wore out, may have destroyed the uniform look. They wear dark, faded cloth cutaway coats with vests and breeches. There can be an unobtrusive trim of nonmetallic braid, applied in lackey-coat fashion. The majordomo has a contrasting vest similarly trimmed. They wear grey or beige hose and black, buckled shoes. If their hair is long enough, it can be pulled back and tied with a string. Otherwise they will have to wear wigs dressed in that manner.

In the third act the servants have been transformed and wear bright, showy, heavily gallooned lackey liveries. Jabots and cuff ruffles are now of lace, their hose are white, their wigs, white tye-bags. The majordomo has, besides a contrasting vest, gold aiguillettes on one shoulder.

SERVANTS HIRED BY NORINA

The libretto divides the servants engaged by Norina into "servants" and "maids," but it helps the stage picture considerably to invent many additional categories. Among the women there may be housekeepers, parlor maids, kitchen maids, and charwomen, while the men may include, besides lackeys, coachmen, grooms, cooks, and gardeners. There should never be less than two in each classification, and the members of each group should be dressed alike, lest they present

Various merchants.

an untidy-looking ensemble. The chorus must have a brand-new, spiffy, and stylish look. That is their raison d'être.

SUPERS

In addition to the singing chorus, the libretto lists "majordomos, milliners and wigmakers, who do not speak." That list can also be extended at will, atlhough one majordomo would seem sufficient in any household. There can be jewelers, dressmakers, milliners, merchants of all sorts, and even some workmen in the process of putting up new draperies, re-covering the walls, and upholstering the chairs. Oriental-rug sellers and assorted animal vendors are not to be sneezed at either. There should be quite a bustle of people at the opening of the third act. That a "wigmaker" emerges from Norina's room indicates that the original production may well have been set in the eighteenth century, for after that time wigs were no longer worn. He can simply be changed into a "hairdresser." These people should represent, as much as possible, caricatures of their trade. Without going overboard, the designer can have some fun here in type costuming.

A production of *Don Pasquale* must always have a great deal of style, and the costumer's contribution can be considerable here.

CHAPTER 10

TCHAIKOVSKY'S *Eugene Onegin*

A cynical Onegin.

It is interesting to contemplate what would have happened if Tatiana had been unable to resist Onegin's pleading and, following the dictates of her heart, had left her husband. We would have been faced with another "Anna Karenina" situation. The duel to which Vronsky challenges Karenin is another analogy between that novel and the opera. These similarities and the coincidence that Tolstoy finished writing his novel in 1877, the same year in which Tchaikovsky composed the opera, make one ponder the advisability of moving the time of action of *Onegin* to the 1870s as well. It would certainly bring the story and the music more closely together.

After giving serious consideration to the advantages of such a shift in time, however, one must conclude that *Onegin* had best be left in the period originally designated by the poet. The differences between Tolstoy's novel and the opera are far more pronounced than their similarities. Over the course of half a century, a significant change of moral climate occurred, bringing about the different solutions to the dilemmas cited above. A sense of honor compelled Tatiana to remain with her husband, despite her avowed affection for Onegin. But Anna Karenina could not bring herself to follow such a course. A sense of honor also obliged Onegin, against his inclinations, to fight a duel, the fatal outcome of which haunted him for the rest of his life. Fifty years later, however, Karenin could decline to pick up the gauntlet of Vronsky's challenge without compromising his honor. In a real-life situation, one might argue that such differences arise simply from diverse personalities. But in a poem or a novel that is so representative of the mores and customs of its time the events should not be moved from the period in which they originally occurred.

Vladimir Nabokov made a painstaking translation of Pushkin's "Eugene Onegin" and also wrote an exhaustive commentary, which was published in no less than four volumes. He even miraculously distilled from the verses a timetable of events, which puts the incidents in the poem between 1819 and 1825 and those in the opera between 1820 and 1825.

To the costumer of *Onegin* falls the important assignment of creating two ball scenes that are visually as different as possible from each other. The first ball is the one Mme. Larina gives to celebrate Tatiana's name day, and it has a distinctly provincial air about it. The second ball, which takes place in St. Petersburg several years later, is a most elegant and sophisticated affair.

A drastic change in the women's silhouette from the 1820s to the 1830s.

In order to accomplish this feat, it is advisable to shift the events in the opera to the period 1823–31, which happens to be the time Pushkin was occupied writing the poem. The fashion silhouette of women in particular changed sufficiently in the interim to make it possible to present a very different picture at the beginning and at the end of the opera (and therefore at the two balls). At the same time this shift enables Tatiana to evolve at some greater leisure from a shy and introspective maiden to the self-assured, elegant society lady. It is not something that happens overnight.

It is not sufficient that the difference between the two balls find expression in the women's costumes only, although they will be the most eye-catching. Men's fashions did not change as drastically between 1823 and 1831 as women's did, but through a few sleights of hand, which will be discussed in detail later on, the costumer will be able to convey the contrast between the two balls in the male attire as well. The term "sleight of hand" is used advisedly, for although a costume historian might frown on such tactics, these mild shifts of emphasis are entirely justified theatrically. Treated with discretion and good judgment, they can be adopted with impunity.

The exhibit of Russian costumes at the Costume Institute of the Metropolitan Museum of Art in New York in 1976–77 provided a grand opportunity to view the clothing of both high society and the peasantry through three centuries. The accompanying book, *In the Russian Style*, with its reports by foreign travellers to Russia, supplies a wealth of information about prevailing tastes and practices. Evi-

Mme. Larina, aged a little for theatrical effect.

dently Russia before the revolution was the "Texas" of Europe, where everyone tried to outdo his neighbor in ostentatious display. This preoccupation naturally influenced the sartorial arts.

The all-pervasiveness of fashion never ceases to astound the students of that phenomenon. Time and again there is evidence that it penetrated to the most remote regions, which one would assume totally beyond its sphere of influence. An emigrant from Russian ghetto life once related to me that she and her friends were at all times aware of, and wore for dress-up occasions, the latest Paris fashions. That the French fashion plates underwent some change at the hands of local tailors and dressmakers is no less demonstrable.

There is no reason to believe, therefore, that young provincials like Tatiana and Olga and their male and female neighbors were not fashionably dressed. Older people, however, tended to cling to fashions of days gone by, an inclination that lasted well into the first quarter of the twentieth century. It is appropriate, therefore, that at Mme. Larina's ball the older guests, of which there are enough to allot them their own music, have an old-fashioned air about them.

The ball in St. Petersburg in the third act must by contrast to Mme. Larina's be as fashionable, ostentatious, and grandiose as possible; truly "in the Russian style."

MME. LARINA

A woman like Mme. Larina, who married young and whose oldest daughter can be no more than eighteen years old, is probably in her late thirties. She may be aged a little for theatrical effect, but she is definitely not an old lady. She cannot possibly be more than forty-two years old.

Madame Larina's "mob-cap."

Among the very few costume references in Pushkin's poem is one made by Mme. Larina, who states that although she always dressed in the latest fashion when she was young, she now wears a "quilted dressing gown and a mobcap." These do seem the proper garments to wear while making jam on a portable stove in one's own garden. Larina is a widow and she would not appear in public except dressed in black, but in the informality of her own home she does not have to be in mourning. Her dressing gorwn is not a mere bathrobe, for she would not receive visitors clad that way. An eggplant-colored garment with black velvet trim and ecru lace edging would be suitable for her.

Her "mobcap" is not really that, although even Nabokov uses the term "faute de mieux" in his translation. In his commentary he explains that he means a gauffered and frilled headdress, "what the English call a bonnet." He could have gone one step further and added: "and what the Italians call a *cuffietta.*" In other words, a soft indoor bonnet like the one Rodolfo buys for Mimi. Mme. Larina's could be a little more substantial and matronly, made out of the same ecru lace that trims her dressing gown.

Long, sheer leg-o'-mutton sleeves over the short puffed ones.

Mme. Larina also wears an apron, for Olga reminds her to remove it before Lenski arrives. She does not wear it for decorative purposes but to protect her dressing gown from jam stains. It should be rather substantial, made of linen or cotton, with a few horizontal tucks near the hem.

At the party Mme. Larina wears a black silk gown of taffeta, moire, ottoman, or some fabric of that genre. Satin is too shiny and velvet too "chic" for her. It was fashionable then to wear over the gown's short puffed sleeves a long, sheer, leg-o'-mutton one. This style was popular for women of all ages but is particularly suitable for older ladies who do not want to expose their bare arms. For the old or demure the gown's frequently low neckline could be filled in with the same sheer fabric, gathered around the neck and ending in a multiple ruffle.

A more elaborate indoor bonnet than the one she wore in the first act may also be fashioned of sheer black fabric and be trimmed with bows and feathers. Her toilette should be finished with short, black lace mittens and a black lace stole.

FILIPIEVNA

Filipievna the nurse, a family retainer, should ideally be an ancient, fragile, almost transparent little woman. Various light-colored or faded cotton prints would be the right choice for her Russian folk costume. Over a floor-length, much petticoated skirt, she wears a three-quarter-length quilted jumper, a garment Nabokov refers to as a "body warmer." Further, she wears a high-necked, full- and long-sleeved peasant blouse, a sizable apron, and two kerchiefs—one tied over the forehead parallel to the eyebrows, the other tied under the chin the way babushkas are usually worn.

OLGA

Tatiana's younger sister, Olga, is sixteen years old, according to Nabokov, which is exactly the impression one gains from her music. The music and the text emphasize her girlishness, her joie de vivre, and, eventually, her flirtatiousness. These are not the characteristics one usually associates with a contralto, but that is how Tchaikovsky conceived her and one must endeavor to make Olga look as girlish as

Somewhere between these two is Filipievna, the family retainer.

)lga and Lenski, the fair-haired ouple.

she is described. Luckily, the fashions of the 1820s are quite helpful in that respect, with their prevailing taste for leaflike trimmings of self fabric at hem sleeves and décolletages creating an airy effect. A light silk fabric, possibly with a small flower motif, is a good choice for her first dress. When she goes for a stroll in the garden with Lenski, she can add a lightweight stole.

Olga, Tatiana, Lenski, and Onegin are constantly juxtaposed in the first act, and their costumes should be conceived as a unit, which does not necessarily imply that they match. Indeed, they may contrast quite sharply, so long as they do not clash. Tatiana and Olga might be opposites in character as well as in looks, but they get along well together, as do Onegin and Lenski. Olga and Lenski obviously harmonize and so, to a lesser degree, do Tatiana and Onegin. He is a loner, if not a misfit, who never really harmonizes with anyone. That he and Olga are not well matched must be quite evident in their second-act costumes. If such juxtapositions are carefully worked out within the overall design scheme, they can do much to aid the performers in their characterizations.

Olga's ballgown has the same characteristics as her first-act dress, with a little more emphasis on the flirtatiousness. A low-cut gown in a sheer fabric, trimmed with matching organza flowers, which can also be used as hair ornaments, will accomplish this feat. She can play flirtatiously with a small fan (they were in vogue then) as well as with a lacy stole.

A pensive Tatiana. (Samuel F. B. Morse, *Mrs. Daniel de Saussure Bacot [Eliza Ferguson].*)

TATIANA

To be the leading lady of an opera and at the same time be called upon to portray a shy and withdrawn young woman like Tatiana seems a contradiction in terms: the character wants to disappear but has to stand out. The solution to such a problem lies in making her look "strikingly simple." Therein must consist her appeal.

One could select for the fabric of her first gown a silk shantung in a light rust color. It should have a modest décolletage or a high neck and, besides the small shoulder puffs, long tight sleeves.

In keeping with her character, Tatiana's hair could be dressed in two or three braided loops at the temple, instead of the curls that were worn there by most women at that time.

The nightgown Tatiana wears in the Letter Scene should receive very careful consideration. The scene is long and emotional, makes demands on the performer's acting ability, and requires a great deal of concentration. If the audience does not quite remember what Tatiana wore in this scene, the designer can congratulate himself on a job well done. To earn such a compliment, he might select a soft, off-white fabric like batiste or a very fine wool muslin, cut the entire garment on the bias, and catch it with a ribbon under the bust, Empire style, but let the back hang loose from a yoke. The long sleeves have some fullness at the shoulder and at the wrist, where they are gathered into a small ruffle on the hand.

A slenderizing hairdo for a buxom Tatiana in her nightgown.

Regardless of whether or not a high neckline is unbecoming to the singer in question, Tatiana's nightgown cannot have a décolletage. If the singer has a short neck and a large bosom, the problem can be solved by letting her loose hair fall on either side of her face. This way the wide surface will be broken and a longer neck suggested. It is the hairdresser's or wigmaker's task to see to it that this seemingly loose hair is actually quite carefully controlled. Tatiana must not be compelled to have to brush the hair out of her face every two seconds. That would prove very distracting.

From Pushkin's poem we know that several days pass before Onegin responds to Tatiana's letter. She should wear a different dress now, as simple as the first one, maybe in a sage green this time. A shawl or stole could serve as symbolic protection of her vulnerability.

Tatiana's first ballgown is perforce more dressy than her previous gowns, but it should not be less simple. Velvet is the ideal choice

Tatiana's "framboise beret" (which does not denote "daytime").

Some decorations the Tsarina might have bestowed upon Tatiana, and some of the hats the other guests might wear to the ball.

here, for it spells "simple and dressy." The color does not have to be a bright one; a golden brown is appealing, combined with a gauzy stole with touches of gold and a simple gold necklace and hair ornament.

At the second ball Onegin asks about "the lady . . . in red . . . with the crimson beret" (or the raspberry beret, depending on which translation one reads). In this instance, we put our trust in Nabokov and settle for a "framboise beret." He discerns a subtle difference between "framboise" and raspberry," the former being more crimson red and the latter more purplish red. It is futile to belabor the point, for names given to colors are necessarily arbitrary.

In 1830 a "beret" was not the type of hat to which that term is applied today. Rather it was somewhere between a "toque," a "turban," and a "beret." Mr. Nabokov erroneously concludes that this must have been an afternoon party because of the mention of a hat. But hats of this sort were worn with evening gowns as well. Tatiana need not be the only person at the ball to wear one, but hers should be the only one in red. It will be just one of the accessories to a fabulous silver brocade gown, including an order sash with whatever decorations the Tsarina might bestow on the wife of one of her husband's favorite generals. A garniture of splendid rubies, long white gloves, and a small bespangled fan will all help give Tatiana an air of the gracious society lady she has become.

In her final meeting with Onegin, Tatiana relinquishes some of the acquired "grand-dame" image, and it is a measure of her inner poise that she can afford to do so. In which part of the palace this scene takes place is not entirely clear, but one may assume that it is in Tatiana's boudoir and hence that she is "en négligée." She could possibly wear a deep rose, fur-edged velvet dressing gown, which opens middle front to reveal a pale green chiffon morning dress underneath. Her hair should be fashionably but simply dressed, and any kind of lace headdress should be omitted, fashionable though they were at that time. In this scene Tatiana should somehow look more stately, young, and elegantly Russian than fashionably French.

Onegin wearing a "Bolivar."

ONEGIN

The costumer will want to set Eugene Onegin apart from the other male characters in the opera. The simplest way to do that would be to dress him in black throughout, but this solution is too facile and would give him too ominous a look. The "sleight of hand" referred to earlier can here be used to good advantage: let Onegin be the only man to wear matching coat and pants while all the other men wear colored tail- or frock coats with lighter pants in acts 1 and 2.

Onegin's suits are in the most somber colors: darkest brown and green, Oxford grey, and navy blue, depending on what fits with the total color scheme of a specific scene.

In his first visit to the Larin family, Onegin wears a frock coat with matching velvet collar and lapels, boots (if he is a tall man), a somewhat lighter vest, maybe of a cotton brocade, a silk stock, and the "Bolivar" hat Pushkin talks about.

To underscore the stern lecture Onegin delivers to Tatiana in response to her letter, he could be costumed in Oxford grey with black accessories for that Confrontation Scene.

In Pushkin's poem Onegin's behavior at the first ball is more clearly motivated than in the opera. Lenski led him to believe that they were going to attend a small family gathering at the Larins'. Instead it turned out to be a huge party with fifty people staying overnight. To make matters worse, most of the guests were all the neighbors Onegin had been trying so assiduously to avoid. No wonder he was furious with Lenski and decided to take revenge by flirting with Olga, who did not atttract him in the least. He could wear here a navy blue tailsuit, again with some velvet touches, and, to emphasize his outrageous behavior, a contrasting brocade vest and a silk stock.

A Russian shirt, ankle tights, and boots for the duel.

haunted Onegin.

Unwittingly, Onegin tries to sabotage the duel with Lenski; he oversleeps and has to get dressed in a hurry. Having failed to secure a proper second, he takes along his valet for that purpose. Accordingly, he could wear almost any old thing that happens to be handy, but that would not be in character and the audience would not get the idea. Instead Onegin should wear his Oxford-grey ankle tights with boots, a white Russian shirt under a very dark great coat with a fur shoulder cape, and a fur hat.

To warrant the comments occasioned by his presence and appearance at the St. Petersburg ball, Onegin should wear here a black tail-suit with a black brocade vest and a black stock. It is attire unorthodox enough for that time to set all the conservative tongues wagging. It is at the same time elegant enough and will accentuate the gaunt pallor of this haunted man.

For Onegin's hapless last meeting with Tatiana, the costumer should not hesitate to repeat the Oxford-grey frock suit Onegin wore four years earlier in the Confrontation Scene, for, in a way, this is a repeat performance with the principal roles reversed. If the audience perceives the symbolism, so much the better; if not, Onegin is still suitably dressed for the occasion, particularly if a full-length, black tiered cape has been added to his costume.

LENSKI

If Pushkin was considered the "Byron" of Russia, eighteen-year-old Lenski is the "Byron" of this opera. In the poem he is described as having "shoulder-length black curls," but in the opera Olga and Lenski come across more as the fair-haired couple and Tatiana and Onegin as the dark-haired one.

Like Onegin, Lenski makes his entrance in a frock coat of a light blue, perhaps, with light grey ankle tights, boots, and a plaid linen vest. To stress his poetic nature, he could wear an open-necked "Schiller collar" and a straw top hat.

At Tatiana's name-day party, Lenski must wear a colored tail-coat. Because he will become so emotional later on, it might be of claret-red velvet, with a brocade vest and fawn-colored pants.

A character's individual traits can be brought out only in subtle touches when a performer is clothed in something as stereotyped as a man's suit. In Lenski's case, for example, his stock should be draped more like an artist's flowing tie, so that he can look like a poet.

Lenski seems fairly fatalistic about the outcome of the duel: "Come what may, it is all for the best" is his attitude. A stage director might want him to look just the opposite from Onegin, something like the image of "slaughtered innocence." He wears boots, very light colored ankle tights, a white Russian shirt, an equally light long cape with a fur shoulder cape, and a fur hat. When he is shot he can clutch his chest and in so doing break a small plastic container with "stage blood," which he carries underneath his shirt. It will very effectively produce instant bloodstains.

MONSIEUR TRIQUET

The old French guest, Monsieur Triquet, whose couplets were considered by some contemporary critics the only worthwhile music in the entire opera, is a very old-fashioned gentleman. He would look well in a dark Empire-style cutaway coat, a flowery brocade vest, knee breeches, a lace jabot, and cuff ruffles. Pushkin endows him with a red wig and spectacles, to which rouged cheeks and a beauty spot might be added. In other words: an ancien régime fop, fussy and very French.

ZARETSKY

In our day, retired, discharged, and even off-duty military personnel can hardly wait to get out of their uniforms and appear in

ʼrince Gremin in "grande tenue" .nd a tiered cape for Onegin's last ʼisit.

ıssorted peasant headgear.

mufti. It was not always so. A uniform was considered a badge of honor, and a man retired from military service never ceased wearing it. Accordingly, Zaretsky, a retired officer and Lenski's second at the duel, should wear a long military greatcoat, boots, and a fur shako.

GUILLOT

Zaretsky, a stickler for protocol in dueling matters, is perfectly justified in taking offense when Onegin brings his French valet, Guillot, as his second to the duel. It was a most inappropriate choice. To bring home the point, Guillot might be costumed in a long livery topcoat with cloth leggings and a cockaded top hat. It is more the attire of a groom than that of a valet, but it is justified under the circumstances.

PRINCE GREMIN

At the hands of *Onegin* librettist Shilovsky, Prince Gremin has become a different man. Pushkin does not spend much time on him but identifies him just the same as a fat, imposing man in his early thirties. He is Onegin's kinsman and contemporary and recalls with him the pranks they shared. Furthermore, he is a general on active duty. In the opera he has become a grey-haired retired general who sings an aria about his devotion to his young wife. He wears a general's colored tailcoat (dark green was a color favored in Russian military uniforms), white pants with a gold stripe, epaulettes, an order sash, and all his decorations. He is in "grande tenue."

THE PEASANTS AT THE LARIN ESTATE

To dress the peasants who come to pay tribute to Mme. Larina, it is tempting to avail oneself of the rich heritage of Russian folk costume in all its colorful exuberance. Unfortunately, they are not in festival attire or even in their Sunday-best clothes. They have been toiling in the field and talk about being tired and footsore. They do not have to look drab, but neither is a riot of color indicated.

The women wear either high-necked, long-sleeved peasant blouses under jumpers of various lengths, or peplumed jackets and full skirts. A variety of kerchiefs, which were often draped over a stiff shape underneath, give the headdresses their contour. The men wear belted Russian shirts, bloomers of rough fabrics, and boots. Some may have loose sheepskin vests. They would carry any headgear (low-crowned soft pillboxes or puffed crowned visor caps).

The peasants at Larina's estate.

THE GUESTS AT MME. LARINA'S BALL

The older female guests wear dark-hued silk or velvet late-Empire gowns with long sleeves, or long sheer sleeves over the short puffed ones, and filled-in décolletages, as mentioned previously when Mme. Larina's ballgown was discussed. All wear soft indoor bonnets trimmed with ribbons and feathers. Many carry dressy stoles and shawls and short gloves or mittens.

Their male companions, some of whom may be in uniform, should all wear knee breeches; black for civilian wear, white with uniforms. The civilian coats are late-Empire cutaway or tailcoats with lapeled brocade vests. With the uniforms some powdered wigs may still be worn. All have gloves.

Among the younger male guests there is also a sprinkling of uniforms, for some officers from a nearby garrison town, including their captain, have been invited to the party. Their uniforms, without decorations except for the captain's, are dark green coats with white pants for infantry officers and white ankle tights and boots for the cavalry.

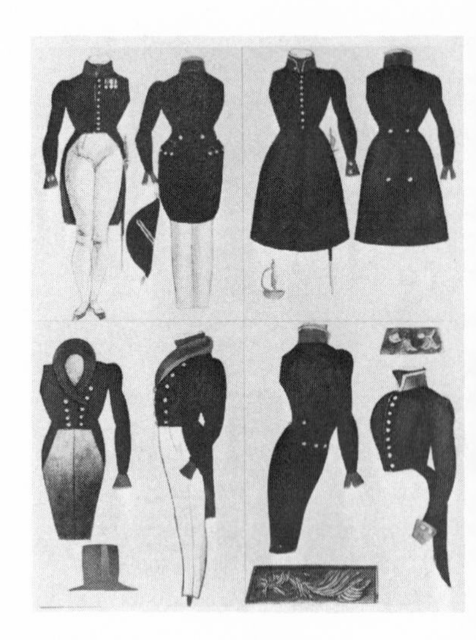

At Mme. Larina's ball: Some officers from the nearby garrison town . . .

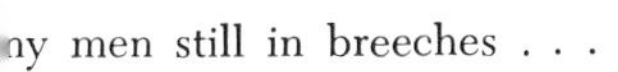

ny men still in breeches . . .

some older people . . .

ıng ladies in ballgowns . . .

ankle tights and dainty black pumps.

The atmosphere at Larina's ball.

The captain has some additional touches of red at his collar and cuffs. The other young men all dress in colored tailcoats with light pants, harmonizing brocaded vests, and stocks. Gloves for everybody.

Fashion plates of the period show that men frequently wore ankle tights without boots, revealing light-colored socks and dainty black pumps. On the opera stage this style is suitable for dancers and, once in a blue moon, for a singing actor with a great sense of style. Experience teaches that, in general, it is wise not to draw any undue attention to feet on the stage. For men, long pants, ankle tights with boots or leggings, or knee breeches are completely acceptable from the eighteenth century onward.

The young ladies will wear a variety of 1820 ballgowns in pastel shades, accessorized with short gloves, small fans, occasional stoles, hair ornaments, and a modest display of jewelry. Shoes are in neutral shades with the lowest possible heels, if any.

If it is deemed necessary to use servants at the Larin ball, it is suggested that they wear identical Russian blouses with black bloomers and boots.

Russian male attire and outerwear for different parts of the day.

THE GUESTS AT THE ST. PETERSBURG BALL

"The difference between the two balls must be as striking as possible," we observed at the beginning of this chapter. The change of silhouette in women's fashions from 1820 to 1830 is enormously helpful in this respect. The waistline, which remained under the bust throughout the Empire era and even beyond, was back to its normal place by 1830. The skirts, which had gradually attained an "A" shape, were now bouffant. It was an entirely "new look," and it is perfectly justifiable theatrically to stretch the duration of the opera's story a little in order to take advantage of a fashion development that will be so helpful to the visual aspect of the production.

Men's fashions had not undergone so drastic a change in those ten years as women's had. In order to achieve the look that is so important for differentiating between the two balls, it is necessary to resort to the sleight of hand earlier alluded to, namely banning the use of colored tailcoats for civilian evening wear and using instead black tailcoats with very light pants, brocade vests, and white stocks. Black tailcoats were already worn then, but not yet exclusively.

At the St. Petersburg ball: elegant uniforms from all branches of the service.

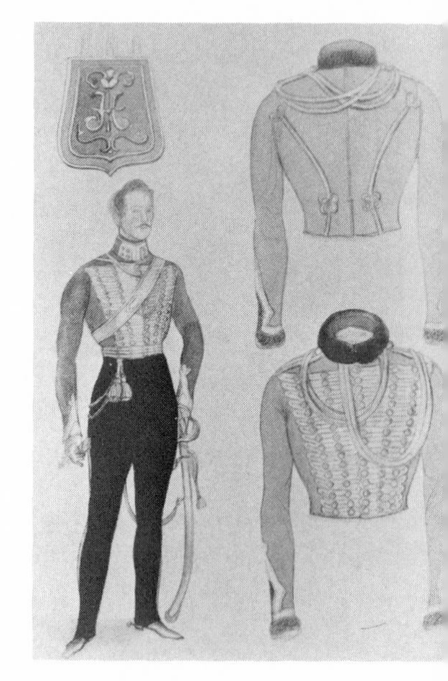

Older men will continue to wear knee breeches on formal occasions for a long time to come. Order sashes and other decorations do not have to be limited to those in uniform. The uniforms themselves run the gamut of the upper echelons of all the military branches, from heavily frogged hussar uniforms with their fur-edged slingcapes, through the attire of generals and admirals and the richly embroidered ambassadors' coats, like the one worn by the Spanish ambassador who is conversing with Tatiana.

The ladies vie in splendor with the gentlemen, but the Bolshoi Opera's idea of dressing them all in white does not seem appropriate. There is no denying its effectiveness, but it reduces a chorus of individual guests to a "chorus line." *Onegin* is too realistic an opera to permit such theatricalities. Brocaded gowns in the 1830 silhouette, in pastel colors for the younger women and darker shades for the older ones, are the right choice for this occasion. When the couples are carefully lined up as to color gradations for the various dances, the effect will still be striking.

There should be an abundant display of glittering jewels, and everyone will wear long opera gloves. Small fans with a certain amount of glitter were de rigueur, but the huge white ostrich fans the Bolshoi ladies sport are entirely out of period.

egant ballgowns for the women.

With the very typical 1830 hairdos a wide variety of hair ornaments made of flowers or feathers were worn, as well as some toque-like hats (mentioned earlier when Tatiana's "beret" was discussed).

There will undoubtedly be a number of liveried servants at such an affair. In that respect also, the Russians were apt to want to outdo the Joneses in a display of richly braided lackey uniforms worn with powdered wigs.

When all these diverse elements are joined together with taste, good judgment, and an equal understanding of the demands made by music and those made by theater, the result should represent the splendid event the occasion calls for.

CHAPTER *11*

GOUNOD'S
Faust

WHILE GOUNOD'S *Faust* takes place in sixteenth-century Germany, the music is unmistakably nineteenth-century French. This discrepancy between the aural and visual aspects of the opera has prompted many a producer of *Faust* in our day to move the action to a period that is closer to the time of its composition. Such sentiments can be appreciated so long as the text is also adjusted accordingly. Accommodations of that type are rarely made, and *Faust* is by no means the only opera to suffer this treatment. In the opera there is but one reference in the text to its sixteenth-century period: upon Mephisto's first appearance he says, "A sword at my side, a feather in my hat, a well-filled purse, a cloak over my shoulder; in short, a real gentleman."

A nineteenth-century English Mephisto. (After Richard Dadd's *Self-Conceit or Vanity.*)

In a recent French production of *Faust* initially mounted for a French audience, both Faust and Mephisto wore grey cutaway suits with matching top hats, as if they had just stepped from the Ascot Scene of *My Fair Lady*. Mephisto did look like a gentleman, but there was no sword, no feather in his hat, no visible purse, and no cloak over his shoulder, despite the fact that he sang about them without batting an eyelash. Producers, stage directors, and designers should not carelessly or contemptuously assume that audiences do not notice such oversights and do not care. A far more salutary solution to the problem would be to set the opera in its sixteenth-century period but base one's research on nineteenth-century French sources, such as Delacroix's illustrations for Goethe's *Faust*.

Librettos are not written for the benefit of designers, who in this case have to content themselves with the slender bit of information, "Time, Sixteenth Century." During those one hundred years, fashions evolved from late Renaissance via pre-Tudor to post-Elizabethan (to use some familiar English historical terms). The costumer might want to settle on a time somewhere in the middle of the sixteenth century so as to take judicious advantage of two styles, using the earlier one for the lower classes, who would naturally tend to lag behind in the matter of fashion, while allowing the wealthier citizens to get a little ahead of themselves in this best of all possible costume plots.

FAUST

The first thing to confront the costumer of the opera is Faust's instant transformation from an old alchemist-philosopher to a young lover. Occasionally two different singers are used for this role, in which case the problem is solved automatically. Most of the time, however, the old and the young Faust are sung by the same performer, and then the magical change has to take place right before the audience's eyes. Elements other than those that relate strictly to costume can help insure the success of this operation. Appropriate stage lighting is essential. In addition, a diversion may be created (one of the oldest tricks in the magician's bag) and Faust may retreat momentarily into a dark area.

The two costumes do not in themselves constitute a real hazard, if one may assume that the old Faust is *underdressed* as the young one. The philosopher's costume usually and correctly consists of a long, dark, ample gown with wide sleeves that must be open at the wrist and comfortably large armholes, which will facilitate easy removal. If the gown is furthermore lined in a smooth-faced fabric, it will not stick to the garment underneath. If the closing of the robe overlaps, bathrobe fashion, the singer will be able to divest himself of this garment in no time flat. Underneath it he wears the young Faust's costume, which has a pourpoint or a doublet with pumpkin hose. If Faust's legs are not too presentable, he may wear "pumpkin breeches" instead. The term "pumpkin breeches" is an invention of this writer. It refers to a combination of pumpkin hose with canions, a tubular extension covering the thighs that became popular in Elizabethan times. A short shoulder cape is in order, as well as tights and slipperlike shoes with a heel, made of fabric or leather.

The difficult part of the transformation lies in dealing with the headgear and wig, particularly if the young Faust also wears a wig. To wear one wig on top of another poses a problem, for the danger exists that in the attempt to remove one, both will come off. Luckily there are some pretty surefire methods of securing wigs short of nailing or gluing them on (the former being rough on the human skull and the latter being ruinous to the wig). If the singer has hair anywhere on his head, long enough to make a pin curl, the day is saved. The use of small hairpins for this purpose is to be preferred over bobby pins. After the wig has been positioned, it can be secured by sticking small hairpins through the wig into the pin curls. Then the wig can come off only by removing the hair pins or by pulling the performer's own hair out of his head. Some additional security may be obtained through the use of matching crepe hair. Once the artificial hair is glued to the temples with spirit gum, the wig can be pinned to it. A wig's close fit at the temples is very important. Now that we have secured young Faust's wig for eternity, it must come as something of a letdown to learn that it is actually better if the old Faust's hair is not a complete wig, but rather hair weft sewn into his hat. The little lecture on securing wigs may stand in good stead on many other occasions, however.

The type of hat favored for old Faust is the one familiar to us from the pictures of Erasmus of Rotterdam. As a matter of fact, there is nothing wrong with making old Faust look like Desiderius Erasmus, except that Faust needs in addition a beard and moustache to make the camouflage complete. His moustache should be wired to the beard, while the sideburns are sewn with a little piece of elastic to the inside of the hat's earflaps. The elastic must be very flexible so as not to restrain the singer's jaw action. Since no glue was used to secure either the beard or the moustache, the performer will be able to remove it all in one fell swoop by grabbing the bottom of the beard and pulling everything upward over his head,

Young Faust also needs a hat. Unfortunately, it is not possible to underdress that. Either the hat is hooked (or Velcroed) to his costume, so that he can put it on quickly or hold it in his hand, or it will have to wait for his next entrance.

Whether or not Faust should have any additional costumes depends entirely on the stage director's approach and on how much money there is available for such an extravagance. The idea of giving him different capes to wear with his basic costume, in order to convey different moods, is a very appealing alternative. For the Garden Scene he exchanges his short shoulder cape for a full-length, more romantic

Making old Faust look like Desiderius Erasmus. (Albrecht Dürer, *Erasmus of Rotterdam.*)

one. It will function again later in the opera. For the Death of Valentin Scene, a very dark cape is appropriate, but Faust should not carry a sword. It is theatrically much more effective if Mephisto forces his sword upon him, although that requires a slight adjustment in the text.

A toga-like drape added to his basic costume will supply the classical feeling needed for the Walpurgis Scene.

In the Prison Scene Faust wears again the "seduction cape" he wore in the Garden Scene. That is the way Marguerite remembers him.

MEPHISTO

No matter what technique is used to materialize Mephisto, once he is in evidence, he is in full attire. We have progressed past the stage of using the more obvious satanic attributes like an arrow-shaped tail, pointed ears, and a red skullcap that comes to a point over the nose and has a single feather sticking straight up in the air. It must be noted that at first Mephisto is not recognized as Satan. His behavior arouses suspicion, and it is soon determined that he is some kind of a sorcerer or even a demon, but no one realizes that he is the devil incarnate. He therefore should not look the part, at least not obviously so. He should be dressed, as he says, like "a real gentleman," predominantly in black with red accents. Since this is the period when slashed fabrics were so abundantly used, it would be a good idea to use black as the top fabric, slash it in all conceivable places, and let the red peek through the slashes. His black shoulder cape can be lined in red and have a fluted stand-up collar. Underneath his large black hat, which is also slashed in red and has red plumes, he can wear a red skullcap, cut with points in front of the ears. His "well-filled purse" hangs on loops from his belt, which also holds his sword. If Mephisto is a tall, slim man, his tights can be mi-parti: one leg red, the other one vertically striped in black and red. If his legs are not of the sort one would want to call attention to, both legs had better be black.

Very few opera companies ever have enough money to have period shoes made. If it is possible to find pump-type cloth slippers with heels, they can be suitably sprayed, dyed, slashed, etc. to be made to look like the real thing. Otherwise, a pair of rosettes sewn on an elastic loop that is slipped over the singer's own black shoes will have to suffice. A pair of black hip boots are also entirely suitable for Mephisto and can do wonders for camouflaging less shapely legs.

In the Garden Scene a long black cape lined in red, again with the fluted collar, is a welcome change. He can wear it with the red side out for the Walpurgis events. In the Church Scene he should look like a demonic monk in a dark, rough-textured, hooded cape.

Valentin and his fellow soldiers in "Landsknechten costumes."

VALENTIN

One way to make certain that Valentin does not get lost among the other soldiers is to move him up a few grades in rank. He is, after all, a leading character: he is the heroine's brother, and he was given an aria to sing, even if it was an afterthought. In the sixteenth century, Germany was not a unified country and consequently did not have a standing army. The rulers of its many states undoubtedly recruited some of the male population, by fair means or foul, to bear arms for them. Much of the fighting was done by professional soldiers, hirelings called "Landsknechten" (in French, transliterated into "Lansquenettes"). The Swiss provided the best hirelings. In the Dutch language the expression "No money, no Switzers!" still exists. (It is the equivalent of "no tickee, no washee.") In the costumes of the Landsknechten, the rage for slashed fabrics reached its height. There were no two alike, and the lack of symmetry in slashing different sections of the costumes made them odd, extravagant, and ostentatious, but quite attractive to behold.

Valentin is a square sort of fellow, and if the Landsknechten style is chosen for his costume, a modified version of it will have to be used. He should do well in a leather doublet with big slashed sleeves and breeches, a big hat with a slashed brim, a large, rough-textured cape, and boots.

The prop department has to provide Valentin with a "breakaway" sword. Through a somewhat intricate mechanism, his sword is rigged in such a way that its blade will break in two when a small lever is pulled. This gives Faust the opportunity to run him through. Another prop of Valentin's should not be forgotten: his "sainte médaille," which he wears on a chain around his neck and which he tears off when he curses Marguerite. The chain must therefore also be breakaway. He should not have to lift it over his head.

If the production is a realistic one, it makes sense to provide Valentin with a battle-worn reproduction of his costume, for his return from the wars.

SIEBEL

The part of Siebel is not so demanding vocally as to make it impossible to find a singer with both the right voice and the right boyish figure. Some of the people who cast operas are curiously unconcerned about or unaware of the appropriateness of a singer's looks for a given part and care only for vocal prowess. To be on the safe side, a costumer had better know how to deal with such a contingency. When carefully fitted, pumpkin breeches can do wonders to conceal female hips and thighs, particularly when worn with a matching doublet under an armhole cloak in a contrasting shade. Armhole cloaks may be a bit fussy for simple Siebel but will cover a multitude of sins.

A pair of tall boots may also add to the lad's manliness. A brimmed beret or a tapered pillbox hat will complete his costume.

WAGNER AND THE SOLDIERS' CHORUS

Wagner is a student, we are told, but in light of the dire future Mephisto reads in his palm, it makes more sense if, like Valentin, he too is a soldier, but a common, ordinary one.

While his attire is being discussed, we may as well occupy ourselves with the costumes of those fellows who will regale the audience in act 4 with the Soldiers' Chorus. It is no doubt the most nineteenth-century-sounding music of the entire score. It conjures up in the mind's eye a regiment of soldiers in frock-coated uniforms with shakos and long pants, as if they had just won a battle in the Franco-Prussian war. Such uniforms would, of course, not fit in an otherwise sixteenth-century setting. That soldiers' uniforms did not exist in sixteenth-cen-

Faust and Marguerite's first encounter.

tury Germany has already been discussed. In this case a compromise has to be reached by dressing the soldiers in identical sixteenth-century costumes, a cloth version of Valentin's maybe, without boots or cape. To distinguish Wagner from the others, he may be given an additional armhole cloak.

Marguerite at the spinning wheel. (Maerten van Heemskerck, *Portrait of Anna Codde, Wife of Pieter Bicker.*)

MARGUERITE

Before meeting Marguerite in person, her vision is seen. It is not absolutely necessary for the vision to be actually visible. Mephisto can point at something up in the wings somewhere, and Faust can wax ecstatic over that sight unseen. If the vision is a projection, however, care must be taken not to make it too specific a portrait of the singer engaged to perform in the opera. Singers have been known to have to cancel rather suddenly. The replacement could well be a colleague of vastly different proportions and even features, in which case the projection would have to be kissed goodbye. Disasters of this kind are amusing only in retrospect. Gounod uses the music of the Spinning-Wheel Song as background of the vision, which makes it imperative that Marguerite look the same in the vision and in the Spinning Scene.

It is curious to ponder why Mephisto picked Marguerite out of the crowd to be the foil for his evil design. She must have had a quality that made her different from the others. Indeed, her Roi de Thulé music gives that impression: she muses, she daydreams, she seems a little out of touch with reality. It is not easy to define such feelings in a costume, but an attempt has to be made. To give the fabric of her simple period gown a sheer overlay of a slightly different shade may be helpful. It will give her dress a faintly ethereal air, which makes it different from all the others. Like many dresses of that time the décolletage reveals the chemise underneath, which also shows in puffs at the shoulder and the elbow. Actually, the sleeves of the gown consist of an upper- and lower-arm section, which are loosely laced to each other, and to the dress, thereby allowing the chemise's long sleeves to protrude. It would be nice if Marguerite could wear a shawl over her dress on her walk from church via the kermess, but sixteenth-century ladies wore no shawls. Amazing though it may seem, shawls had not been invented yet. Capes and armhole cloaks were being worn in great profusion, and the choice for Marguerite's crossover is a lightweight hooded cape to complement her gown.

Marguerite usually wears a headdress or a coif, and her hair is plaited in one or two braids, as was the habit for unmarried women. One might want to go a step further and make her the only one with long hair. It will be an additional distinction that sets her apart.

A Marguerite with braids.

From the jewel casket that Mephisto deposits on her doorstep, Marguerite chooses three distinct items with which to adorn herself: earrings, a necklace, and a bracelet. These, as well as the other contents of the casket that may be visible to the audience, must have a definite period look about them and not be merely a bunch of junk jewelry, as is so often the case. The metal must be gold colored and the stones in jewel tones. No silver or platinum settings, no diamonds or rhinestones. Only French pictures of that period show women wearing earrings, and those were quite modest. For stage purposes a somewhat larger pair may be needed. Clip-on earrings are the most practical, if not the most secure. A thin rubber band around the earshell is safest. The audience must not realize how the earrings are put on. Putting on a necklace with a chain that has to pass underneath braids can have its hazard. It had better have a sizable hook and eye or a strip of Velcro for easy closing. Necklaces that can pass over the head are awkward and make the pendant fall too low. A jeweled pendant on a chain, or several chains, is most suitable, but pearls have such a subtle beauty that they do not carry across the footlights. A "clamp" bracelet, although historically not correct, works best in this case. Otherwise, it must either be large enough to pass over the hand or have a hinge and an easy-action clasp. The time spent to rehearse this scene to make it come off without a hitch should not be considered wasted. Embarrassing scenes have been witnessed in which something or everything went wrong, because of nerves (the Jewel Aria is only seconds away) and lack of preparation.

The Church Scene is sometimes set after the death of Valentin. In that way the curse first uttered by Valentin is then carried further by Mephisto, which gives the entire piece more dramatic cohesion. For Valentin's death and the Church Scene a dark, hooded cape is appropriate for Marguerite.

Realistically, Marguerite would wear in prison the now-ragged version of whatever she happened to be wearing when she was first taken there. Somehow, that does not seem to fit either the action or the feeling of this scene as it develops. A loose garment with wide, hanging sleeves, made of a homespun fabric and belted with a cord, is more suitable.

It seems a good idea if Faust protectively puts his cape over her. It will accidentally also serve in her forthcoming ascent to heaven. For that feat to come off, the cape has to be hooked surreptitiously to the back of each shoulder.

A dour Martha Schwerlein. (Tobias Stimmer, *Elsbeth Lochmann.* Detail of a double portrait, 1564.)

MARTHE

Dame Marthe Schwerlein, or Schwertlein, as her name is in the original, is what the Germans call "die komische Alte" of this opera (the comic old lady), and she is the only comic relief in the entire piece. She is a lusty old dame, not too upset by the unexpected announcement of her husband's death and immediately ready to take up with a new suitor. Her costume should be in a warm color: maroon or dark mauve. She wears a large apron, a full-length armhole cloak, and one of those matronly coifs that abounded in this period.

THE KERMESS SCENE

A kermess, or country fair, always brought all sorts of people from the surrounding countryside to the town to sell their wares. A circus or amusement park atmosphere prevailed, which attracted gypsies, jugglers, soothsayers, magicians, sideshow characters, pickpockets, and the customary assortment of unsavory characters. In other words, to use a tired phrase, people from all walks of life.

The "waltz," or rather peasant dance, has Breugelian overtones. The artist's paintings of feasting peasants are a good guide for the

The Kermess attracted men and women from all walks of life.

A Kermess with Bruegelian overtones. (Bruegel, *The Peasant Dance.*)

general look of this scene, particularly in their display of some bright color touches in an otherwise subdued palette. This makes it possible to create a cheerful-looking scene while avoiding a riot of color, which does not seem suitable here.

THE WOMEN

The padded roll around the hips is the one feature that, except in Spain, gives all sixteenth-century women's costumes a similar silhouette regardless of their social status. For the more affluent this style developed into the farthingale, while the simpler folk just gathered several skirts over those rolls. Rich ladies wore skirts to the floor, with a little train, but lower-class women showed their ankles and more. They all had the tendency to pick up the overskirt, revealing the one underneath, but for different reasons. The rich caught the overskirt with a cord or a chain and thus showed off a brocaded underskirt. Their poorer sisters did it to get the clumsy thing out of the way and gain more freedom for working. Sometimes the overskirt got tucked up all around like a peplum. Tight-fitting bodices occasionally had a pointed waistline, but more often they were straight. They presented a many-layered look with varying necklines, of which the top

Lower-class women showed their ankles. (From a pamphlet redrawn by Antony Formschneyder, Augsburg, 1540.)

layer was the lowest, while the bottom one often reached the neck. One of the layers invariably had long sleeves, which might be rolled up for working purposes. Women were rarely without head coverings, which took a great variety of forms.

Aprons worn by burgher ladies and their maids were long and seemed relatively narrow over the voluminous skirts. They were sometimes gathered at the waist, sometimes pleated, and sometimes pulled straight over the waist without any gathers, which produced a peculiar stuffed effect.

THE MEN

It is always easier to discover what rich people wore in times gone by, for they commissioned their portraits from the fashionable painters of their day, while the common man depended on those artists who were interested in depicting characters and local scenes. Since that sort of art was not very lucrative, it tended to be scarce. Although few pictures exist of the working man in his daily pursuits, enough of them remain to give us some idea of the clothing of laborers and middle-class citizens. They dressed essentially like their richer neighbors but used much coarser fabrics and omitted all the trimmings.

The slashed fabrics in particular, which were all the rage then, are seen on wealthy men, occasionally on artisans, and, oddly enough, on soldiers, who may have slashed their own fabrics. In expensive fabrics paintings reveals that those slashes were raw edged. A nervous man these slashes were prefabricated. A close examination of contemporary could always occupy himself by picking at his slashes.

The working man's doublets, pourpoints, and jackets were longer than those of the upper classes and showed very little of the pumpkin hose underneath.

Full-sleeved shirts, more or less closely gathered at the neck and wrists, were worn by all classes, but the quality of the fabric naturally varied with the wealth of the wearer. Shoulder capes and armhole cloaks were widely worn by everyone, the latter often trimmed or lined in fur. A great variety of beret-type hats were popular throughout the century.

Everybody sported hose and slipperlike shoes. Boots of varied lengths are also observed.

THE WALPURGISNACHT SCENE AND BALLET

The Walpurgisnacht Scene was always part of *Faust*, but the ballet was added much later in order to make the opera acceptable for l'Opéra, where such things were obligatory. The Walpurgisnacht music fits perfectly into the score, but the ballet has a totally different character. It might be wise to treat it as a separate entity.

The music of the scene reminds one of the weird creatures that inhabit the paintings of Hieronymus Bosch, which are recommended as a point of departure for the costumes. That means a lot of body stockings and leotards suggesting nudity, although dyed in odd colors and with grotesque extensions and headgear. For the mythological and classical characters that are mentioned, like Cleopatra and Helen of Troy, it is helpful if they can be identified by the audience despite an often crowded and dimly lit stage. Distinctive headdresses, easily recognizable as Egyptian or Greek, will achieve this. The rest of the costume can consist of a body stocking plus suitable drapery to adorn "the face that launched a thousand ships."

CHAPTER 12

STRAUSS'S *Die Fledermaus*

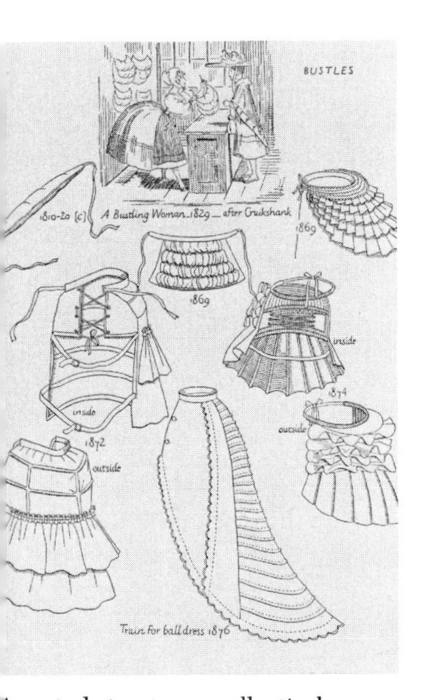

Assorted structures, collectively called "bustles," to give the amassed fabric some stability.

THE WORLD PREMIERE of *Die Fledermaus* took place in 1874, when ladies wore bustles, a fashion phenomenon that came about as follows: After the hoopskirts of the 1860s had reached their greatest volume, that mass of fabric gradually started to be pushed toward the back, where it was eventually gathered up in large, looped draperies, while the front was draped into the so-called swag. In order to give this amount of fabric some stability, it had to be supported underneath by pads, by petticoats that had a back panel of tiered ruffles, or by collapsible wire structures. Oddly enough, the result of all this drapery proved to be a very attractive and distinctive fashion, which maintained itself, through various mutations, for almost twenty years. It is ideally suited to the story and the music of *Die Fledermaus.* One has only to recall productions in which the time was advanced to 1890, 1910, and modern times, and this conviction is confirmed.

Those who have heard people rave about Max Reinhardt's production of *La Chauve-souris* in Paris in the 1930s have met this enthusiasm with some scepticism: Might not the passing of time have blurred their memory? Maybe so, yet, in his autobiography, the great fashion and stage designer Erté recalls Reinhardt's production with equal admiration. Mr. Reinhardt had the clever idea of mixing among the guests at Orlofsky's party dancers and singers in about even

Tipsy couples when it comes to the "Dui-Du" chorus.

The return of the "Watteau" back for negligees.

numbers, who had been trained to act like guests instead of like *dancers* and *singers*. As a result the audience never knew who was who, and there was almost constant dancing in the second act. Furthermore, Reinhardt borrowed from Meilhac and Halévy's play *Le Reveillon*, whence hails *Die Fledermaus*, the notion of preceding the ball at Orlofsky's with a supper there. In his staging this became a hilarious party with the guests eventually dancing on top of the dining-room table. When later in the opera it came to the "Dui-Du" chorus, couples were tipsily hanging around each other's necks in a slow whirl. When only the music dances, while the guests merely stand around the stage, as is so often the case, the audience is apt to respond to Orlofsky's repeated utterance, "I am so bored!" with the sigh, "Brother, you and me both!"

ACT I

The curtain rises on a room in the Von Eisenstein ménage, in the middle of the morning. Consequently, Rosalinde is seen for the first time in an elegant negligee. People of the 1870s believed that they were experiencing stylistically a second rococo period. In women's fashions this was noticeable in, among other things, the return of the

Maids' costumes also had bustles.

Replace the tennis racket with a feather duster for the perfect parlor-maid's attire.

Watteau back, but this time around the feature was applied mostly to negligees. These were ornate and elegant garments and just the right thing for Rosalinde on this occasion.

Maid's costumes also adopted the bustle silhouette, but otherwise remained quite simple. In keeping with their social status, they avoided the intricate draperies. The maid Adele, the only other important female character in *Die Fledermaus,* is not so simple as all that. In the first place she is a parlor maid and hence a few notches above the common servant. She has a sister who dances in the Opera-Ballet, and she also boasts a very sick aunt. In short, she is an important character and deserves to be costumed accordingly, while staying within her class. One way to accomplish this is to give her that simple maid's dress in a striped or dainty plaid silk fabric, with a calf-length skirt, three-quarter-length sleeves, and a "sweetheart" neckline. A tiny maid's cap and laced shoes are also in order, but the pièce de résistance is her white organdy bib apron, of which the skirt part has been draped into a swag, while the apron strings have blossomed forth to form a cascade of loops atop her bustle. In this way she remains a maid, but a chic and perky one.

Alfred, Rosalinde's would-be lover is, according to the original playbill, Orlofsky's singing teacher, not the man of means one might assume. He should look like our idea of a nineteenth-century Italian opera singer, in a short velvet cutaway jacket and a fancy vest. If his figure permits it, his pants may be in a harmonizing plaid. He should also have a flowing tie and an artist's broad-brimmed hat.

The same playbill tells us that Rosalinde's husband, Von Eisenstein, is a "rentier," a man of leisure, who lives off the income of his investments. To him money is no object. He wears an elegant three-piece suit. The coat may also be the short cutaway type that was so popular then. A variety of neck- and headgear is possible for him, depending on what is most becoming to the Eisenstein in question. His collar may be of the stand-up or turned-down genre, his necktie a four-in-hand or a bowtie, and his hat a low-crowned, soft-brimmed felt one, or what was later to become known as a "homburg." A top-coat is optional.

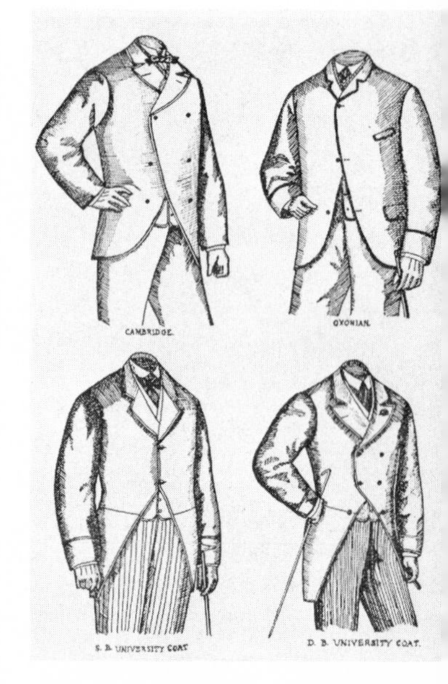

Various possibilities for Von Eisenstein's daytime-wear. (P. Cunnington and Cecil Everitt.)

Eisenstein's change into formal wear later in the act will constitute a considerable quick-change problem, which can be solved in the following manner: Instead of a shirt he wears a shirt front, to which collar and tie are attached. The collar opens in the middle back, where it overlaps and fastens with a snap or with Velcro. The shirt front is sewn into a backless vest, which in turn has been attached in front to the waistband of the pants. This procedure has rendered the fly opening of the pants unusable. Therefore the middle-back seam of the pants must be provided with a zipper closing. The shirt, collar, tie, vest, and pants of the tailsuit have been rigged in like fashion. In this way the quick change can be effected in a matter of seconds.

With formal wear, black vests were fashionable then. But they tend to make everybody look like a headwaiter. Traditional white evening vests are suggested instead.

When he leaves the house with Falke, Eisenstein wears with his evening suit an opera cape and a "chapeau claque" (opera hat). If time is lacking for him to change into his opera pumps, no one in the audience will be any the wiser so long as his daytime shoes are also black, and so long as he promises to change into his pumps at intermission.

Dr. Falke, a more formal dresser than Von Eisenstein. (Fashion plate.)

Dr. Falke, the "Batman" of this operetta, is a notary. This is a profession hardly known anymore in this country, except for the Notary Public, usually your friendly corner druggist, who, besides dispensing drugs for whatever ails you, will, for a quarter, also notarize any papers. In Europe, however, the notary's profession is closely allied with that of the lawyer. Ergo, Falke is a man of some substance and officialdom, and, accordingly, a more formal dresser than Eisenstein. With his dressy morning suit he can wear a top hat, maybe a topcoat, and spats. Sometimes Falke appears at Eisenstein's already in tails, as if he is all set to go to the party. That does not seem to make much sense, but if it is done anyway, his opera cape should be a substantial one. Falke has been known to perform quite a "bat" routine with that cape.

When Alfred puts in a second appearance, he will, by donning Eisenstein's dressing gown, convince Frank, the prison director, that he is the master of the house. If we have seen Eisenstein in the same garment earlier in the scene, this bit of business will be much more effective. It is entirely reasonable that Eisenstein would have decided to put on this leisure garment upon his return home. If Eisenstein and Alfred are of very disparate height and girth, the choice is either to make a virtue of the dressing gown's ill fit on Alfred or to use two identical dressing gowns, which may strain the budget unduly. Whatever the decision, the garment should be handsome and substantial, with quilted collar and cuffs, frog closings, and a sash with tassels; a matching quilted smoking cap, also with a tassel, tops it off. The short smoking jacket that is sometimes used instead is completely inappropriate here.

As mentioned previously, it is always a good costuming habit to differentiate as much as possible between various characters. It helps the performers in their characterizations, while preventing visual ennui. As far as Frank's costume is concerned, the Teutonic predilection for uniforms, even on civil servants, should be exploited by dressing him in a simple double-breasted uniform frock coat with matching pants and one of those typically Austrian shakos with a slightly conical crown. If he is accompanied by the two prison guards who will escort the criminal to jail, they should wear shorter, drabber, single-breasted versions of Frank's uniform.

For Alfred–Von Eisenstein, a dressing gown is better than a smoking jacket.

The role of Dr. Blind, the lawyer, is open to different interpretations. He may in his bumbling way affect some pretensions of officialness, in which case he would be properly clad in a black frock coat and top hat, or he can be more a shyster lawyer, in a long, loud, plaid inverness, with a pince-nez and a bowler hat. This kind of costume will also stand in good stead in the last act, when Eisenstein disguises himself as Blind. Naturally, he will require a complete suit under the inverness, lest he be left standing in his underwear on that occasion.

ACT II

A nasty habit has been sneaking up on us, namely the casting of a man in the part of Orlofsky, although Strauss intended it to be

A choice of approaches for Dr. Blind.

A blasé Orlofsky. (Orest Kipronsky, *Portrait of Evgraf Davydov.*)

"eine Hosenrolle." Whoever has seen the part interpreted by men and women must perforce reach the conclusion that Strauss was right in the first place. Only a woman can give this role of a very rich, blasé young show-off the charm it absolutely requires. Aside from that, it is so unsatisfying musically to have one more male voice in a cast that is already a bit top-heavy on that score. Orlofsky's part provides exactly the right amount of mezzo sound to establish a vocal balance.

For Orlofsky's costume a Hussar uniform can be very attractive, provided that the lady in question is not too hippy. Otherwise, one of those extravagant court costumes the Russian nobility was so fond of strutting around in on festive occasions will serve the purpose very well. Orlofsky certainly should not wear tails. Ivan, his personal servant, is usually dressed in a Russian blouse, bloomers, and boots, which is all right, so long as it is all high-class stuff. The Russians did not skimp on their servants' attire; it tended to be on the sumptuous side.

Adele (now Olga) arrives at Orlofsky's in a gown she "borrowed" from Rosalinde. It is important that at one point during the first act the audience see Adele with that gown, even if she only carries it over her arm in a quick stage crossing. In general one should be leery of bits of stage business that show the stage director's or designer's

A Hussar uniform for Orlofsky. (A general's uniform of the Life Guard Hussar Regiment.)

Adele in Rosalinde's doctored-up ballgown.

osalinde as a Hungarian countess.
\ *Lady of St. Petersburg.*)

brains at work, but with respect to Adele's gown, something has been devised that comes across to the audience very well: Adele intimates that Rosalinde's gown is not quite flashy enough for her parlor maid's taste. As she crosses the stage with Rosalinde's gown over her arm, she suddenly spots a lace tablecloth, grabs it, and exits. In act 2 that tablecloth will have been added to the gown, as a swag in front, while the ends have been looped up, thus making her bustle look even more bustley. This has the additional advantage of making Adele stand out from the crowd, not a bad idea for a leading character.

Ida (or Sally, as she is sometimes called), Adele's sister, must also be noticed in a minor sort of way. One might reflect upon the fact that she is a ballerina and carry elements of that into her ballgown as well.

Rosalinde must have played a Hungarian countess on a previous occasion; otherwise it is difficult to figure out where she dug up that outfit on such short notice. Luckily, audiences do not fret about these things but are content to accept them at face value. It is not easy to get worked up about the Hungarian costumes Rosalinde has displayed in various *Fledermaus* productions, the trouble being that there is rarely anything "Hungarian" about them. "What constitutes a 'Hungarian' costume?" one might well ask. Anything that the audience will

A sling-cape and a shako: the Hungarian touches used by Mlle. Hortènse Schneider.

An ample display of jewelry.

identify as such, although we must in this case regretfully eliminate all regional peasant wear. It should be a Magyar court costume of rich brocade or velvet, trimmed in fur with a court train. A sling cape and a fur shako with a feather stick-up also have a Hungarian feeling about them. Mlle. Hortense Schneider, a famous performer of Offenbach's time, did very well with them in her role in *La Grande Duchesse de Gerolstein.*

Rosalinde needs an elaborate mask, preferably something with feathers on it, and white gloves, which for evening wear at that time had progressed from the wrist-length version of the 1860s to halfway up the forearm. She is not the only one to wear gloves though. In act 2 everyone, regardless of gender, has a pair.

The ladies of the ensemble should be resplendent in an array of lovely bustle ballgowns, in pastel shades. Some fans may dangle from their wrists, there is an ample display of jewelry, and there are dainty arrangements of flowers and feathers in their hair.

A word must be said about women's hairstyles of that period, which complement the dress fashions to such an extraordinary degree. They seem to have bustles all their own. With all the curls, puffs, and braids that were piled on, it is quite evident that a lot of postiches must have been used that match the wearer's own hair color. This

An array of bustle ballgowns. (Fashion plate.)

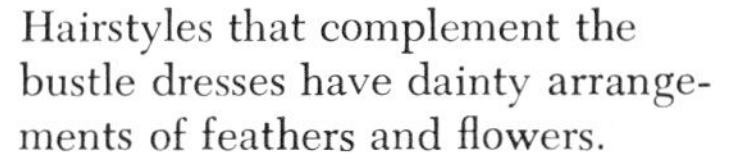

Hairstyles that complement the bustle dresses have dainty arrangements of feathers and flowers.

A few men in uniform to brighten things up.

practice should be emulated in trying to re-create these hairstyles. It is much more difficult to do than using wigs, but at its best it is much more successful.

Eisenstein, who is now "Marquis Renard," Frank (Chevalier Chagrin), Falke, and the bulk of the chorus wear evening tailsuits. These differed somewhat from our modern evening wear, in cut as well as in the style of their accessories. Eisenstein and Frank might sport some decorations in keeping with their appropriated titles, and, as usual at such parties, a few men in uniform will tend to brighten things up a bit. Orlofsky can be expected to have some smartly liveried servants around the house.

The aforementioned original playbill of the *Fledermaus* premiere lists among the male chorus a number of individual guests: an Egyptian (he should wear a fez with his tails), an American (obviously with a ten-gallon hat, cowboy boots, and a string tie), a "functionary from the embassy" (he might just as well be promoted to full ambassador and be dressed accordingly), an English lord (the jeweled garter of the Order of the Garter and black satin knee breeches are obligatory for him), an Italian marquis (a Garibaldi shirt will look cute on him), and a German baron (he can sport a Bavarian jacket). All these local touches add to or partially substitute for their tailsuits.

The original ballet in this act was a sort of United Nations, consisting of representative national dances in the following order: Spanish, Scottish, Russian, Polish, and Hungarian. Here the costumer can amuse himself by producing native costumes of the respective countries, but with an 1874 silhouette.

Often other dance music from Strauss's prodigious output is used instead. Whatever the choice, the ballet costumes must be in the period of the rest of the opera. This may seem an obvious and redundant observation, but it is exactly in this area where productions often lose all sense of homogeneity.

Distinctive evening wraps of the bustle period.

ACT III

This act make few new demands in respect to costumes. Frosch, the drunken jailkeeper, wears the uniform already described in act 1 for Frank's assistants, except that Frosch's should be in considerable disarray, owing to his besotted condition. A large keyring with some oversized keys may be dangling from his belt.

Adele, Ida, and all the other ladies now have complementary outer wraps over their ballgowns. Evening wraps of that period are very distinctive: they are half cape, half jacket, and longer in front than in back in order to accommodate the bustle.

At times Rosalinde appears in this act in a street dress with a hat, which implies that she went home and changed. Whatever the reasoning may be behind this, it does not make much sense. Rosalinde should also be in an evening wrap, but one of more substance than the others.

CHAPTER 13

MOZART'S

Le Nozze di Figaro

the Count had found Cheru-
no . . . (Gravelot, Illustration
ur *La Prude*.)

FOR ANYONE WHO is curious to know how the first performance of Mozart's *Figaro* was costumed, I have sad news: no one seems to know. We are familiar with the names of the singers who performed the principal parts, and, from their many portraits, we know what they looked like, but there is no record of how they were costumed for their roles in the opera. Even Michael Kelly, the first Basilio–Don Curzio, who in his memoirs reminisces about that first performance, makes no mention of costumes, not even his own.

Although this is regrettable it should not come as a surprise. The premiere of an opera based on a popular contemporary play, which required costumes that were neither very lavish nor unusual, would hardly stir the chroniclers ino a frenzy of costume reportage, nor would it prompt the singers to want to pose in costume before the fashionable painters of their day. In Mozart's voluminous correspondence there is no reference to the visual aspects of his operas. He evidently gave the matter no thought.

Luckily, Beaumarchais, the author of the play from which da Ponte so deftly distilled the libretto for the opera, was very much concerned with the looks of his plays, so much so that he prefaced *The Barber of Seville* as well as *The Marriage of Figaro* with a character-by-character costume description. Then as now, it was an un-

The styles advocated by Beaumarchais for his play, as depicted in the gravure after Van Loo's *Conversation Espagnole*.

usual thing for a playwright to do, and there is no evidence that he persuaded the actors in his plays to follow his suggestions, not even the members of his own troupe.

Beaumarchais advocated for his plays costumes in "the old Spanish style," and he gives us a very good clue of what he means by pointing out that an engraving called "Conversation Espagnole," after a painting by Carle Van Loo, is exactly what the Countess-Susanna-Cherubino scene (in the opera, act 2, Cherubino's aria) should look like. The costumes depicted in this engraving are used in many eighteenth-century historical presentations. They are a mixture of seventeenth-century styles, seen through eighteenth-century eyes. There is nothing particularly Spanish about them from our point of view. We have a very different notion of a "Spanish" look.

For the court audience to whom the play was presented, the subject matter of *Figaro* was a little too close for comfort, dealing as it did with the revolt of the lower classes against the nobility. That may have prompted Beaumarchais to move the action back in time somewhat. Illustrations of contemporary editions of the play by such famous illustrators as St. Quentin and Chodowiecki, as well as pictures of the actors in costume, show the men in some sort of seventeenth-century dress but the women costumed entirely in the fashionable

'ashionable dress for the women, watered-down seventeenth-century tyles for the men. (Chodowiecki's llustrations for Beaumarchais's *'igaro.*)

dress of the day, with only an occasional Medici collar thrown in for good measure.

In our day the eighteenth century is pretty much accepted as the appropriate setting for *Figaro*, but maybe this period should be questioned. There is so much talk in this play (and in the opera no less) about "Le Droit du Seigneur" that one might consider setting the opera in the time when this feudal law held sway. When the play was written, however, this medieval convention had been out of practice for about 150 years. First it was converted into a tax and then it disappeared completely. Beaumarchais used it merely as a device to strengthen his plot. The need to put the action back in time in order not to shock the audience no longer exists. That leaves the option of costuming the opera in modern dress. There are some compelling arguments in its favor: it was done so in Mozart's own time, and for a long while thereafter the costumes merely changed with the prevailing fashions of the day. Transposed to modern times, the story might be more relevant to young audiences. And does not Mozart's music transcend all time? Arguments against such a move have more validity, however. The conflict of the master-servant relationship, which dominates the plot of the opera, has no relevance today. Figaro won that battle long ago. Nor do some of the eighteenth-century theatrical conventions come off very well in modern dress. How does a pageboy of the Cherubino variety fit into a modern setting, and how appealing would he look in knickers or short pants? There is also the eighteenth-century predilection for situations involving mistaken identity. Even when such episodes are set in a period framework, they are hard for modern audiences to accept, and they tax the ingenuity of our stage directors. In modern dress these intricacies would become entirely implausible.

The late eighteenth century of Louis XVI is particularly suitable for Mozart's *Figaro*. It is a time when the rumblings of revolt are clearly discernible, as they are in the play and in the opera. It is a period, furthermore, that is close to composer, librettist, and playwright alike. Because it affords such a variety of dress among persons from different walks of life, it is eminently suited to point up the situations as they arise in the opera.

The locale of the opera is "three leagues from Seville," and the town is frequently mentioned in the text. The costumes must therefore have their Spanish flavor, although there is little Spanish music in the opera. The best source for Spanish costume styles of that period is no doubt the painter Goya, who in his various oeuvres, but particularly his tapestry designs, depicted men and women of all strata of society.

Members of the upper classes wore pretty much the prevailing

European fashions. National characteristics found expression mostly in hairstyles and headdresses, particularly for women. For the middle classes, servants, and peasants, the rule is: the lower the social rung, the more regional the costume.

The Marriage of Figaro is a long opera and benefits from as many visual changes as can be reasonably applied. Each act takes place at a different time of the day, which is a great help in this respect. Wherever it is in character, the singers should be suitably attired for *the morning* in act 1, *the early afternoon* in act 2, *the late afternoon* in act 3, and *the evening* in act 4.

SUSANNA

> BEAUMARCHAIS: Her costume in the first four acts is a very chic white bodice with a short peplum and skirt, and a toque [since then named "à la Susanne" by our milliners]. In the festivities of the fourth act the Count puts on her head a toque with a long veil. In the fifth act she wears the long ample dress of the Countess and no headdress.

Susanna is one of the most important characters in the opera. She does more singing and spends more time on stage than anyone else. It would become tedious, therefore, to see her in the same costume throughout three acts. In keeping with the early hour and the informal nature of act 1, I like Susanna to be somewhat "en négligée," in a corset bodice, an underskirt, a short bed jacket, and a dainty version of a mobcap. Skirt, jacket, and cap are in white by the very fact that they are underwear, but the corset can be of a pastel shade.

The "hat" Susanna is trying on in front of the dressing table is not a hat at all. The sprig of orange blossoms that brides attached to whatever headgear they might be wearing was then referred to as "chapeau de la mariée" a term that Figaro abbreviates to "chapeau" and that da Ponte, who evidently was not familiar with the custom, translated into "capello." What Susanna needs, then, is a small bridal wreath made up of orange blossoms and tulle. The bridal veil is attached to that; for a chambermaid I prefer a hip-length veil to the long one Beaumarchais talks about. Neither here nor at the moment in act 3 when the Count puts the veil on Susanna is it necessary for her to remove the cap she is wearing. "Mobcaps" in all their many variations were worn constantly, and by women of all standings, as a regular part of dress. Additional headgear was simply superimposed. In Susanna's case I would like to establish the cap, in conjunction with an apron, as her "chambermaid" trademark. She should never be without these two items, except when she is disguised as the countess.

A sprig of orange blossoms attached to her cap constituted Susanna's "chapeau de la mariée." (Hippolyte Lecomte, *Costume de Suzanne dans le mariage de Figaro.*)

A polonaise for Susanna.

A baigneuse. (M. A. Parette, *Provoking Fidelity.*)

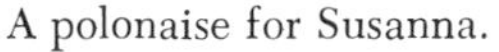

Susanna's first exit in act 1 is in response to the Countess's bell. She would not attend milady in her underwear, and when she returns we see that she has put a polonaise on over the underskirt and corset and added an apron. The skirt part of the polonaise was tucked up by tapes inside (the English term for the garment consequently was "tuck-up"), and it was open in front to reveal the stomacher part of her corset. She keeps this costume throughout the second act and part of the third.

When Susanna makes her second entrance in act 1, she carries two prop-costume items: a lace cap with a separate ribbon and a dress. The lace cap is the Countess's. It is a baigneuse (originally a bathing cap, as the name implies), an elaborate lace affair. The ribbon is to be laced through it. The ribbon is important, because Cherubino steals it away from Susanna and produces it again in the second act. To whom the dress belongs is not made clear, but my preference is for it to be a prop copy of the dress the countess has chosen to wear to attend the wedding of her chambermaid. Susanna has taken it to press it or probably to sew a stitch or two. It is also a very good idea to use this dress as a cover for the hiding Cherubino. It somehow implies that Cherubino is hiding from the Count under the Countess's skirts, a bit of symbolism that appeals to me.

If the audience gets it, *tant mieux*. If not, there is no harm done.

One would like to see a bride in her wedding dress for the first time at the actual ceremony, particularly in *Figaro*, where so much suspense has been built up concerning the possibility of the event's never materializing. Alas, the construction of the third act does not make that possible. Scenically the situation is awkward enough, when, after the relative intimacy of the Letter Duet and the Flower Chorus, with the ensuing denouement of Cherubino's disguise, a sort of ceremonial room has to be produced for the wedding ceremony. The drawing of some drapes usually accomplishes that feat satisfactorily, but one cannot drop a wedding dress on Susanna from the flies, "deus ex machina" fashion. She has to change into her wedding dress right after the sextet, when it is apparent that the Count's efforts to prevent the wedding have been successfully foiled. Only the wedding veil will be added at the ceremony.

The apron as a fashion item.

Although the custom of dressing brides in white did not develop until the third quarter of the nineteenth century, I propose to follow Beaumarchais's suggestion and grant Susanna this symbol of virtue and purity she so richly deserves. Modern audiences expect a bride to be in white. By making this concession to contemporary custom, one furthermore avoids the sin, discussed at some length in my introduction, of devising a situation that necessitates adding footnotes of a costume-historic nature to the program.

Susanna need not be without her trademarks, the cap and apron, when she is in her wedding gown. Like caps, aprons then were not simply utility items; on the contrary, they were considered articles of great luxury. Many museum collections preserve precious examples of this eighteenth-century fashion.

In the last act, when shadowy figures slip in and out of pavilions in semidarkness, it is often difficult to determine who is who on the stage. When, in addition, the Countess and Susanna are draped in voluminous dominos, as is the custom, confusion reigns supreme. It is very important that the audience know who is the Countess and who is Susanna, even when they are disguised as one another. There is a foolproof way of establishing their identities. In the last act Susanna and the Countess should wear very similar, but not identical, summer evening dresses. With her costume, the Countess wears a lace mantilla (without comb) and a fan; whereas with hers, Susanna wears her trademarks, the cap and apron. Directly after Susanna's aria these accessories are exchanged in full view of the audience. In that way everybody knows who is who. There is not much time to effect this exchange, but it can be accomplished in a matter of seconds and it is eminently worthwhile. The place where the exchange

Susanna in a summer evening gown Act 4. (Hippolyte Lecomte, *Mme. Dugazon dans le role de Nina.*)

has to take place is clearly indicated, since throughout Susanna's aria Figaro observes her and recognizes her as his bride, while shortly thereafter he mistakes her for the Countess. It is a curious oversight on Beaumarchais's part that he wants the Countess and Susanna in each other's costumes at the beginning of the act, which makes no sense. On occasion one actually sees the Countess and Susanna in each other's clothes, with the result that the Countess forgives her husband in Susanna's costume, which I find unforgivable. In the unhappy event that the Countess and Susanna are of very different stature, it may be necessary to resort to the use of dominos of sharply contrasting hues.

THE COUNTESS

> BEAUMARCHAIS: She is dressed in the first, second, and fourth acts in a comfortable negligee and without hair ornament. She is supposed to be indisposed and keeps to her room. In the fifth act she wears Susanna's dress and high hairdo.

In the opera there is no mention of the Countess's alleged indisposition, but, being a noble lady, she is entitled to be one act behind the others in dress, remaining "en déshabillé" for a considerable time, as was the wont of elegant ladies and gentlemen of that day. Their clothes were elegant but cumbersome; the daily hairdressing was so involved that they could hardly be blamed for wanting to remain comfortable as long as possible. That many a nobleman had his portrait painted wearing a dressing gown, with only a day cap to cover his clean-shaven head, attests to the social acceptability of this kind of undress. The Countess's "comfortable negligee" Beaumarchais talks about is just that. Basically it is a very ample floor-length chemise, open middle front, with a drawstring neckline, the forerunner of the "robe à la française," when the fullness started to be pushed backward and arranged into the plis Watteau. It has sleeves, can be decorated as elegantly as one likes, and is worn over an elegant corset-bodice and no less elegant flounced underskirt. Beaumarchais notwithstanding, I would not hesitate to give the Countess some kind of head covering with her negligee. Women were rarely without one then. It could be another baigneuse like the one Susanna carried in act 1.

negligee for the Countess.

Although only three years have elapsed since she married her "Lindoro," there is a world of difference between the gay and fun-loving Rosina of the *Barber of Seville* and the sad and serious Countess of the *Marriage of Figaro*. This change must also be reflected in her costumes.

To participate in the festivities connected with the marriage of her chambermaid, the Countess should be elegantly gowned, but not so formally as for a state occasion. She already wears this dress upon her first appearance in act 3, to put, as it were, her stamp of approval on the wedding plans. The Count, on the other hand, puts off dressing for the occasion as long as possible. He does his utmost to prevent this wedding from ever happening, so why dress for it?

From the dress that covered Cherubino in act 1, we were able to see that the Countess was going to wear a beautiful brocaded robe, consisting of a bodice with elbow-length sleeves and a very full skirt. Both bodice and skirt were open middle front, revealing a richly decorated stomacher in the bodice section and an underskirt of an identical or harmonizing fabric. If the back of the bodice continued downward in the stately plis Watteau, it was a "robe à la française"; if not it would have been a "robe à l'anglaise." The sleeves would have ended in that most flattering trimming: three tiers of scalloped lace, called "engageantes."

A "robe à l'Anglaise" for the Countess. (Antonio Rafael Mengs, *Queen Marie Louise of Parma.*)

It is no coincidence that a pin is referred to in this opera on several occasions: Susanna seals the rendezvous note with a pin, which the Countess pulled from her dress. The Count pricks his finger on the pin and sings about it; Figaro notices the incident and remarks about it to Susanna. Barbarina, who is supposed to return the pin to Susanna, loses it and sings an aria about it, while Figaro replaces the lost pin with one he pulls from Marcellina's gown.

To be talked and sung about as often as that, a pin surely must have been a prominent accessory to women's dress of that day, as indeed it was. The aforementioned stomacher was pinned to the corset. The bodice of the robe was in turn pinned onto the stomacher. Skirts over paniers, robes over skirts, fichus, hats, and bonnets—a lot of items had to be prevented from shifting around, and they were all held in place by pins. Until fairly recently the use of pins for such purposes could be observed in nuns' habits.

The spectacular and flattering high white wig of this period is a suitable finishing touch for the Countess's third-act costume. In keeping with the character and the mood of the wearer, as well as the intimacy of the occasion, it should not be overloaded with feathers or strings of pearls (not to mention bonnets or hats), as it sometimes was.

As discussed previously, her last-act dress is a light, summer evening gown, similar to Susanna's, with a lace fan and a mantilla in lieu of the baigneuse.

The flattering high wig. (Portrait présumé de la Princesse de Lamballe.)

rcellina in a caraco.

ry Spanish Marcellina. (Ignacio
ia Barreda, *Donna Maria*
ero.)

MARCELLINA

BEAUMARCHAIS: Her dress is that of a Spanish Duenna, of modest color, a black bonnet on her head.

In a sense, Marcellina is one of the most interesting characters in the opera, for she shows *character development*, something quite unheard of in the theater of the eighteenth century. At first a bitter and aggressive old maid, she becomes a wise, contented, and understanding matron. One would expect such a drastic change to be expressed in her costumes as well, but the only Marcellinas I have ever seen receive their due costumewise were the ones I have costumed.

Since she claims to be of noble birth and lives in the castle, she might as well usurp some of the privileges of nobility and appear in the first act in a negligee. Only in her case, everything should be a bit overdone and hence look comical. Her "robe de chambre" is twice as ample as the Countess's and her baigneuse three times as high. There are too many frills and ribbons everywhere. She wears too much rouge and too many beauty spots. She is making a fool of herself, and it should show.

In acts 2 and 3 I like her in a caraco, that peculiar eighteenth-century garment that added to a relatively short skirt a cut-off plis Watteau. It is the perfect costume for an older woman who dresses too young for her age in hope of catching a man.

After the sextet, however, comes the metamorphosis: This poor woman, who was forsaken by her lover and whose child was stolen, unexpectedly regains her son and belatedly gets a husband. The need for competition with a younger rival suddenly removed, she can now afford to appear as Beaumarchais describes her, in a dignified dark gown with a black lace cap in the Spanish fashion. Her wedding veil should also have a matronly look, which can be achieved by tying it under her chin.

In the last act she may wear a lace shawl to protect her from the evening chill.

BARBARINA AND THE FEMALE CHORUS

BEAUMARCHAIS: Barbarina's dress has a brown, tight bodice, with decorative edging and silver buttons. The skirt [is] of a strong color and [she wears] a black feather headdress, like the other peasant girls at the wedding.

Whereas a modified version of Beaumarchais's description seems fine for the chorus (except that black feather headdress), I like Barbarina a little more girlish. After all, precocious though she may be, she is supposed to be only thirteen years old. If her bodice is of a somewhat younger color than dark brown, and the color of her skirt not quite so "strong," that goal will have been achieved. She should have a dainty apron and mobcap as well, or maybe a snood with a little bow in the middle. That depends on how "Spanish" we are going. The silver buttons can go to the highest bidder.

Compared to some, *Figaro* is not an expensive opera to costume, but if any money is going to be splurged it surely will not be for the chorus. And yet, the chorus needs a change of costume, in my estimation. In act 1 Figaro hastily rounded them up, interrupting whatever they were doing: milking the cows, cleaning the stables, thrashing corn, or killing pigs. In other words, they are in their workday clothes of rough-textured fabrics in earthly colors, with straw hats and sabots (which were naturally left outside). In act 3 they are in their "Sunday-best" attire, as Beaumarchais describes.

Some of the peasants have learned a little dance for the occasion, and there you have the entire fandango. No ballet if I can help it. Nor do I believe that the Almavivas would have some of *their* friends over to attend this affair, as some stage directors seem to think. What the score clearly indicates, but what is never used, is a village band preceding the wedding procession. I cannot imagine what else the crescendo and diminuendo of the Wedding March is supposed to indicate. The fact that the musicians march off again, while the rest of the procession stays onstage, should be no deterrent. They may be dressed much like the other peasants and be of various shapes and sizes. They would be a great visual addition to the scene, I believe.

CHERUBINO

BEAUMARCHAIS: His rich costume of the first and second acts is that of a page of the Court of Spain—white with silver embroidery, the light cape of blue over the shoulder, and a hat bedecked with plumes. In the fourth act he wears the bodice, skirt, and headdress of the peasants who bring him. In the fifth act, an officer's uniform, a cockade, and a sword.

A French Cherubino. (Hubert Drouais, *Comtesse du Barry*.)

The costume described by Beaumarchais is consistent with his harking back to an earlier period. In the eighteenth century, pages would probably wear such a costume only for ceremonial occasions. Usually, and correctly, Cherubino is costumed as a late eighteenth-century young nobleman, and it must be said that that costume, with

Spanish Cherubino. (Antonio
fael Mengs, *The Prince of*
turias.)

its cutaway coat, jabot, and vest, is particularly helpful in concealing a singer's female attributes. In Cherubino we see Count Almaviva as a young boy, and his feelings toward women, and their reaction and attraction to him, do much to explain the attitude and behavior of Almaviva as a grown man.

In keeping with the idea of the division of time, Cherubino should not be in full attire in act 1. None of the inhabitants of the castle should be. If figurewise a shirt and breeches are not a good solution, I would not hesitate to put him in a dressing gown.

A page does not enter his mistress's rooms but fully clothed; thus, we see him in act 2 in a light-colored cutaway coat with vest and breeches and a full shirt, since he will presently take off coat and vest in order to be disguised as a girl. Although the text does not ask for it, it is nice to put him in a dress, presumably Susanna's. Experience has taught me that what works best in this instance is a sleeveless bodice sewn onto a peasant skirt. Both are open middle front, and there are ties at the waist to pull it all together. It is very easy to put on and the effect is instantaneous and total. A comically large mobcap is another necessary ingredient. The advantage of using a dress is that it advances the basic idea of this scene, which is so often overlooked. On the one hand, Susanna and Cherubino are fooling around at leisure, having a wonderful time, while the Countess is only mildly amused. She is nervously pacing up and down, correctly anticipating disaster at any moment. In this context also, Susanna's baffling statement, "Madame qui non è . . ." makes sense.

Cherubino's third-act disguise as one of the peasant girls can be a very simple one: his own shirt, a very large mobcap, the flounce of which half hides his face, and a peasant skirt on a drawstring, the ties of which are held by Cherubino. When Antonio unmasks him, he lets go of the ties and suddenly stands there in his pageboy breeches. When he is not a replica of the other peasant girls, it is more logical that the Countess should single him out.

Except for the use of some eighteenth-century theatrical conventions, like the frequent asides and the predilection for mistaken identities, *Figaro* is a pretty realistic piece. Cherubino's ability to produce a complete officer's outfit at a moment's notice does not make any sense under the circumstances. If we are nevertheless loath to forego this handsome military display, here is a way out of the dilemma: In the eighteenth century, as now, only enlisted men wore uniforms that were government issue. Not only did officers supply their own outfits, but there was, unlike today, considerable leeway in choice of style. Cherubino's military appearance can gain much by having an improvised air about it, which can be accomplished in the following manner: Add to his previous costume a metal breastplate, worn underneath the coat, a military sash, a baldric, boots, epaulettes, gauntlets, and the tricorn with cockade that Beaumarchais calls for. Add as a finishing touch a large cape, and you have as dashing a military outfit as one can wish for, without resorting to the absurdity of producing a uniform.

Costumewise, famous actors spurned Beaumarchais's intentions. (Dugazon as Figaro. Drawing after a contemporary lithograph.)

FIGARO

BEAUMARCHAIS: Figaro wears the suit of a bourgeois Spanish dandy [a majo]. His head is covered with a snood or net [and a] white hat, a colored ribbon around the crown, a silk kerchief around his neck, vest and breeches of satin, with buttons and buttonholes fringed in silver, a wide silk sash, garters tied with tassels that hang on each leg, jacket of striking color, with large lapels matching the vest, white hose, and grey shoes.

From Beaumarchais via da Ponte to Mozart, the personality of Figaro has been modified more than that of any other character in the play. Not only have the revolutionary speeches gone by the boards, but much of the bravado and many of the "Jack-of-all-trades" elements, so evident in the play, have been toned down considerably. Except for the sentiments expressed in his last-act aria, Figaro emerges as a happy-go-lucky, somewhat two-dimensional character. To follow suit his costume requires some modifications as well. Beaumarchais's desire for the use of "the old Spanish style" evidently did not apply to his leading man. The description fits that of an overdressed eighteen-century majo. Stripped of its exaggerations it is entirely suitable for the opera's Figaro.

The reasons advanced for not dressing Susanna in her wedding dress from the start do not apply to Figaro. He is all set to get married from the very beginning and dresses for the occasion in his Sunday-best suit. Only he gets into it in stages. In the first act, when he is measuring the room on hands and knees, he is in his shirt sleeves, with breeches, a sash, and the snood that has become almost as much of a trademark for Figaro as the barber pole. It was a very popular eighteenth-century Spanish costume accessory for men and women. No reason that Figaro should not have it.

In act 2, when he barges into the Countess's bedroom without knocking, ostensibly to dress her hair, he adds a vest and is thus in typical hairdresser's attire. To appear before the Count to have judgment passed and subsequently to get married, he adds the majo jacket, with its square lapels matching the vest and its little puffs at the shoulder. In act 4, when he hides in the bushes to spy on a "faithless" bride, he adds one of those large cloaks Spaniards were so fond of wrapping themselves in.

utilitarian hunting costume for
lmaviva in act 2.

egant and to the manner born:
maviva in act 3.

THE COUNT

BEAUMARCHAIS: His first- and second-act dress is a hunting outfit of the old Spanish style, with calf-high boots. From the third act till the end, a magnificent suit in that style.

Like the Countess, the Count has also changed a great deal in the few years that have passed since, in *The Barber of Seville*, he found it necessary to disguise himself successively as "Lindoro," a drunken soldier, and a music teacher, in order to press his suit with Rosina.

In an opera that might be subtitled "A Study in Frustration," the Count is the most frustrated of all. He firmly believes in his God-given right to be a philanderer, by virtue of his noble birth. Now not only does he find this right challenged, but he is forced to relinquish it. He is constantly tricked into situations wherein he is humiliated and left with nothing but the cold fury he expresses in his third-act aria. Neither Almaviva nor the Countess seems to have a sense of humor; on the other hand, both of them retain their dignity. Almaviva is an elegant man, dressed in excellent taste and in every sense to the manner born.

As was mentioned earlier, it was the habit of eighteenth-century nobility to spend considerable time in a state of semi-undress. In the case of men this meant an elegant floor-length dressing gown, often with a matching vest, and a day cap to protect their shaven heads from the cold. It is the ideal costume for the Count in act 1, not only because of the early hour of the day, but also because it is somehow suggestive of the gentleman's amorous frame of mind. The hunting costume is thus reserved for the second act and part of the third.

What was said of uniforms when discussing Cherubino's military dress was even more true of hunting costumes. Noblemen with sizable estates and a great deal of money might outfit their hunting crews with uniforms bearing their colors, but the Lord of the Manor was free to wear whatever he chose. A hunting costume is mostly utilitarian in nature, even in eighteenth-century terms, made of a combination of wool and leather. Green is the hunting color par excellence, and it can look very elegant when combined with a brown suede vest, boots, and gauntlets. A tricorn and sword are also in order. The hair is in a natural color. The jabot and shirtsleeve ruffle in this case require only a very modest lace edging.

In the third act, preferably after the sextet, when the wedding has become inevitable, the Count puts on his gala suit. It consists of a velvet or brocade cutaway coat. The vest, usually handsomely em-

Fashionable undress for a philandering Count. (John Singleton Copley, *Portrait of Nicholas Boylston.*)

broidered, is of a contrasting but harmonizing fabric. The breeches usually match the coat, but if the Count is a short or stocky man, breeches that match the vest will make him appear taller and slimmer. A sword, white hose, and buckled shoes are part and parcel of such a suit, as is a white-powdered queue wig. At that time tricorns were often worn indoors as well, but singers hate hats, so we will omit one here.

In the last act an additional large cape will fully equip the Count for any amorous eventualities.

As Chief Magistrate, the count might don a judge's robe and wig for the Judgment Scene in act 3. Personally, I think he would not bother to do so just for his valet.

DR. BARTOLO

BEAUMARCHAIS: Short black buttoned suit, large wig, turned-back cuffs, a black belt, and, when he goes out, a red cape.

We know from certain illustrations that the costume Beaumarchais prescribes for Bartolo makes him look like a wizened Lord Fauntleroy, which does not express the character of the blustering doctor very well. Members of the clerical, judicial, and medical pro-

A "soutanelle" for Don Basilio.

fessions invariably dressed in black, and since we know that Bartolo is a well-to-do physician, there is no reason not to dress him in a nice black cloth or velvet coat and breeches of that period. Instead of the red cape, I prefer to give him a red vest, to emphasize his choleric disposition. A full-bottomed grey wig of the type we are used to seeing on J. S. Bach will suit him well. He also wears a black tricorn, black hose, and a black cape. He came all the way from Seville and may carry a cane. The same costume will suffice to carry him through the four acts.

DON BASILIO

BEAUMARCHAIS: Black hat with turned-up brim, soutanelle, and long cape, without cuffs or ruff.

Beaumarchais attacked the nobility of eighteenth-century France through the person of Almaviva, the clergy through Don Basilio, and the judiciary through Don Gusman. Evidently he was satisfied to make his point with fairly low exponents of each group. Almaviva is a big fish in a small pond, and Don Basilio is not even an ordained priest, but a lay brother, a member of a low religious order entered into in the eighteenth century by all sorts of people for various reasons, religious fervor rarely being one of them. Lay brothers' costumes varied widely. One version was the long cassock with the padre shovel-hat, as we are used to seeing Don Basilio wear in *The Barber of Seville*, but the costume somewhat incorrectly described by Beaumarchais was more common. Originally this was a short cassock ("soutanelle" means little cassock), which gradually changed to a black cloth suit, at the back of which a short cape, a kind of vestigial choir robe, was attached. They wore black skullcaps and black hose and had their own white tonsure wigs, which curled around the skullcaps. Black clerical tabs with a white edging were used in lieu of a jabot.

Although Basilio appears in the first act and might participate in the "undress" vogue I favor, I do not think that his character permits such a departure from the formal. Some stage directors like to make a really shady character out of Basilio, including his torn and dingy clothes. Although is he socially no more than a servant, and admittedly poor, I have mixed feelings about such caricaturization.

DON CURZIO

> BEAUMARCHAIS: Don Gusman Brid'oison's costume is the robe of a Spanish judge, but not as full as that of our state attorneys, almost a cassock. A large wig, a neckband or ruff Spanish style, and a long white staff.

In the opera Don Gusman becomes Don Curzio and, in the process, loses his social significance. Da Ponte entirely omits the point that judgeships are a negotiable commodity. Nor is Curzio made out to be quite as inane as Gusman. He is merely Almaviva's stuttering echo.

We do not have to quibble here about the fullness of Curzio's robe. I agree that it should not be too full. He is too skimpy a character for that. He wears a judge's wig and white tabs. No staff.

ANTONIO AND THE MALE CHORUS

> BEAUMARCHAIS: His suit is that of a Spanish peasant, with loose sleeves hanging behind, a hat and white shoes.

For his second-act appearance, Antonio is in his working clothes: a rough shirt with rolled-up sleeves, an equally rough pair of breeches, a gardener's apron, and, on top of a kerchief, a straw hat that has seen better days. He is in his stocking feet: either he left his sabots outside or he carries them in his hands.

Originally the roles of Bartolo and Antonio were sung by the same performer, and the speed with which he had to change costumes must have been the neatest trick of the week. In our days of affluence we can usually afford one singer for each part and hence Antonio can appear in the Wedding Scene as well as in the finale. He is indeed a more likely person to give Susanna away than Bartolo. Antonio is, after all, her uncle. For that occasion he too is naturally in his Sunday-best outfit, a modified version of Figaro's costume in a more subdued color.

What was said about the female peasants is equally valid for the men. In act 1 they are dressed in rough-hewn working clothes, variations of Antonio's second-act costume, each according to his trade. In the Wedding Scene they are all dressed up for the occasion, in costumes similar to Antonio's: breeches, boleros, sashes, kerchiefs under hats, snoods, or stocking caps.

The village band I insist upon is similarly clad.

There is every reason to believe that the Count has some lackeys in his service. They should be dressed in the traditional lackey uniforms of that day, with white wigs.

CHAPTER 14

WAGNER'S *Tannhäuser*

WE ARE INCLINED to think of fashion in terms of clothes only, while in fact it is a phenomenon that touches everything in which man is involved, from ailments to zeppelins. It should not come as a surprise, therefore, that there are fashions in music, in opera, and in opera production. The desire for a change of style in an opera production is essentially no different than our yearning for a new hat. It is based on our dissatisfaction with the status quo and our eternal optimism that what is new will also be better.

We disassociate ourselves almost violently from the fashion that is passé, for while on one hand we welcome what is new, we are also reluctant to relinquish what is old and familiar, no matter how unsatisfactory it proved to be, in exchange for something unfamiliar, unproven, and therefore threatening, if not hazardous. Our repudiation of the old serves here to bolster our faltering morale. After some time has passed, however, and the new fashion proves not to be the panacea we hoped for either, we can afford to look back, not in anger, and reevaluate our forsaken loves to find that they were not bereft of virtue after all, and that we can appreciate them again in a new perspective.

The story of *Tannhäuser* is set in the thirteenth century, and from manuscript illuminations, mosaics, and statuary of that era, we

The feeling of the Venusberg Scene. (Richard Dadd, *Come unto These Yellow Sands.*)

have a pretty good idea of how people dressed at that time, even allowing for highly stylized renderings. The costumes are simple and beautiful, but very ill suited as visual interpretations of Wagner's music. Without going so far as moving the setting to a somewhat later period, as was almost invariably done in Wagner's own time, it is necessary to adapt the thirteenth-century styles in a manner that is more flattering to the body and more in keeping with Wagner's music, which seems to demand a far richer ornamentation.

THE VENUSBERG SCENE

Of the many things that are difficult to present successfully on the opera stage, orgies are no doubt the most difficult. To read the stage directions, particularly those of the Paris version, is embarrassing enough. To see them carried out can be a real trial. Yet it should be possible in this day of multimedia presentations to choreograph a ballet that suits both the musical and the theatrical intent. An adaptation of the kind of scene one can observe today in a discothèque seems almost sensuous enough for the purpose. Choreographed acts of wholesale copulation are somehow rarely satisfying visually.

Richard Dadd, *Titania Sleeping.*

Besides Venus and Tannhäuser, who in this scene present a *tableau vivant*, the stage is populated by naiades, the Three Graces, amorettes, young men, nymphs, bacchantes, satyrs, and fauns. Two paintings by the Victorian English painter Richard Dadd, *Come unto These Yellow Sands* and *Titania Sleeping*, painted at almost the time of the *Tannhäuser* genesis, capture the feeling of this scene particularly well. They demand almost complete nudity, but that state—be it real or faked—is not difficult to achieve with a corps de ballet. It is interesting to observe, although not surprising, that early productions of this opera show the female dancers clinging to their fashionably bouffant skirts.

Despite the scantiness of the characters' attire, the designer will want to differentiate between the various types that inhabit the Hörselberg: sea-nymphs may be adorned with a bit of seaweed here and there; regular nymphs are often endowed with gossamer wings; bacchantes may sport some attributes of the fruit of the vine; and amorettes, which are cupids, usually have wings also, and bows and arrows to boot. The distinction between fauns and satyrs is small if any. Both of them are half-goat, half-man, with hairy legs and hoofs, goatees and horns. How ordinary "young men" got mixed up in this crowd is a mystery. There must have been a scarcity of male Greek mythological characters. A scanty loin cloth and a wreath in their hair should do nicely for them.

The raison d'être for the Graces, who do not appear in the Dresden version, is to give the bacchanale some sort of a plot. Afraid at first of being swept up in the frivolous proceedings, they eventually bring them to a halt by persuading the amorettes to shoot everybody in sight with their tranquilizing darts. If these ladies are so moralistic, they really do not belong in the Venusberg in the first place. Once they are there, however, they should be dressed in long Grecian gowns (far less revealing than the other costumes), made of a fabric that drapes well, like a silk jersey, in white or pastel shades. Their hairdos should also be in the Greek style.

An eighteenth-century "amorette." (Hippolyte Lecomte.)

VENUS

The challenge of a "tour de force" attracts many an opera singer, be it, in the female repertoire, the three heroines in *Les Contes d'Hoffmann*, Cassandra and Dido in *Les Troyens*, or Venus and Eliasbeth in *Tannhäuser*. The merits of such an undertaking need not be weighed here. It is evident that the visual difference between the two characters should be considerable; one is a seductress, the other, a saint. There is also no lack of time to accomplish a thorough transformation. The singer, on the other hand, may want the characters to look somewhat similar, to insure that the audience appreciates that the same performer is doing both parts. Any attempts in that direction must be nipped in the bud.

Although in Greek mythology Venus is usually visualized as a blond goddess, in this opera she should be a dark, sultry woman, more in the Delilah category. She could also be a flaming redhead.

It is to be expected that a seductive lady like Venus would show a considerable amount of exposed skin. The problem this may present if the singer in question is not svelte is solved most satisfactorily by building her a nude leotard with a solidly boned foundation, which will give her the best support and the best figure possible. The leotard can furthermore be cleverly shaded. Once this is accomplished, all sorts of chiffon drapery can be attached to the foundation in an alluring peek-a-boo manner, exposing what can be exposed to good advantage and concealing that which best remains covered up.

It is helpful if Venus's changing moods also find expression in her costume. There are several ways this feat can be accomplished, but the success of the endeavor will depend on the skill of the

Venus: „Mein Ritter! mein Geliebter! Willst Du fliehen?

Landgraf: „Drängt es dich, dein Herz mir endlich zu erschließen!
Elisabeth: „Blick mir ins Auge! Sprechen kann ich nicht."

Wolfram: Blick' ich umher in diesem edlen Kreise, welch hoher Anblick macht mein Herz erglühn!"

Tannhäuser: O Walther der du also sangest, du hast die Liebe arg entstellt!"

Wolfram: „O du, mein holder Abendstern!"

Tannhäuser: Bleib fern von mir! die Stätte wo ich raste, ist verflucht!"

Presented as "absolutely authentic" costume reproductions, these illustrations leave nothing to the imagination as far as Venus is concerned.

singer. In a fit of emotion, she may grab a brightly colored piece of chiffon, which happens to be draped on the couch, and toss it over one shoulder. Or some panels of her gown may have a bright facing that can subtly be brought to the fore with her changing mood. Things of that nature require careful rehearsing but are worth the time spent on them, for they can greatly support the musical and emotional expression.

It is not recommended that Venus be made to look like a 1930 Jean Harlow–type siren in a bias-cut white satin evening gown.

ELISABETH

It is implied, after the fact, that Elisabeth was informed of Tannhäuser's return, which is the reason she "joyfully greets these halls" on this occasion, after having shunned them ever since his departure.

Elisabeth is a pure and saintly lady, and one likes to visualize the pure and innocent as being blond. There is a lot to be said in favor of that, although pictures of earlier performances show

Garments for both men and women were abundantly lined in fur. Chinbands and crowns were frequently worn.

her occasionally as a brunette. Elisabeth's hair may be long and flowing. The chin band, which is such a frequent and typical part of the medieval woman's headgear, can be unflattering to a prominent "soprano chin." Singers do not like to have things going on around their faces anyway, but it cannot always be avoided (consider, for example, the costume of a nun). Such chin bands must always be cut on the bias, in order to maintain an impression of being drawn tightly around the face without impeding the singer's opening of her mouth.

The wearing of crowns by the nobility seems to have been a much more common practice than it was in later times, when it became the prerogative of royalty only. A vestige of the old custom survives in the English coronation ceremony, in which the attending nobles don crowns at the moment the king is crowned. So, Elisabeth shall have her crown even though she is only a Landgraf's niece.

Her costume has to be an adaptation of the rather shapeless fashions of the thirteenth century. A princess-line gown of a light gold cloth with long, fitted sleeves may have a band of jeweled embroidery at the decolletage, descending in a panel middle front to the hem, as well as around the wrists. A cape of a darker gold, edged with a wide ornamental band, is attached with a jeweled ornament to each shoulder. The fabrics of her costume must not be too heavy. Elisabeth must appear youthful.

If the third act does not represent an out-and-out winter scene, it should at least have a strong autumnal feeling. Accordingly, the costume Elisabeth wears for her prayer must convey that atmosphere. She should wear a wide-sleeved, light grey velvet mantle with a head covering, half hood, half shawl, in a darker shade of grey. This garment will establish the virginal, saintly impression that is required and will at the same time be very becoming, particularly if the ends of the hooded shawl, draped over one shoulder in front and in back, almost touch the floor in front and trail in the back.

If Elisabeth is actually visible in the funeral procession, she should be completely in white, with a medieval coif like a nun's.

Elisabeth's costume has to be an adaptation.

TANNHÄUSER

Wherever Tannhäuser dwells, he should give the impression of not belonging. Yet when his friends see him again for the first time, Biterolf remarks that he is dressed like a knight. The costume he wears on this occasion is the same one he wore in the Venusberg Scene, for he is magically transported from one scene to the other. Since he cannot possibly be in "shining armor," what designates him as a knight must be the quality of his clothes. It must also not appear as if he made love to Venus in his travelling clothes. Most tenors who sing Tannhäuser are no shrinking violets, and it takes some doing to make them look like the irresistible lover he evidently was. One successful solution may be the choice of a light-colored cloth tunic in a warm shade, its length to be determined by the height of the performer and the presentability of his legs. A shorter tunic would be preferable. It is ample, but the fullness is carefully controlled by an ornate girdle. The oval neckline and dolman sleeves have a decorative border. The tights are in a harmonizing darker shade. In addition he wears a capelike drapery in a dark warm color, a deep magenta perhaps, consisting of a half circle approximately ten feet long with a decorative border along the curved edge. At a foot and a half from the straight edge, the drape is attached to the back of one shoulder, passed under the opposite arm, and brought to the front, where the drape's end joins the point of departure at the shoulder, to be held there with an ornament or a clasp. Such an arrangement has to be adjusted according to the performer's height. A draped cape of this type has special advantages in this case: it is enough out of period, although not outrageously so, to make Tannhäuser stand out from the others. It is also very flattering to the figure.

Young men clean shaven, older men with beards.

Much time has elapsed between Tannhäuser's arrival and the singing contest, so that a change of costume is warranted. The tunic can now be ankle length and the cape of a more elaborate fabric with all-over motives.

Men's hairstyles of that time are shown to be pageboy length, curly, rolled under at the nape of the neck, parted in the middle, or combed straight back, always without bangs. A hair ornament that looks like a jeweled circlet or a small flower wreath is frequently depicted. Flower wreaths tend to look silly on grown men, but the circlets are perfectly acceptable, particularly for the singing contestants, who, incidentally, also carry small harps.

Tannhäuser with a beard.

Contemporary pictures show young men as clean shaven and older men with short beards and hairline moustaches if any. In the famous Manessische Manuscript, Tannhäuser is nevertheless shown with a beard, although he is obviously a young man. When in modern times these facial adornments happen to be fashionable, it is more difficult to persuade performers to shave them off for theatrical purposes than the other way around, regardless of the legitimacy of the request. Here a goodly amount of tact and diplomacy will serve the costumer in good stead, along with the stage director's putting his foot down, for it is not a matter of common sense but rather an emotional issue.

Hunting attire per se did not exist in the thirteenth century.

Short tunics worn by the lower classes. (Dutch costume plate.)

Dolman sleeves, a typical feature of thirteenth-century costume.

Tannhäuser's pilgrim costume is a tattered version of what the other pilgrims wear (to be discussed below).

WOLFRAM

If one were to costume the Hunting Scene from *Tannhäuser* in a historically correct manner, it would, but for the women, look like a modified version of the Wartburg Scene, for hunting attire per se did not exist in the thirteenth-century, nor for a long time thereafter. Short tunics were worn only by laborers, peasants, and shepherds, and the sole concession made to the comfort of men on horseback was a slit to the waist in the middle front and rear of their long robes. But such authenticity would not serve the visual logic of this scene, nor our concept of what a hunting scene looks like. That pertains to Wolfram's costume and to all the others involved in the hunt.

Indulging in a bit of obvious symbolism, one might assign the color blue to this true and self-effacing young knight, but it should be a greenish blue for the hunt. He wears a sleeveless, calf-length, belted cloth tunic over dolman sleeves and tights of a harmonizing shade. Dolman sleeves, mentioned earlier, were a very typical feature of thirteenth-century costumes for men and women. In order to use them to good advantage, a fitted bodice lining is required to control the fullness.

Short leather boots were in fashion in the thirteenth century and are suitable for Wolfram, so long as he is a tall man. If he is not, the top of his boots should be raised and the hemline of his tunic lowered until they overlap. This will avoid a horizontally cut-up effect, which is undesirable.

Men's headgear, mainly small, consisted of soft, low pillboxes, short hanging caps with a rolled brim indented in the middle front, linen coifs that tied under the chin and had an almost babyish effect, and conical hats with loose strings under the chin that looked amazingly like coolie hats. The men's hat most frequently seen was apparently a band of widely pleated fabric around a dome-shaped crown, sometimes with a pompon on top. These hats gave a crownlike impression, the more so because, like all men's hats of that time, they were not set deep in the face but seemed to rest atop the curly hair, suggesting that it had a great deal of body. Wolfram and the other singers should naturally get the hat that suits their features and character best.

A nineteenth-century interpretation of medieval hunting clothes. (Richard Dadd, *Robin Hood.*)

Like the other knights, Wolfram carries a sword on a leather belt low around the hips. Falconers were frequently seen with one or two gauntlets, which would suit Wolfram as well.

For the singing contest, Wolfram may wear a blue velvet, full- or calf-length tunic with dolman sleeves and ornamental bands at the neck, wrists, and hem. His costume should be simple, but the color can stand out. If he is in blue, no one else should be.

An additional much darker blue cape, with a shoulder cape and a side closing, as is the medieval fashion, will serve Wolfram for the four scenes in the third act in which he participates without having a chance to change costumes: Elisabeth's prayer, Tannhäuser's return, his visit to the Venusberg, and Elisabeth's funeral.

THE OTHER MINNESINGERS

Among the four other Minnesingers, only Walther von der Vogelweide and Biterolf have any solo lines, and, accordingly, any chance to establish a character. Walther, whose short aria was omitted from the Paris version, echoes Wolfram's sentiments and should visually be a variation of him, both in the Hunting and the Wartburg scenes. Biterolf is quite a bit more aggressive in his utterances, and one might be inclined to dress him in chain mail but for the fact that this is a "Singers' War," where voice and harp are the only weapons,

Assorted male headgear.

A "Landgraf Hermann"–type and lady guests. (Dutch costume plate.)

and any type of armor would be out of place. However, some metal studding applied as a trimming to a tabbard over a dolman-sleeved tunic should give him a martial air in the Hunting Scene as well as in the singing contest.

The hunting attire of Reinmar von Zweter and Heinrich der Schreiber, the two remaining Minnesingers, may be a variation of the costumes described for Wolfram, the Landgraf, and the members of the ensemble. At the proceedings in the Wartburg they stand out from the other guests only because of the lighter color of their tunics, the fillets in their hair, and the harps they carry under their arms.

LANDGRAF HERMANN

The custom of lining garments with fur was most prevalent in medieval times and seems particularly appropriate here for the Landgraf. Fur used as a lining would naturally show only where a slit in the garment revealed it, or where a border was turned up. A calf-length, dark green woolen tunic with dolman sleeves, edged in fur at the wrist and at the hem, worn under a three-quarter-length, fur-lined hooded cape is right for him. His boots should be high enough so that no tights will be visible. A nobleman's crown adorns his brimmed hat. He wears gauntlets and carries a sword.

As the host of the singing contest, the Landgraf should wear a long brocaded robe under a fur-lined cape, which is slit at the shoulder and covers one arm. The cape has a wide ornamental border, and some heraldic bearing can be applied as well. His crown should not be too ostentatious. He is not a king. On his shoulders rests an ornamental chain.

Assuming that all the participants in the funeral procession are dressed in black, the Landgraf will wear on that occasion a costume very similar to his previous one but entirely in black this time.

A shepherd boy with dogs. (Dutch costume plate.)

THE SHEPHERD BOY

He, or rather she, wears a beige, knee-length tunic of a thin wool fabric. It is very full and belted and has a matching hooded shoulder cape and tights. There are leg wrappings with leather thongs.

THE PAGES

There are four singing pages, who introduce the singers, and a number of identically dressed super pages, who usher the noble guests to their seats. They wear tabbards, which were at that time not yet rigid, with a coat of arms in front. Also a brief, long-sleeved, belted tunic, tights, and a linen coif that ties under the chin.

THE FEMALE CHORUS

While the score of *Tannhäuser* identifies only "noble ladies" in the chorus, the libretto divides them into higher- and lower-rank nobility, the former designated by that untranslatable German title *Fürstin*, which indicates "princess of the realm" as opposed to "princess of the blood," a king and queen's daughter. (The corresponding male term is *Fürst.*)

The libretto indicates that the "young pilgrims" who appear in the last act are also women. It even goes so far as to reassure us that "they need no beards."

Whether or not a distinction is to be made between courtiers of higher and lower ranks is up to the stage director and the size of the chorus. The "princesses" could wear more elaborate crowns and capes in addition to their gowns, while the noble ladies wear gowns, sleeveless over-robes, and coifs. The use of fur could also be limited to the higher-ups.

Elisabeth seems to be all by herself. There is no mention of any ladies-in-waiting, not even so much as a solitary "Inez"-type confidante.

The Singers' War is a joyous but also a solemn occasion. The subject being sung about is love, which in the Middle Ages was a very elevated and very serious matter. It is an occasion for a display of rich, warm colors. The use of the mi-parti division of garments is a fashion novelty of the time that can be put to good use here, as can the application of heraldic devices on fabric, such as diagonal stripes or zigzag bands. All this will provide variation to the princess-line gowns. The use of dolman sleeves is particularly suitable when over-robes are used. Bands of fur or embroidery are appropriate at the wrists, the décolletages, etc. The coifs were small, inevitably with a band under the chin, but the hair was frequently long, flowing, and curly.

Ballet slippers dyed to match the gowns are the only suitable footwear here.

THE MALE CHORUS

Among the singing men, the score identifies Thuringian counts, knights, nobles, hunters, and pilgrims.

Originally the pilgrim's costume was simply a utilitarian travelling robe with a hooded shoulder cape. Since pilgrims went to holy places to do penance, it stands to reason that their attire was dark and of the utmost simplicity. They went barefoot, tied a cord around their waist, used a tree branch as a cane, carried a shoulder bag, and wore a broad-brimmed felt hat to protect them from the sun and rain.

The shrine of St. James of Campostello was one of the places frequented by the pilgrims. In penance, they would eat scallops there, the cockle shells of which they would, after a completed pilgrimage, affix to the pelerines of their robes (*pelerin* is French for pilgrim) and to the upturned brims of their hats. These shells of St. James became the pilgrims' trademark. To this day, a gourmet ordering Coquilles St. Jacques may be heard humming the Pilgrims' Chorus from *Tannhäuser*.

After this elaborate discourse on the origin of the pilgrims' garb, it must be noted that in this instance the application of all those shells upon the pilgrims' return from Rome may not seem in keeping with the mood of the opera. It seems more prudent also to substitute sandals for the pilgrims' bare feet. The old pilgrims should be bearded.

A pilgrim with cockleshells on his hat.

The pilgrims' robes used to be of various lengths, which is fine if the stage director and designer decide that they want them to look like a motley crowd. If a solemn, dignified impression is the aim, uniformly long robes are preferable, a choice that might also be considered in view of the fact that some of the hunters have to overdress as pilgrims.

The hunters' costumes may all be variations on Wolfram's and the Landgraf's: cloth and wool tunics of various lengths (but not below calf) with leather and suede for trim and belts. Dolman sleeves and over-tunics are appropriate here also. The mi-parti principle can be applied here too, by making garments half in cloth and half in leather of the same color. Falconers' gauntlets and calf-length boots are suitable as well. Swords, spears, hunting knives, and bows and arrows are the usual hunting tools. The colors for the hunt may be browns, greens, and terras—warm earthy tones that are not too somber. They must contrast markedly with the drabness of the pilgrims' robes.

Since the guests at Wartburg castle usually enter as couples, it seems logical to coordinate their costumes as such.

It is necessary to differentiate between Thuringian counts, nobles, and knights without resorting to armor. The use of heraldic devices can be helpful in this respect. The Thuringians might bear their coat of arms on the chest or on the shoulder of their capes. Another emblem may identify the nobles, a third one, the knights. The Thuringians can all have capes and crowns, the nobles, capes and hats, the knights, over-tunics and hats. In concept, if not in execution, men's and women's costumes were very similar at that time. It may seem redundant to mention that the length of the men's robes and tunics should be established according to the performer's height, age, and girth, but simple rules like this are the most frequently sinned against.

It is important and not difficult to simulate the very distinctive men's footwear of this period. A band of fabric cut on the bias is pulled tightly around the sole of a slipper and closed with a middle-front seam. The band is wide enough in front to cover the instep, but tapers from there on to be no higher than the heel in back. A box pleat in the middle front will be held down on the foot with a single lacing or a buckle.

THE SUPERS

The score makes no mention of supers at all, but a libretto of one of the opera's early performances mentions six pages, Trabanten, and feast marshalls. The pages have been dealt with while discussing their singing counterparts. Trabanten are "men at arms," and if anyone is going to be in armor, it should be they. Their tights and sleeves can be chain mail under cloth tunics with an heraldic emblem, a gorget and helmet, gauntlets and halberds.

Feast marshalls are "masters of ceremony" who wear long tabbards with a chest emblem over a belted tunic. On their heads they wear a short hanging cap with a rolled brim. They carry a staff.

The number of supers can be extended endlessly, according to the size of the production and the conception of the stage director. It has been noted elsewhere that the use of vast numbers of supers is no cure-all. It often creates more visual problems than it solves.

CHAPTER 15

PUCCINI'S

Tosca

THE RESEARCHER WHO scans Giacosa and Illica's libretto of *Tosca* for costume clues will reap a meager harvest. The time and the place are given (June 1800, Rome), the sacristan informs us that poor priests wear dirty collars, and we also learn that Angelotti is in "prison garb." It seems that Cavaradossi has a pocket somewhere, from which he produces a miniature of Tosca, who has black eyes and brown hair. The Marchesa Attavanti, on the other hand, has blue eyes and blond hair and owns a fan with her coat of arms on it. Finally, Scarpia has a pocket that holds a watch. That is the entire yield.

The sketch of a gown worn by Sarah Bernhardt as "La Tosca."

Not so easily daunted, we turn next to Sardou's *La Tosca* for further enlightenment. Alas, the results of that search prove equally unrewarding. We do obtain a more precise date of the events: June 16 and 17 to be exact, and we read that it was very hot in Rome those two days. It turns out that Angelotti, who has cut off his beard and moustache, was not in "prison garb" after all, but rather "disguised as an artisan." Cavaradossi, we are told, wears a hat, a topcoat, a jacket, and boots. He has a beard and a moustache and combs his hair "à la Titus." According to Sardou, all this is most revolutionary and suspicious, for in Rome the nobility still dresses in knee breeches and powdered wigs. Tosca, who made her entrance in church carrying flowers and a staff, sings the cantata in "full evening dress." Sciaronne is "very elegantly attired." So much for Sardou.

Luckily we have a few pictures of the original actors in costume. It is not surprising to see that the gowns worn by Sarah Bernhardt, who created the role of "La Tosca," are 1900 adaptations of 1800 styles. What does seem odd is that she should choose to jump to her doom on such a hot day in a hooded coat heavily trimmed with fur. Pierre Berton, the first Scarpia, looked about like the Scarpias we are used to seeing, but Monsieur Dumeny (his first name is never given), the first Cavaradossi, presented from the neck up a strictly "1900" look. He had no beard, sported a tiny curled-up moustache, and wore his hair in a crew cut. I wonder whether they changed his lines to match his appearance. Whatever was or was not done, *we* have done our homework. Now we shall sort it all out, use what makes sense and is relevant, and discard the rest.

Sardou's first Scarpia looked like the ones we are used to seeing in the opera.

La Tosca (Sarah Bernhardt) ready to skip town on a very hot day in ermine-trimmed discomfort, while M. Dumeny, as Cavaradossi, presented (from the neck up) a "1900" look.

ACT I

The idea of Angelotti in prison garb is not a happy one. Historically there was no such thing as a prison uniform in 1800, particularly not in Italy, which as a nation did not exist, and especially not in Rome, a city-state which at that time changed rulers every few months. But even if such a uniform had existed, the distance between Castel Sant' Angelo and Sant' Andrea della Valle is too great for Angelotti to have covered it undetected in such garb. The play offers here some interesting insights: Angelotti tells Cavaradossi that he managed to make his escape by obtaining workmen's clothing and mingling with the artisans who were doing some repair work necessitated by the French occupation.

Castel Sant' Angelo was in fact one of Europe's most notorious prisons. Conditions there were so bad that even fifty years after these events, the English government sent a commission to investigate and make a report. Prison cells had only a hole in the top, for entrance, exit, and food supply. There was no sanitation of any kind. When the French troops occupied the city, they were ordered to put doors in the prison cells. I suppose that the "repairs" the workmen were making after the departure of the French consisted of removing those doors again.

Prison management then was thoroughly corrupt everywhere. One could live in a prison in relative comfort, depending on how much money one had. The little barter Cavaradossi undertakes in the last act, trading his ring in payment for the delivery of a letter to

A more likely disguise for "Angelotti." (Vien fils, *Portrait of Frion.*)

Cavaradossi enters wearing a cape. (Ingres, *Portrait of François-Marius Granet.*)

Tosca, is only a small example of the prevailing custom of bribery. Surely a wealthy and loving sister like the Marchesa Attavanti would not let her brother languish in prison. The play's suggestion for Angelotti's disguise is a perfect one. Rough and worn breeches, hose, shirt, and vest in shades of grey and brown are the proper clothing for him.

Whether sacristans were ordained priests or laymen evidently depended on the importance of the church in which they served. Accordingly, Father Eusebius (that's the sacristan's name in the play) can wear a black cassock and skullcap. I like him to wear a dark work apron, which he can remove later on. It must contain large pockets. If he participates in the procession, he will need a white surplice for that event.

The sacristan is surprised not to find Cavaradossi in church, although the reason for the painter's absence is not given in the opera. His entrance will gain validity if it is made evident that he was indeed on an errand (fetching a piece of brocade, it says in the play, to serve as a background in the painting).

I would like to take advantage of the fact that no mention is made in the opera of the prevailing temperature by giving the two male leads capes to wear. I would not go so far, though, as to light

Cavaradossi in ankle tights and boots or in hose and breeches.

a huge fire in Scarpia's fireplace, as I have witnessed in an otherwise distinguished production at Covent Garden.

The way Cavaradossi describes himself in the play is perfectly correct except for the beard and the moustache. At that time, no man, conservative or revolutionary, French or Roman, was anything but clean shaven. But a hairstyle "à la Titus" was very much *en vogue*. Even women adopted for a while the wind-blown aspects of that coiffure. If Mario is tall enough, boots over fawn-colored ankle tights will look very good on him. If he is not a tall man, he will do better in knee breeches with hose of the same color, or in ankle tights with matching cloth gaiters. It is too early in the nineteenth century to wear long pants. His light-colored tailcoat has a high collar and wide lapels, while his fancy vest has a stand-up collar and lapels as well, the latter partly covering the lapels of his coat. His shirt collar has points that almost touch his cheeks, and his cravat is wrapped several times around his neck. He has a choice of different hat shapes to find the one that suits him best. In church, naturally, he will remove his hat, but the temptation to omit the hat altogether for this reason must be resisted. A gentleman would not venture outside the house without a hat any more than he would wear it inside a church. A large cape slung over his shoulder in

Roman toga fashion was de rigueur then and makes for a dashing entrance. After getting rid of cape, hat, and coat, Cavaradossi should put on the painter's smock that is lying or hanging near the easel. It is a good idea to keep the smock unbuttoned, so that he can easily reach into his vest pocket for Tosca's miniature. When Mario changes into his smock we see his shirt sleeves, as we will again in acts 2 and 3. They are quite full, set in from a dropped shoulder, and gathered at the wrist into a plain cuff without ruffles or pleating. Coat sleeves were so long then that the shirt cuff never protruded.

Cavaradossi in his painter's smock. (Ingres, self-portrait at the age of twenty-four.)

The chemise dresses of the Directoire era are not the sort of garments that flatter the figure of any Tosca I have ever seen or costumed. By the time these styles had evolved into the fashions of the Empire period, they had become more tailored, more manageable and more becoming. I propose to use the later style for Tosca's three costumes.

In theater classics as well as in opera classics an element of surprise no longer exists as far as the plot is concerned: most people in the audience have seen the work many times before and are familiar with its story. Instead, we have an "element of anticipation." Especially in an opera where the heroine's first entrance is heralded by her offstage voice, this sense of anticipation can be very keen. No diva wants to disappoint her audience in this respect. Everyone hopes to create an impressive entrance. In Tosca's case, a spectacular hat has become the favorite object with which to achieve this strived-for effect. Successive Toscas seem to have chosen poke bonnets bedecked with ostrich plumes, not unlike those worn much later by the *Merry Widow*'s can-can ladies from Maxime: Lou-lou, Clo-clo, and Frou-frou. The whole thing went a little far when a certain Tosca could not get through the church door with her bonnet and had to make her entrance from the wings.

Tosca with a turban and a stole. (Andrea Appiani, *Ritratto di Marianna Waldstein.*)

Floria Tosca is a many-faceted character. She is very young, very much in love, very devout, very jealous, and very much a diva. All these elements must find expression in the way she looks, which poses no problem except for that hat. It expresses the "diva" aspect of her character but gets in the way of everything else, particularly the lovemaking. Her remark "My hair is quite disheveled . . ." becomes meaningless if her hat is so large that Mario cannot come close enough to dishevel anything. Nor is it esthetically helpful if her tall bonnet makes her tower over a medium-sized Cavaradossi. My choice for Tosca's head covering, which is, of course, a must in church, is an elaborate lace stole, which will rest lightly on her hair, frame her face pleasingly, and drape elegantly over one shoulder.

osca with a bonnet and a spencer.

For her costume I opt for a spencer, a minature tailcoat. Spencers came in many variations, but I like them cut exactly like a man's tailcoat, with a collar and lapels, and even a miniature vest. The "tail" part, which starts in true Directoire style, right under the bust, can do wonders to minimize figure problems below the waist. Underneath the spencer is a simple silk or mousseline gown with a little train. It may seem redundant to mention that the flowers Tosca carries must harmonize with her gown, but the prop and costume departments do not always get together on such matters. I have seen some lulus. My favorite colors for Tosca's first-act costume are in the yellow family. They set off her dark hair very well and are light, warm, sunny, and "jealous" colors.

From the end of the eighteenth century through the first quarter of the nineteenth, women wore low-heeled or even heelless shoes. Not all women look good in them and they make some feel even worse. If the shoes are unobtrusive—which on the stage is a good idea most of the time anyway—and match the costume, a little heel will do no harm, as long as it is kept as low as possible. In the case of a very short singer, I would rather resort to the use of platform shoes, which will not show underneath a long skirt anyway, than use very high heels, which alter the wearer's stance and gait so drastically. Many a short Cavaradossi might wish that he could avail himself of this device.

It is true that Directoire ladies occasionally carried the tall staff that has become one of Tosca's trademarks. But it is the sort of accessory whose successful application is predicated on slow and stately movements, which is very much out of keeping with Tosca's character, emotions, and music. After it has given Tosca her diva's entrance, it gets in the way and certainly does not fit the mood of her exit. I would relinquish it gladly.

Cavaradossi's first aria and the ensuing duet with Tosca focus on the contrast between her dark-haired, black-eyed beauty and the blond and blue-eyed Attavanti-Maddalena. What is to be done if the Tosca in our cast happens to be blond and blue-eyed? There are several possibilities for dealing with such a contingency and only one "impossibility." The impossibility lies in pretending that it does not exist and ignoring it. That is an insult to the audience's intelligence. The possibilities are threefold:

1. The Marchesa can become the one with brown hair and black eyes. One sees many depictions of Maddalenas with dark hair. However, such a switch would necessitate changing the text, which is no simple matter and is something people are generally reluctant to do.

2. Tosca can wear black contact lenses and a brown wig. That would constitute the most thorough and satisfying solution, but for a reluctance to fool around with contact lenses.
3. One can hope that the blue eyes will not be noticeable from a distance and settle for the dark wig only.

Dark hair has a tendency to "wash out" light-colored eyes, but Tosca's hair does not have to be really dark. Experience has taught me that dark henna, a sort of mahogany color, looks very good on grey- or blue-eyed people. I have used it successfully on blue-eyed Rosinas, Figaros, Carmens, Escamillos, and the like.

The "choirboys" who next put in their boisterous appearance consist of four groups, according to the score. They are: priests, lay brothers, religious students, and choirboys. After a while the sacristan urges them to get into their vestments, which indicates that they entered wearing their daily clothes: black cassocks in the case of the priests and lay brothers; 1800-style boys' suits of the school-uniform type for the two other groups. The vestments are purple cassocks, white surplices, and skull caps. To undertake a complete costume change for this entire chorus is going to be an unwarranted expense. If the budget is not prepared for such an outlay, the students and choirboys may wear their purple cassocks right away (or red ones if those are more readily available) and then for the procession add surplices to the cassocks. Many a time when costuming *Tosca* on a mail-order basis have I received the message: "Do not bother about the boys' choir. We are getting those from the local church."

Italian peasants in church (Francesco Scaramuzza, *Il baliatico*), and a nun (Giacomo Ceruti, "Il Pitocchetto," *Ritratto di Monaca*).

A black-clad Scarpia is the tradition, and I consider it a good one, not only because he is a sinister and menacing character, but also because he is in his uniform as Chief of Police. Over a three-piece, black cutaway suit he wears a voluminous black cape with a multiple-tiered shoulder cape. Black boots, black gauntlets, a black bicorn, a sword, and a white powdered wig complete the outfit.

Spoletta and the other secret agents (there must be at least four of them, but there may be more) are not in uniform, or they would not be "secret" agents. They wear simple, dark cutaway suits with boots, tye-bag wigs, and tricorns. I prefer not to give them capes, for it makes them too obviously conspiratorial. I think of them as a scruffy bunch.

The score is quite specific about who the churchgoers are and at which moment they enter. They are listed as follows: peasants, shepherds, artisans, burghers, and nobles. I would not mind adding some children and, if the stage is large enough, some nuns and some military. In other words, the sort of people one might ordinarily expect to attend such an occasion. Among a mixture of people like this, one naturally would find some more fashionably dressed than others, which in this period implies pre- and postrevolutionary styles.

The only participants in the procession mentioned in the score, beside the choirboys, are a cardinal and the Swiss Guard. A cardinal officiating at a Te Deum Mass wore white vestments trimmed in gold and silver. Swiss Guards were exclusively in the service of the Pope. What they are doing in Sant' Andrea della Valle is not clear, especially since there was no Pope in Rome at that particular time. However, we shall not quibble. Their bright blue, yellow, and red sixteenth-century costumes, with the breast plates, morion helmets, and halberts, are a welcome touch of color in the procession. Space permitting, I would not overlook the chance of adding some bishops, monks, and lay church officials to the procession.

ACT II

In order to convey a relaxed, "at-home" atmosphere, Scarpia is occasionally shown in his apartments in his shirt-sleeves. In class-conscious Europe such a notion would have been totally unacceptable. Only persons of the lower classes could be found in their living quarters in shirt-sleeves. A hundred and fifty years later that still held true. Scarpia might wear an elegant dressing gown at home but would never appear in his shirt-sleeves.

Whether Scarpia is planning to go "downstairs" to attend the festivities in the palace is not made clear in the opera. It would be reasonable to assume that he would have done so had not urgent business interfered. It would be equally reasonable to assume that at such a state occasion he would have worn a dress uniform, still black, but jazzed up with silver braid or embroidery and a silver brocade vest. With his black knee breeches he now wears black hose and buckled shoes.

Why Sciarrone, of all people, should have been singled out in the play for a costume description, while far more important characters were not, is a puzzle. My guess is that he was played as a fop and therefore merited elegant attire. In the opera he is merely Scarpia's aide, a glorified flunky, and his costume can be a simple cutaway uniform coat, with matching plastron, vest, ankle tights, and boots. Neither he nor any of Scarpia's flunkies are really villains either and should not be costumed as such.

The room in which Cavaradossi is tortured is not a torture chamber, although it is called that in the score. Palaces do not usually have torture chambers. Prisons do. It is worth reflecting that

Empress Josephine in an Empire gown with sleeves. (Jean Louis David, *Le sacre de Napoleón* [detail].)

in the play the torture scene takes place in Cavaradossi's own house. It is unlikely that *he* had a torture chamber. Roberti evidently carried the torture instrument with him. It would be nice if the audience could see it hanging from his belt.

Although Roberti is an executioner, he should not wear the black hood with two holes in it that is usually associated with his profession. He would wear that only for public executions. He is not going to execute anyone now; he is just going to apply a little pressure. It would be perfectly satisfactory to see him costumed in rough black breeches and leggings, a rough, very dark shirt, a sleeveless black leather jerkin, and a belt.

The interrogating judge is a "fiscal" one because the word *fiscale* in Italian means inquisitional. He wears black judicial robes and hat. The court clerk is in an abbreviated version of the same.

For Tosca, the type of Empire gown we know so well from David's famous painting of the *Sacre de Napoleon*, where the Empress Josephine and her court ladies wear it, is favored. It consists of a gold-embroidered white gown with short puffed sleeves and frequently a short, gold lace Stuart collar. Long sleeves are seen on the *Sacre* gowns, for bare arms were not allowed in church, but such sleeves were not usually part of that kind of court costume

Queen Carolina, Tosca's patron, in a similar dress without sleeves. (Mme. Vigée le Brun, Portrait of Queen Marie Caroline of Naples.)

'osca's "garniture." (François
;erard, Portrait of Queen Marie
;aroline of Naples.)

very disturbed Cavaradossi with
air "à la Titus." (Ingres, *The
:ulptor Paul Lemoyne.*)

and they are not required here. Over the gown the so-called court mantle is worn. It is actually a train set on a halter, made out of velvet or brocade and trimmed in gold. The train is usually quite long and may be carried with a loop over the wrist. It is a regal, formal, and very flattering garment. The use of the court mantle omits the need for an additional evening wrap, which is a nuisance anyway.

Tosca needs quite a bit of jewelry with that gown. A garniture consisting of a tiara, necklace, earrings, and bracelets is to be hoped for. Yet discretion has to be exercised. Not everyone can successfully "carry" so much jewelry. Opera gloves often belong with such a costume.

More often than not, Cavaradossi is brought out in this act dressed only in his shirt, ankle tights, and boots. Most singers I have observed in the part look much better with an additional vest, worn unbuttoned. It will do much to camouflage a waistline that has gone "the way of all flesh."

The pins that will penetrate Cavaradossi's skull are placed at the temples and the nape of the neck. We know, therefore, exactly where blood will drip on his shirt: on both shoulders and the middle back. There is no need to make a bloody mess of his shirt, as some over-zealous people from the art department tend to do. If the vest is worn, it will have to be bloodied as well.

ACT III

Although the opening music of this act depicts the serene awakening of the city of Rome, it conveys a sense of desolation and despair that fits entirely with Cavaradossi's mood and colors the entire stage picture.

The sentinel and guards, including the sergeant, wear subdued uniforms not unlike Sciaronne's but with tricorns.

The jailer's costume is a greyed version of the executioner's: a rough shirt, breeches, leggings, a leather vest, and belt, all in greys and earth tones.

Tosca is dressed in a travelling costume. Her statement to Cavaradossi that she gathered her money and jewelry makes it evident that she went home and had the opportunity to change into something more suitable for the journey. A simple long-sleeved gown with an ample, harmonizing hooded cloak are appropriate as well as striking for this scene. The colors must not be too flamboyant.

Some stage directors like Tosca to fling the cape at Spoletta at the last moment, in order to impede his advance toward her. If

A travelling costume for a departing Tosca. (Costume Parisien 1811–1812.)

Italian military costumes around 1800. (Detail of an Italian military band.)

such is the case, the use of a cape is inevitable. Capes do have certain drawbacks, though. They tend to hinder free arm movement in such a dramatic scene and restrain action. For those who feel that way about capes, the solution lies in the use of a cape-coat. It too may have a hood and should be tailored in front but ample in back and have long, fitted sleeves. Furthermore, this type of garment does not require an additional gown underneath.

For the firing squad, I recommend bright uniforms with powdered wigs and tricorns. I obviously differ with those who feel that the costumes in this scene should match the somberness of the occasion. On the contrary, I think that they should be as gay and as "make-believe" as the execution is supposed to be. It will render the horror of the reality doubly poignant.

CHAPTER 16

VERDI'S *La Traviata*

[S]arah Bernhardt as Marguerite [G]autier in a bustle costume.

It adds to our romantic notion of a masterpiece to believe that, although it was initially badly received by the audience, it subsequently became a brilliant success. In the case of *La Traviata,* it was the composer himself who spread the word that the premiere of his new opus was a fiasco, and the use of contemporary costumes is traditionally cited as at least a contributing factor to this unhappy event. Fortunately, there are always scholars around who take nothing at face value and who like to do a little digging in order to unearth the real story. What they discovered was nothing short of amazing. The premiere of *La Traviata* on March 6, 1853, in Venice was not really the disaster the composer would have us believe. Many in the audience, including some of the critics, liked the opera quite a bit. Nor is it true that the costumes were contemporary. They were in the period of Louis XIV, designed by the Venetian artist Bertoja.

To find the reasons for these misstatements and misconceptions is not within the scope of this book. It is true, though, that Verdi would have liked the opera costumed in modern dress. The idea of a modern story in a contemporary setting evidently intrigued him. But the producers of the opera seem to have considered such a daring innovation hazardous. The composer was persuaded to abandon these notions, and there is no evidence that he put up a big fight over it. All the same, one cannot help wondering what motivated the producers to move the story back in time almost two hundred years.

The play *La Dame aux camélias* by Alexandre Dumas *fils*, on which Piave based the libretto for the opera, had a modern production in Paris in 1852, which proved an enormous success, albeit a "succès de scandale." The play had had great difficulty reaching the stage. Twice the censor forbade its production, first in 1849 and again in 1852. Only considerable diplomatic maneuvering by Dumas *père*, and eventually even the personal intervention of Emperor Napoleon III, succeeded in bringing the play before the footlights. Several factors helped to insure its success: first, a book by the same author on the same subject, which had previously made a decided impact on the public, hence whetting the audience's appetite; then, the leading character herself, whose short but notorious life was still vividly remembered; and finally, the censor's ban, inevitably the best publicity a play can receive. Once the ban was lifted the public flocked to the theater. Under these circumstances the play could not fail to be a hit, whether or not it had any intrinsic merits. It must be said that its merits were considerable.

The "scandale" part of the success was the realistic and sympathetic portrayal on the stage of a social problem: that of the courtesan. Nothing like it had ever been attempted before, and it had about the same shock value as the presentation of nudity or the performance of sexual acts on the stage today. Because music has the power to heighten the impact of a dramatic situation, it is possible that a theme that is merely shocking on the legitimate stage becomes emotionally overwhelming in an opera. Since the operagoing public, always more conservative in its taste, had shown no great penchant for social documents set to music, it is rather surprising that the producers even considered the subject matter of *La Traviata* to be suitable for their repertoire, and one can appreciate their desire to soften the blow—and protect their investment—by shifting the scene of action to an earlier period. Distance thus diffused the harsh lines of reality. It must be remembered, furthermore, that with *Rigoletto* Verdi and his collaborators had only recently discovered what havoc a nervous censor could wreak. No wonder that all involved sought safety in distance.

The fashions of 1848: charming but sedate.

The second half of the nineteenth century was the great age of the *demimonde courtesan*, that by-product of the industrial revolution, so *La Traviata* could appropriately be costumed in any given time within this fifty-year span. The year 1848, in which the play was written, and which would seem the logical time for the opera also, found France in great political turmoil. This upheaval did not find

Elegant abundance expressed in the painting of Empress Eugenie and her court ladies. (Franz Xavier Winterhalter, 1855.)

expression in the fashions of the day. They were sedate and bourgeois, not bereft of charm by any means, but without that feeling of elegant abundance that colors the music of the opera's first act. Nor did they evoke the atmosphere of dark foreboding that pervades Flora's party in act 3. The fashions worn at the turn of the 1860s do have these prerequisites. The prevailing mood of the Second Empire, then at its zenith, found expression in nothing quite so ostentatious as the circumference of women's skirts. At that time the skirts had reached such dimensions that the use of a cagelike structure was needed to support the volume of fabric and spread it out. Initially, stiffened petticoats reinforced with whalebone sufficed for this purpose, but as the width and volume of the skirts increased, cane, and later steel, frameworks were required to achieve the desired effect. If these contraptions were virtual firetraps at their worst, at their best they conveyed a feeling of great elegance and grace, unequalled at any other period of fashion. They gave the unique impression that the wearer was floating rather than walking. The famous painting by Franz Xavier Winterhalter of the Empress Eugenie and her court ladies, painted in 1855, portrays particularly well the "elegant abundance" that I favor for Violetta's party in act 1. With the large tiered and ruffled skirts went tight-fitting, long, pointed bodices, wide, off-the-shoulder décolletages, and tiny sleeves or "berthas." The long white opera gloves, which we now associate with elegant evening attire or ballgowns, were not worn then for such occasions, although they had been before and would be again later. Instead, short lacy gloves or mittens were de rigueur at that time.

The hair, invariably parted in the middle and slicked down with Macassar oil, was caught in a low chignon or dressed with long ringlets covering the ears. There were hair trimmings of a rather dainty nature, consisting of flowers, feathers, and ribbons, pushed fairly far out of the face or caught at the nape of the neck. Since hair covered most of the ears, earrings were relatively small. Necklaces were somewhat more substantial, and the bare arms supported an abundance of bracelets of various shapes and sizes. Evening footwear consisted mostly of pumps with a little heel.

The use of a quantity of hoopskirts on the stage is not an unalloyed blessing. They were no unalloyed blessing in real life, when they were fashionable and universally worn. When one examines the early photographs that put in their appearance just then, it is astounding to see how universally they were worn—by princesses and pauperesses, by young and old, from morning till night. As a result, people had plenty of opportunity to learn how to deal with them. Women learned how to balance them with agility and how not to bump into things. Men learned how to maneuver around them in their social intercourse with women and how not to set matters atilt. The embarrassment that ensued when hoopskirts went out of control has been an endless source of inspiration for contemporary cartoonists. Such a situation has been very humorously exploited in the musical comedy *The King and I*, when the Siamese court ladies are ordered to appear gowned in western fashion, hoopskirts and all, at a banquet given by the king for an English diplomat. From the hoopskirt point of view, the event proved a debacle.

Very few opera companies have either the time or the money to train an entire cast of soloists and choristers in hoopskirt deportment, assuming that there is a person around who can teach it. It is better therefore to abandon the hoops altogether and to use in their stead petticoats made of synthetic horsehair, a fabric that can be purchased by the yard and from which it is possible to construct petticoats of great width and equal flexibility. Occasionally, when the size of the stage does not permit the crowding of a lot of full-skirted women onto it, or in the case of a touring company where compactness is of the essence, it is advisable to move the period of the opera to a somewhat later date, that of the 1870s, for instance, when the fullness of the skirts had been pushed back and

Fashionable coiffures.

Dainty hair ornaments.

Pants had become somewhat baggy. (Frenchman of the Second Empire, after Disderi.)

gathered up into the bustle. Sarah Bernhardt as Marguerite Gautier and Maria Callas as Violetta Valery are two celebrities who have had great success in these roles in costumes of the bustle period.

Men's fashions of the 1860s do not match the women's in elegance. Pants had become somewhat baggy, sleeves long and wrinkled. Everybody looked a little as if he were wearing his older brother's castoffs. It is not a tremendous problem, really. Men's fashions of the fifties are beautiful in tailoring and detail. To suggest that they be used instead is a very justifiable theatrical and artistic liberty to take.

ACT I

It is the costumer's task to aid performers in the characterization of their parts by providing the most typical attire for the kind of person the actors wish to impersonate. In the case of Violetta, the costumer asks himself how he will get the point across, via the costumes, that Violetta is a courtesan, a lady of easy virtue. There is, in fact, no way to make this clear at all, costumewise. It is possible to single out a streetwalker in a crowd because of her cheap, vulgar, loud, and provocative dress, but it is not possible to detect a courtesan in this way. To be sure, both women are prostitutes, but in the case of the courtesan, she is also ambitious and has brains. She may have wit and taste to boot. The real-life Alphonsine Plessis, who became notorious as Marie Duplessis, famous as Marguerite Gautier, and immortal as Violetta Valery, was, regardless of her morals, a creature of exquisite taste. Her salon, furnished entirely in Louis XV style, was filled with precious objets d'art, and her personal appearance reflected her good taste no less. So it should be in the opera. There should be nothing gaudy about her—no masses of camelias, feathers, or lace. In the first act, Violetta should be the most simply dressed and most elegant of all the women on the stage, but a more vivid color than the traditional white seems to harmonize more with her first-act music. Even a display of jewelry can be reserved for act 3, when she has a good occasion and a special reason for wearing it. In the first act, one camelia strategically placed is all that is needed for decoration—and to be given to Alfredo.

If Violetta behaved like a lady, her guests were no less well mannered. In the play the milliner Prudence, who has been omitted from the libretto, remarks on this upon entering the party. "My goodness," she says, "such elegant goings-on, such hand kissing, such fine manners . . ." or words to that effect. Last but not least, there is Verdi's music, which depicts a gay and lively party, certainly not a

A gay and lively party. (Winslow Homer, *A Cadet Hop at Westpoint.*)

rowdy orgy. We have here, then, a company of pretty young women in beautiful ballgowns, one more elegant than the next, dressed every bit as expensively as their hostess. They are not Violetta's poor relatives, as they so often look to be onstage. Their skirts are just as voluminous, and their gowns may be even more elaborate.

If the minor characters in this opera—Flora, Annina, the baron, Gastone, etc.—are only sketchily drawn, the chorus is a completely anonymous crowd. Attempting to give them more than token individuality is a mistake, does not further the opera's action, and is most distracting. Circumstances once compelled me to use for the first-act-chorus costumes a set of ballgowns in various shades of three related colors, but identical in design. This is not to be recommended as the ideal solution, but it was a perfectly satisfactory one, and a great deal better than a group of gowns of ill-assorted design in equally ill-assorted colors.

The only other women mentioned by name in the opera are Flora and Annina, who share a feeling of great benevolence toward Violetta. Aside from that, we are allowed a good deal of leeway in the interpretation of their characters, and, consequently, in the way we make them look. One can visualize Flora, for instance, as somewhat older than Violetta, in her late twenties maybe, with red hair, dressed

For men, white tie and tails. (Contemporary fashion plate.)

Older men continued to wear knee breeches. (Contemporary fashion plate.)

in shades from lavender to purple. Good natured, materialistic, and shrewd, she has the situation with her elderly lover, the Marquis d'Obigny, well in hand. Both have their little escapades, but she is discreet about hers and makes him pay through the nose for his. As far as her taste is concerned, we shall have ample time to discuss that when we visit her establishment in act 3.

There is no doubt that Annina should be an elderly, motherly woman, if only for the simple reason that no self-respecting courtesan would employ a young maid who might attract her mistress's lovers' roving eyes. Annina is the one stable element in Violetta's life, the one who sticks by her through thick and thin. Thus, she can be dressed in one basic costume with changing accessories to suit the different circumstances. Some stage directors like to have Annina onstage in the first act, notably when Violetta has her fainting spell. It is an excellent idea, for otherwise we see her for the first time in act 2, in travelling clothes no less. Since she has not previously been alluded to, the uninitiated might wonder who the devil she is! Since Annina's status is somewhere between chambermaid and housekeeper, she does not necessarily have to be dressed in a black maid's uniform, but might wear a simple grey wool dress of the period with a high neck, a Peter Pan collar and long, tight sleeves. To this are added in the first act a fancy cap and apron. Aprons were then by no means the exclusive trademark of the serving classes, but rather a housekeeping adjunct of all middle-class women. Caps were around-the-clock head coverings for older women of all classes and for servants of all ages.

The appropriate evening attire for men was then what it is today only for very gala occasions: white tie and tails. With the tailcoats older men frequently wore knee breeches, and one may assume that at a gathering like Violetta's there would be quite a few of their vintage present. Younger men could rarely afford to maintain establishments like Violetta's or Flora's. If no one else, at least the Marquis d'Obigny should wear a pair of knee breeches, accompanied with black hose and pumps.

If the chorus is a large one, it is pleasant to have a few men in uniforms to break the monotony. A few modest decorations are also appropriate on uniforms and tailcoats alike. But no rows of medals or order ribbons. This is not a diplomatic ball. So as to stand out from the crowd, Dr. Grenvil might wear a black vest with his tails. Soon that would be fashionable anyway. Lackey costumes had undergone some subtle evolution since the days of Louis XVI, but they remained basically the heavily braided cutaway coats, vests, and knee breeches of the period, with white hose, jabots, and pumps.

Powdered wigs were becoming optional. White gloves were a must with all male evening attire, for master and servant alike. The lackey uniform must harmonize with the decor.

When the guests return from the dining room for their "Thank you for a lovely party" chorus, the men may now carry their topcoats or evening capes over their arms and their top hats in hand, while the ladies have now donned evening wraps or shawls. Most likely they would not have entered the room in these outer garments, but their doing so provides a welcome visual change and hence is theatrically justified.

For lackeys, powdered wigs were becoming optional. (Contemporary fashion plate.)

ACT II

The breakup between Mlle. Duplessis and M. Dumas *fils* (the play was semi-autobiographical) was caused by reasons far more realistic than those advanced in the play and in the opera: his lack of money and her infidelities. It is also interesting to note that, where we are inclined to point to Giorgio Germont's demands for Violetta's sacrifice as a prime example of Victorian morality, at least some contemporary critics found them not credible. Violetta, psychologically constituted as she was, had been faithful to Alfredo just about as long as a prostitute can be expected to be faithful; on a deeper level she may well have welcomed this parental intervention, which does not contradict her love for Alfredo or her despair at the parting.

If the first act displayed an air of rich elegance and frivolous gaiety, act 2 should have a feeling of sunshine and serene charm . . . and some make-believe simplicity. As could be expected of Violetta, her "Petit Trianon" was no hovel. It cost plenty of money and should display the good taste that is as much Violetta's trademark as her camelias. It tells us a great deal about Alfredo also that he seemed to have no inkling how much it cost to maintain such a modest little summer place in the manner to which "Madamigella Valery" was accustomed.

A Germont-like Alexandre Dumas *fils* (the play was semi-autobiographical). (Achille Devéria.)

Leisure clothes as we know them today did not exist in the nineteenth century, but we must attempt to make Alfredo and Violetta look as informal as possible in their costumes. It says in the libretto that Alfredo has been hunting. As a result he invariably appears in riding breeches and boots. Aside from the fact that boots were worn for horseback riding then but rarely for hunting, they tend to make a not too tall Alfredo look even shorter. There is no further significance to the hunting reference anyway. Alfredo might just as well have been birdwatching or gone out for a stroll. Do not hesitate, therefore, to put him in a light summer suit, with a plaid

Leisure clothes did not exist. (W. Verschoyle, *Croquet at Countryhouse*, 1862.)

Hunting attire without boots. (Contemporary fashion plate.)

vest perhaps, and a Byronesque open-neck shirt filled by a flowing ascot tie (rather daring). His planter's wide-brimmed straw hat will provide welcome relief from the stereotyped top hat. Brown congress gaiters go well with such an outfit. Those who cannot tear themselves away from the "hunting suit" idea do not have to fret either. A style of pants called "ankle tights," which are riding breeches without a flare at the hip, was also fashionable then for hunters. Instead of boots they were worn with calf-length cloth gaiters. If this style is chosen, it is a good idea to have ankle tights, vest, and gaiters of the same color, topped by a darker single-breasted coat worn unbuttoned. This is optical illusion at its best and will make any Alfredo look as tall and slim as possible.

Violetta is frequently done up for this occasion like a southern belle, in a garden-party dress with a big straw hat. It is a notion to be spurned emphatically. She must look disarmingly simple, although very attractive. Papa Germont must be able to do a real double take upon seeing her for the first time, because she looks so totally different from what he expected. This objective can be accomplished by taking advantage of a relative novelty of the contemporary fashion scene, the separate shirtwaist and skirt. They are the ideal garments for Violetta on this occasion. Granted, some care

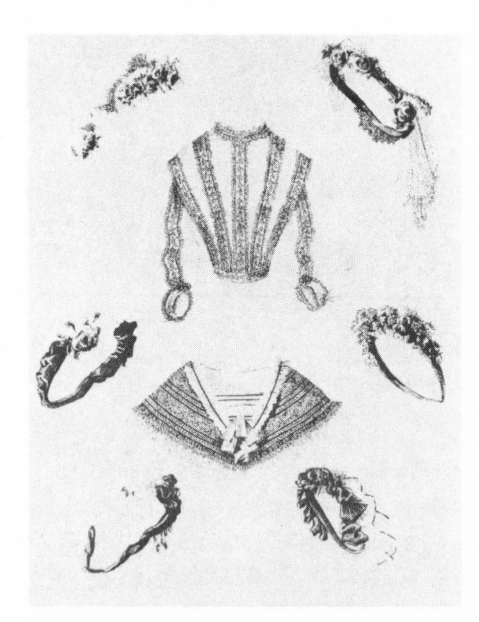

Blouses, a novelty of the contemporary fashion scene.

A dark frock coat for Germont *père* and a cloth livery coat for Giuseppe. (Contemporary fashion plate.)

and good judgment have to be exercised in the design of this costume, so that Violetta can look tall and slim and not cut in half. If the blouse and skirt are of the same color, though not of the same fabric, the problem is already half solved. With a skirt and blouse of contrasting colors, a bolero or shawl that matches the skirt will do the trick and change the horizontal line into a vertical one.

Alfredo's father should wear a dark frock coat of a summer-weight fabric, pants of a somewhat lighter shade, and a contrasting but harmonizing vest. The conservatism of his attire and the soberness of its coloring must be stressed—not only because of his character and his age but also because he is from the provinces and does not dress in the latest Paris fashions. People were much more inclined then to "dress their age," although there is no reason for Germont *père* to be a very old man. A dark stovepipe hat, gloves, and a cane complete his costume.

Annina is in the same dress she wore in act 1, but instead of the cap and apron, she now wears a dark straw bonnet tied under her chin and a large paisley shawl around her shoulders. Large shawls enjoyed enormous popularity then, and women of all stations had them in quantity and quality according to their wealth.

Giuseppe, the servant, may wear a dark cloth cutaway livery

A large paisley shawl for Annina.

coat with metal buttons, knee breeches, and a striped vest. Anything less formal would be out of place. If the vest has long black sleeves and a back, the coat can be omitted.

The messenger who delivers Violetta's letter is most likely a farmer. A farmer's smock and cap, rough pants, and stocking feet are just right for him. His sabots are left outside, assuming that this is an indoor scene.

ACT III

No two parties could be more different in atmosphere than Violetta's and Flora's, but they are rarely made to look different enough. If Violetta's taste harks back to the rococo style of Louis XV, Flora's apartments are strictly "1860 modern"—all cast iron, neo-Gothic, dark and gloomy, but very expensive. The music of this act is so nervous, so ominous and full of foreboding, that the drama that ensues in reality is almost anticlimactic. Having witnessed Alfredo's reaction to Violetta's letter, Father Germont seemed to have concluded that there was going to be bloodshed, and his appearance at Flora's party is perfectly justified on these grounds. By the same token, he should wear exactly what he wore in act 2: he is not an invited guest but is crashing the party because he fears that something terrible is going to happen. Changing clothes would rob his entire appearance of its motivation.

The idea of turning Flora's party into a *bal masqué* is a godsend. For the costumer to have to devise a second set of ballgowns, equally lavish but very different in feeling from those of act 1, is a most thankless task. But, what is more important, from the audience's point of view it becomes very repetitious. The notion of repeating the first-act costumes is entirely out of the question. Realistically, this type of woman would not appear in the same gown in virtually the same company, while from a theatrical point of view these costumes do not at all reflect the mood of the third act's music. Luckily there is a mention of "maskers" among the guests, and that saves the day. If some of the guests are to be masked and costumed as "gypsies and matadors," as it says in the libretto, then all of them might as well be. Costume balls were much in vogue at that time, as anyone who ever leafed through contemporary fashion magazines like *Godey's Fashions* will know. They fairly abound in suggestions for fetching costumes to wear to such occasions. In order to conform to the mood of the situation and to the music, the silhouette and palette of the women's costumes must be tightly controlled. What is to be avoided is the impression that the guests had been let loose

A look as if the guests had been let loose in a costumer's establishment.

in a theatrical costumer's establishment, there to indulge their fancy-dress whims. It was always the habit to adopt for masquerade costumes the prevailing fashion silhouette, regardless of the costume's historical origin. It is helpful as well to choose a theme for the party. For instance, the ladies might come as famous mistresses of kings. Violetta might be "Diane de Poitiers," Flora, "Mme. de Pompadour." For the male guests, dominos are suggested, to be worn over their tailsuits. Dominos are hooded, wide-sleeved, loose garments, adapted from monks' habits. They were the accepted "cop-out" dress for those who did not want to bother with a full-fledged costume. Though usually black and white, they may also have a color. In this instance, subdued shades that harmonize with the women's costumes are in order. The dominos' ample sleeves do not make them practical garments to dine or play cards in. It is reasonable to assume that the guests would have removed them when they went to dinner and never put them back on again.

The Spanish interlude in this act is the entire basis of the masquerade. It is a planned improvisation. The lady guests who participate in it can temporarily add mantillas and/or Spanish shawls to their costumes. Gastone dons a toreador's bolero, cape, hat, and sash, while for the chorus toreadors, a cape and hat are enough. Picadors don't wear capes, so these gentlemen have to settle for the picadors' bolero and wide-brimmed felt hats with red pompons. The

Fancy-dress costumes had the same silhouette as fashionable gowns. (Contemporary fashion plate.)

Violetta in act 3. (Comtesse de Castiglione.)

section of the Spanish interlude that deals with the saga of Piquillo usually produces a bevy of dancers. It is not surprising, for it is very "dancy" music. It should be noted, however, that neither the score nor the libretto breathes a word about dancers. It is therefore entirely up to the stage director and his helpmeet the choreographer what to make of this. I believe that it should have the same air of improvisation about it as the rest of this episode; better to use some of the guests who have decided to act out this little story than a corps de ballet imported for the occasion.

Sometimes an unexpected dramatic occurrence in what was supposed to be a happy and festive occasion can be made to seem doubly poignant by the contrast between the sad event and the gay and colorful surroundings. Such is not the case here. The music of the gypsy chorus and the matador song have for me a feeling of false gaiety. From the moment Alfredo goes to the gaming table there is no longer any doubt of what is afoot. If ever nervous tension was translated into music, this is it. The mood can be matched in the costumes through a sense of somber opulence. In considering the most appropriate costume for Violetta in this act, it is worthwhile to reconstruct her emotions as she was preparing to go to the ball. Combined with a sense of grief and loss there must also have been a feeling of release and relief at being able once again to indulge her hedonistic bent and her craving for luxury and splendor, all of which she had to forego while living with Alfredo. She selects, therefore, a gorgeous black gown, because she is mourning her loss, and because it is a splendid background for the garniture of diamonds, consisting of a tiara, earrings, necklace, brooch, and bracelets the baron gave her as a "welcome back" present. Flora's lackeys wear no powdered wigs. Their livery complements the decor of the salon.

Negligees too sturdy for a dying Violetta.

ACT IV

In these, her dying moments, we wish Violetta to give the impression of utmost frailty. It is not always easy to achieve this. Nightgowns and negligees of the period are no help at all in this respect. They give an impression of sturdiness and solidity, in silhouette as well as in the choice of fabric, which renders them unsatisfactory to the mood and the music of this act. Their heaviness is due in part to the haphazard heating methods of that time, which made the wearing of sheer clothes in drafty rooms and corridors a health hazard. One might be able to get away with the use of authentic clothes of that type, if the Violetta were a very frail woman, but most Violettas are made of sturdier stuff, or they would never get through the first act.

The costumer's task of creating a "frail" Violetta can be achieved through the use of limp fabrics, such as crepe-back satin and silk chiffon. An ideal color for her in this act is mauve, a greyish lavender. The sleeveless nightgown is made of lavender crepe-back satin (used on the crepe side), covered with pale grey silk chiffon. If the singer's arms do not permit total exposure, a small shoulder cape or bed jacket of a harmonizing shade may be used to cover them. The reason for the sleeveless nightgown is to facilitate putting a negligee over it when Violetta gets out of bed. That operation should look as effortless as possible. Putting on one sleeve on top of the other can be somewhat of a struggle, which is to be avoided here. If the sleeves of the negligee are cut raglan style, slipping into them will be even easier. The negligee is made of a double layer of chiffon, the bottom one lavender, the top one pale grey, like the nightgown, possibly with some simple lace trimming. It should be a very sheer, very ample, and very lovely garment.

Since Violetta has been in bed and under the covers for a while, it is necessary to hide the wrinkled condition of her nightgown, a touch of verismo not warranted here. Annina can usually mask Violetta's arising successfully by holding up the negligee spread out in

More springlike attire for Germont, father and son. (Contemporary fashion plate.)

front of her, for her to get into. It is all a matter of careful rehearsing. A pair of unobtrusive slippers or mules should be placed strategically near the bed so that Violetta can slip them on almost unnoticed.

Annina still wears the same dress as in the previous acts, but now with an everyday cap and apron, in contrast to the Sunday-best ones she wore in act 1. Upon awakening she has a large, dark knitted shawl around her shoulders.

Whether or not Dr. Grenvil, Alfredo, and Father Germont should wear their outer garments when they enter Violetta's room can best be determined by thinking through the position of each individual who enters. There is no doubt that at this time of the year they *would* be wearing topcoats or capes. Dr. Grenvil, although he is Violetta's devoted friend, is a professional man. He knows that this is a terminal case and so he comes early, possibly the first visit of his daily rounds, to see how close to the end she is. It is doubtful that he would remove his cape-coat for that purpose. It is a black garment worn over a black frock suit. Professional men like doctors and lawyers continued to favor black clothes. His top hat, gloves, and little black doctor's bag may be put on a side table. When Dr. Grenvil enters for the second time, he has been apprised by Annina that the end is near. He takes the time now to doff his outerwear and leave it outside.

Alfredo, in a subdued travelling suit, should give the impression that he "ran all the way." He rushes in and tosses the hat and coat, which he removed while running up the stairs, on the nearest chair.

Father Germont is not in such a hurry to enter. A sense of honor, duty, and maybe guilt, brings him here, but it is going to be a painful visit for him. He leaves his outer garments outside and enters in a frock suit, similar to the one he wore in act 2, but of a wintery fabric and even darker color.

GLOSSARY

F = Female, M = Male

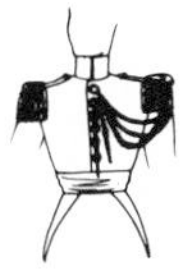

Aiguilette: A cord, partly braided, hanging at one shoulder and around the armhole of a uniform or livery. The ends usually have metal tips. It is worn in a variety of ways.

Ancien régime: French for "the old order," especially the one in power before the French Revolution. The term is also applied to the mode of costuming of that era.

Ankle tights: Three-quarter-length tight pants, often with a strap under the foot, usually worn with boots or leggings.

Armhole cloak: In the sixteenth century, an ample, sleeveless, three-quarter-length coat, its fullness often set onto a yoke. Frequently trimmed with a large fur collar and lapels extending down the entire length of the coat. M

Baigneuse: Originally a bathing cap, as the name implies, it developed in the eighteenth century into an elegant indoor head covering. It had endless variations, each with its own name. F

Baldric: In the seventeenth century, an elaborate belt worn diagonally over one shoulder, to the waist and below. Sometimes it served as a sword belt. M

Bandoleer: *See* Baldric

Bata: An Andalusian woman's gown of the late nineteenth century, with a princess-line bodice to the hip and a full skirt with a train, covered with ruffles.

Bertha: From about 1830 to 1860, a collar or border around a gown's wide décolletage.

Bias cut: Fabric cut on the diagonal of the grain.

Bib apron: An apron attached in the middle front to a flat piece of the same fabric, which covers part of the bodice. It may have shoulder straps at the top edge or may be pinned to the bodice. F

Bicorn: A man's hat of which the brim is turned sharply upward at two sides. Late eighteenth and first quarter of the nineteenth century.

Bolero: A short jacket not reaching the waist, and usually not closing middle front. It can be with or without sleeves. M, F

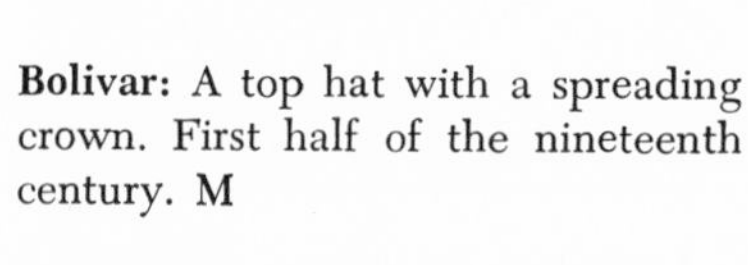

Bolivar: A top hat with a spreading crown. First half of the nineteenth century. M

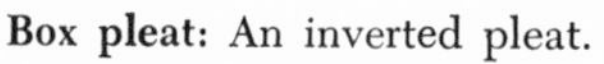

Box pleat: An inverted pleat.

Canions: In Elizabethan times, a garment covering the thighs. In the late seventeenth century, knee ruffles worn particularly with petticoat breeches. M

Capote: A small hat worn off the face and tied under the chin, popular in the "bustle" period. F

Caraco: In the eighteenth century, a hip-length garment with a "sack" back. F

Changeable fabric: A weave of which the woof is of a different color than the warp, resulting in an iridescent-looking fabric that will seem to change colors depending on where the light strikes it.

Chapeau: Short for "chapeau à bras," a tricorn or bicorn carried under the arm. Now a ceremonial bicorn, like an ambassador's.

Chapeau claque: Opera hat with a collapsible crown. M

Chemise dress: Late eighteenth-century dress omitting paniers and worn with a wide sash.

Chignon: A coil of hair at the nape of the neck. F

Circlet: A simple headband worn in ancient and medieval times. F, M

Clerical tabs: A rudimentary "falling band" worn with a cassock when not officiating. Eighteenth century.

Cockade: A rosette, usually decorating a hat. M, F

Coif: A linen head covering, medieval in origin. F, M

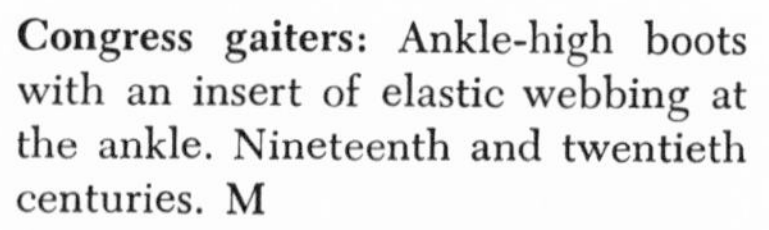

Congress gaiters: Ankle-high boots with an insert of elastic webbing at the ankle. Nineteenth and twentieth centuries. M

Court mantle: In Empire fashions, an elaborately decorated velvet train starting just below the bust and supported by halters.

Crested helmet: Of Greek-Roman origin, a military helmet with a raised section on the crown, often topped with feathers or a brush. Popular in the nineteenth century and still used by honor guards on ceremonial occasions.

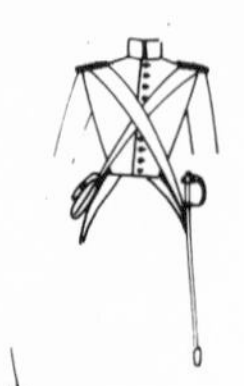

Cross-belt: Two shoulder belts, one over each shoulder, crossing middle front and back over a uniform coat.

Cuff ruffle: In the late seventeenth century and the eighteenth century, the shirt-sleeve protruding beyond the coat-sleeve's cuff. Frequently of lace. M and sometimes F for hunting coats.

Cuffietta: A soft indoor head covering, worn throughout the nineteenth century. F

Day cap: In the eighteenth century, a covering for the shaven skull in lieu of a wig. M

Dolman sleeve: A sleeve narrow at the wrist but with an exceedingly deep armhole, sometimes extending to the waist. F, M

Domino: An ample hooded masquerade costume, based on a monk's habit. F, M

Doublet: A tight-fittting, padded torso covering, worn during the fifteenth, sixteenth, and seventeenth centuries. M but occasionally F as a riding habit.

Dropped shoulder: Fashionable in women's dress of the 1830s, when the shoulder width was extended down the upper arm, thus narrowing the armhole and restricting the arm motion.

Empire hairstyles: Called "à la Titus." An imitation of ancient Greek and Roman hairstyles during the Empire period. F, M

Engageante: In the eighteenth century, a triple lingerie ruffle, facing and protruding beyond the sleeve's flounce, just below the elbow. F

Entre deux: A lace insert.

Espadrille: Spanish peasant's footwear with a rope sole.

Farthingale: A framework used in the sixteenth century to hold out a woman's skirt. French, Spanish, and English farthingales existed, each with a different silhouette. The one illustrated is the English "drum farthingale."

Fichu: A usually transparent triangular neckerchief covering a dress's décolletage.

Fillet: Man's headband in ancient Greece, worn by women in the eighteenth and nineteenth centuries.

Fontange: A high cap of lace or linen, trimmed with loops and supported by a wire frame. Late seventeenth century. F

Frogs: A looped coat fastening, made of braid or cord. F, M

Full-bottomed wig: Late seventeenth, early eighteenth century, curly shoulder-length wig, parted in the middle. M

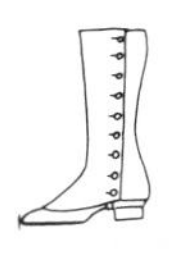

Gaiter: A cloth or leather covering extending over the top of the shoe and around the ankle or higher. Usually with a strap under the instep. F, M

Gallooned: Trimmed with galloon, a decorative flat braid. M, F

Gauffering (Goffering): An intricate gathering of fabric, used in the nineteenth century on women's indoor caps, for example.

Gorget: A metal collar, part of the armor. M

Greaves: Greek and Roman soldiers' shin protectors, reaching from the ankle to the knee.

Halberd: Originally an ax on a long pole. Still used as a symbol of office, e.g., by the Vatican Swiss Guard.

Hanging cap: (Also bag cap or stocking cap.) A long, tubular head covering, gathered at one end and often finished with a tassel or a pompon.

Hanging sleeve: A loose oversleeve slashed to let the undersleeve come through. It appeared in many forms and lengths. Fifteenth, sixteenth, and seventeenth centuries. F, M

Hoover collar: A high, stiff, turnover collar. M

Horsehair tail: A switch of horsehair attached to the side or the top of a dragoon's helmet.

Incroyable: A fop of the French Revolution, boasting the elegance of ill-fitting garments.

Jabot: Originally a ruffle at either side of the neck opening of a man's shirt. The accepted men's neckwear throughout the eighteenth century. F also in the nineteenth century.

Jerkin: A close-fitting, short-skirted jacket, often sleeveless, worn in the sixteenth and seventeenth centuries. M

Justaucorps: Late seventeenth century. Man's close-fitting, long, square-cut coat.

Kilt: A wraparound, knee-length skirt. M

Lapel wig: *See* Full-bottomed wig

Legging: A cloth or leather leg covering of varying length. See gaiter. M, F

Leg-o'-mutton sleeve: A sleeve extremely full at the arm's eye, tapering toward the elbow, and tight at the underarm. 1830 and 1890. F, but in children's smocks also M.

Love lock: A lock of hair separated from the rest of the hairdo, to fall on the shoulder. Sometimes with a bow at the end. Seventeenth century. M

Medici cap: A widow's coif with a wired edge, named after Maria de' Medici. Seventeenth century. F

Medici collar: A lace collar over a wire frame, spreading around the décolletage and framing the face. F

Merveilleuse: In the French Revolution, a woman's exaggeratedly careless dress, the female equivalent of an Incroyable.

Mi-parti: In medieval times, the geometrical color division of a garment, so that sections of one side are of different color than the corresponding section of the other side. Mostly M but occasionally F.

Mitten: 1. A glove without separate finger coverings except the thumb. F, M. 2. A dressy glove without fingers. F

Mobcap: An indoor head covering consisting of a circle of fabric shirred around the head a few inches from the edge, producing a puffed crown and a ruffled edge. Eighteenth century. F

Moiré: Watered silk.

Morion helmet: A crested, brimmed, sixteenth-century helmet, still worn today on ceremonial occasions by the Papal Swiss Guard.

Mousseline (Muslin, Mouselaine): A thin, soft, cotton fabric.

Norfolk jacket: A jacket (usually tweed) with two vertical bands front and back, underneath which a belt passes. M

Open seams: A peek-a-boo effect achieved by revealing the fabric of the underclothes through partly joined sections of the top fabric of the costume. Fifteenth, sixteenth, and seventeenth centuries. M, F

Opera gloves: Long, usually white gloves worn with a ball- or evening gown. Their length varied greatly at different periods.

Order sash: A grosgrain or moiré ribbon, part of a high-ranking decoration, worn across the chest on gala occasions. F, M

Ottoman: A ribbed silk fabric.

Padre shovel-hat: A low-crowned hat whose large brim is rolled up at the sides (but occasionally at the front and back). Worn by priests.

Pancake hat: A flat-brimmed, low-crowned hat. F

Paniers: Eighteenth-century side-hoops to extend the skirt's width.

Pelisse: A coatdress, originally fur lined. F

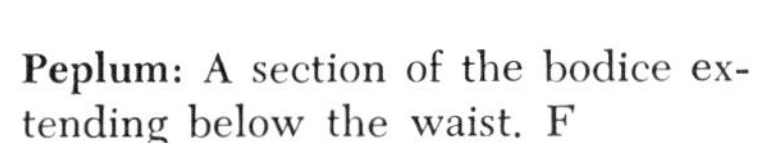

Peplum: A section of the bodice extending below the waist. F

Plastron: The superimposed front panel of a military coat, often of a contrasting color.

Plis Watteau: The pleats of a dress extending from the back of the neck and becoming part of the skirt. Eighteenth century.

Point d'esprit: Dotted net.

Poke bonnet: A hat with a stiff, off-the-face brim. Nineteenth century. F

Polonaise: A dress whose skirt has been pulled up in places (usually with inside tapes), revealing the underskirt. Eighteenth century.

Postiche: A false hairpiece. F

Pourpoint: A forerunner of the doublet. M

Prince Albert coat: A frock coat. M

Princess dress: A long, close-fitting dress cut in vertical panels. The skirt and bodice are not separated at the waist. Late nineteenth, early twentieth centuries.

Pumpkin hose: Short, puffed breeches. Sixteenth century. M

Puritan hat: A flat-brimmed hat with a conical crown. M, occasionally F.

Queue wig: A wig gathered at the nape of the neck with a bow or braided into a tail. Eighteenth century. M

Raffia: Fiber of the leaves of a palm tree, used for decorative purposes or woven into a strawlike material.

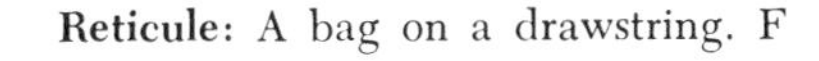

Reticule: A bag on a drawstring. F

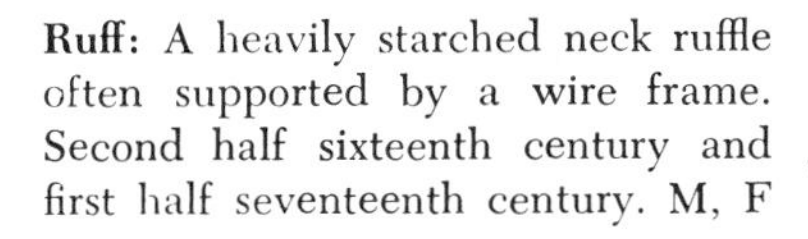

Ruff: A heavily starched neck ruffle often supported by a wire frame. Second half sixteenth century and first half seventeenth century. M, F

Sack coat: A hip-length jacket. M

Schiller collar: An open-neck shirt collar. M

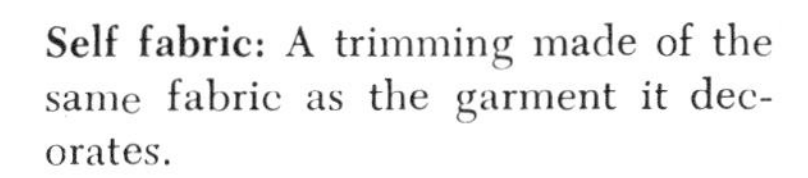

Self fabric: A trimming made of the same fabric as the garment it decorates.

Shako: Nineteenth-century military headgear with a cylindrical crown and often a visor brim.

Shantung: A China silk.

Shift: An undergarment worn next to the skin. F

Shirtwaist: A garment giving the appearance of a shirt but constructed like a dress bodice.

Sling cape: Short military jacket of a hussar's uniform, often fur edged, worn diagonally across the back like a shoulder cape.

Smoking cap: A pillbox hat worn with a dressing gown or a smoking jacket. Often trimmed with a tassel.

Snood: A net to catch long hair. M, F

Spats: *See* Gaiters

Square-cut coat: Long-skirted eighteenth-century coat. M

Steinkirk: Early eighteenth-century cravat, loosely tied, the end frequently pulled through a buttonhole.

Stick-up: An ornament at the top edge of a shako.

Stock: Nineteenth-century neckwear. M

Stocking cap: *See* Hanging cap

Stomacher: In the eighteenth century, a triangular piece of fabric, often lavishly decorated, pinned to the front of the corset. The gown's bodice was in turn pinned to the edge of the stomacher.

Straw boater: A stiff-brimmed straw hat with a flat-topped oval crown. F, M

Stuart collar: *See* Medici collar

Sunburst pleating: Fabric pleated on the diagonal of the grain, with each pleat starting exceedingly narrow at the top and gradually widening toward the bottom.

Surplice: A white linen or lace clerical garment worn during a service, over the cassock.

Swag: The front drape of a bustle skirt.

Sweetheart neckline: A décolletage starting close at the neck, then spreading outward and dipping toward the cleavage.

Swing tacking: A way of joining bodice and skirt with long, corded stitches on the inside of the garment.

Tabbard: In the thirteenth and fourteenth centuries, an ample, wide-sleeved garment. M

Tailor-made: A woman's skirt and jacket made by a man's tailor following the principles of male tailoring.

Tiered shoulder cape: Several shoulder capes in rows of varying lengths on top of each other. F, M

Tonsure wig: An eighteenth-century clerical wig with a tonsure.

Tye-bag wig: A queue wig of which the tail is caught in a small rectangular bag, mainly for military. Eighteenth century. M

Visor helmet: A metal helmet that covered the entire head and often the neck as well. A hinged visor, perforated in order to permit vision and breathing, covered the face. The visor could be raised. The shape of helmet and visor varied widely. Fifteenth and sixteenth centuries. M

Weft. In wigmaking, a string to which strands of hair are attached.

Wing collar: A stand-up collar of which the middle-front corners have been folded back.

BIBLIOGRAPHY

Adami, Giuseppe, ed. *Letters of Giacomo Puccini.* Translated by Ena Makin. Philadelphia: J. B. Lippincott Co., 1931.

Anderson, Emily, ed. *The Letters of Mozart and His Family.* London: Macmillan & Co., 1938.

Anelli, Angelo. *Ser Marcantonio.* Paris: Imprimerie Hoquet, 1813.

Besade, Léon de la. *Le Droit du Seigneur.* Paris: Rouveyre, 1878.

Bestetti, Carlo, ed. *Abbigliamento e Costume nella Pittura Italiana. Barocco e Impero.* Rome: Edizioni d'Arte, 1964.

Bleiler, Ellen. *Aïda.* New York: Dover Publications, 1962.

———. *Don Giovanni.* New York: Dover Publications, 1964.

Boehn, Max von. *Die Mode.* Munich: F. Drückmann, 1925.

Busch, Hans. *Verdi's Aïda.* Minneapolis: University of Minnesota Press, 1978.

Cali, François. *L'Art des conquistadors.* Paris: B. Arthaud, 1960.

Colle, Doriece. *Collars, Stocks, Cravats.* Emmaus, Pa.: Rodale Press, 1972.

Cunnington, C. Willet, and Cunnington, Phillis. *The History of Underclothes.* London: Michael Joseph, 1951.

Cunnington, C. W.; Cunnington, P. E.; and Beard, Charles. *A Dictionary of English Costume, 900–1900.* London: Adam & Chas. Black, 1960.

Curtis, Mina. *Bizet and His World.* New York: Alfred A. Knopf, 1958.

Davenport, Millia. *The Book of Costume.* New York: Crown Publishers, 1948.

Echagüe, José Ortiz, ed. *España, tipos y trajes.* Madrid: Publicaciones Ortiz Echagüe, 1963.

Erté. *Things I Remember.* New York: Quadrangle, 1975.

Gili, Gustavo, ed. *El traje Español en la época de Goya.* Barcelona: Editorial Gustavo Gili, 1962.

Goldovsky, Boris. *Bringing Opera to Life.* New York: Appleton-Century-Crofts, 1968.

Grout, Donald Jay. *A Short History of Opera.* New York: Columbia University Press, 1947.

Harding, James. *Gounod.* New York: Stein & Day, 1973.

Heingold, Margaret Bauer. *The Baroque Theatre.* New York: McGraw-Hill, 1967.
Houston, Mary G. *Ancient Egyptian, Mesopotamian, and Persian Costume.* London: Adam & Chas. Black, 1920.
Hughes, Patrick. *Famous Mozart Operas.* New York: Citadel Press, 1963.
———. *Famous Puccini Operas.* New York: Citadel Press, 1959.
Kahane, Eric. *Un Marriage Parisien sous le Directoire.* Paris: Editions "Le Carousel," 1961.
Kinderen Besier, J. H. der. *Spelevaart der Mode.* Amsterdam: Querido's Uitgevers Maatschappij, 1950.
Koslinskov, V.; Berman, E.; and Kurbatovoy, E. *Ruskiy Kostyum 1750–1917.* Moscow: Vserosiyskoe Teatralynoe Obshchestvo, 1960.
Krehbiel, Henry Edward. *A Second Book of Operas.* Garden City, N.Y.: Garden City Publishing, 1917.
Kybalova, Ludmila; Herbenova, Olga; and Lamarova, Milena. *A Pictorial Encyclopedia of Fashion.* New York: Crown Publishers, 1968.
Leloir, Maurice. *Dictionaire du costume.* Libraire Gründ, 1951.
Marais, Jean. *Histoires de ma vie.* Paris: Editions Albin Michel, 1975.
Maupassant, Guy de. "Le Rosier de Mme. Husson." In *Oeuvres complètes.* Paris: Librairie de France, 1943.
Merimée, Prosper. *The Loves of Carmen.* New York: Pocketbooks Inc.
La Merveilleuse histoire de l'Armée Française. Paris: Editions G. P., 1947.
Murger, Henry. *Scènes de la vie de Bohème.* Le livre club du libraire, 1958.
Newman, Ernest. *Stories of Great Operas.* New York: Alfred A. Knopf, 1929.
———. *More Stories of Great Operas.* New York: Alfred A. Knopf, 1943.
Onassis, Jacqueline, ed. *In the Russian Style.* New York: Viking Press, 1976.
Pushkin, Alexsandr. *Eugene Onegin.* Translated and annotated by Vladimir Nabokov. Princeton, N.J.: Princeton University Press, 1975.
Rat, Maurice. *Théâtre de Beaumarchais.* Paris: Editions Granier Frères, 1964.
Roulin, Dom. E. *Linges, Insignes et Vêtements liturgiques.* Paris: P. Lethielleux, 1930.
Rütz, Hans. *Wolfgang Amadeus Mozart.* Munich: Verlag C. H. Beck, 1950.
Sardou, Victorien. *La Tosca.* English version by Robert K. Evans. Boston, 1958.
Wilcox, R. Turner. *The Mode in Hats and Headdresses.* New York: Charles Scribner's Sons, 1948.
Working Friendship: The Correspondence between Richard Strauss and Hugo von Hofmannsthal. Translated by Hanns Hammelmann and Ewald Osers. New York: Random House, 1961.
Vilimkova, M. *Egyptian Ornament.* London: Allan Wingate, 1963.
Waugh, Nora. *Corsets and Crinolines.* London: B. T. Batsford, 1954.
Weaver, William. *Verdi Librettos.* Garden City, N.Y.: Doubleday & Co., 1963.
Wechsbert, Joseph. *Verdi.* New York: G. P. Putnam's Sons, 1974.
Wendel, Friedrich. *Die Mode in der Karikatur.* Dresden: Paul Aretz Verlag, 1928.

PICTURE SOURCES AND CREDITS

All drawings are by Leo Van Witsen unless otherwise noted. All photographs not provided by museums and archives were taken by William Greene, Jack Neubeck, Robert Stoeckle, and Whitestone Photos.

Aïda 1, 2 (top): Historical Archive of G. Ricordi & C., Milan. 2 (bot.): Museo Teatrale alla Scala, Milan.

Albert Herring 23: From *An Edwardian Holiday* by John S. Goodall. (A Margaret K. McElderry Book.) Copyright © 1978 by John S. Goodall. Reprinted by permission of Atheneum Publishers and Macmillan, London and Basingstoke. 24: (r.) *An Edwardian Holiday*. 25: (top) *Victorian Fashions and Costumes from Harper's Bazar: 1867–1898*, by Stella Blum. Dover, New York, 1974. (bot.) Fashion plate from *The Delineator*. Butterick Publishing Co., New York. 26: *The Delineator*. 27–29: Suffolk Photographic Survey. 30: (top) *An Edwardian Holiday*. (bot.) Suffolk Photographic Survey. 31–33: Suffolk Photographic Survey.

Ariadne auf Naxos 34, 35 (bot.): Devonshire Collection Chatsworth. Reproduced by permission of the Trustees of the Chatsworth Settlement. 35 (top): Bibliothèque Nationale, Paris. 36–37: Biblioteca Nazionale Universitaria, Turin. 38: Metropolitan Museum of Art. Dick Fund, 1932. 39: Reprinted by permission of Boosey and Hawkes. 40: Reproduced by courtesy of the Trustees of The British Museum. 41: *Personnages de Qualité*, by Roger-Armand Weigert. Éditions Rombaldi, Paris (n.d.). 42: (top) Library of Brooks Van Horn Costume Co., Inc., New York. *Costumes de Théâtre de 1600–1820*. Imp. Lith. de Delpèche, Paris (1824?). (bot.) *Personnages de Qualité*. 43: *Costumes de Théâtre de 1600–1820*. 44: (top) Bibliothèque Nationale, Cabinet des Estampes, Paris. (bot.) Victoria and Albert Museum, London. 45: *Costumes de Théâtre de 1600–1820*. 46. (top) Ashmolean Museum, Oxford. (bot.) *Personnages de la Comédie Italienne*. Les Éditions Braun & Cie, Paris (n.d.). 47: (top) *Personnages de Qualité*. (bot.) Victoria and Albert Museum, London. 48: (bot.) *Personnages de Qualité*. 48 (top)–49: *Costumes de Théâtre de 1600–1820*.

Barber of Seville 50: Museo del Prado, Madrid. 52: (top) *The History of Lingerie in Pictures*. Fairchild Publications, New York, 1952. (bot.) Museo del Prado, Madrid. 53: (l.) Museo del Prado, Madrid. (r.) Reproduced by courtesy of the Trustees, The National Gallery, London. 54: (top) Museo del Prado, Madrid. (bot.) Banco Urquijo, Madrid. 55: (top) Museo del Prado, Madrid. (bot.) Courtesy, Museum of Fine Arts, Boston. 56: (top) Pinacoteca di Brera, Milan. (bot.) Private collection. 57: (top, l.) *Galerie des Modes et Costumes Français*. Librairie Centrale des Beaux Arts, Paris (n.d.). (top, r.) Reproduced by courtesy of the Trustees, The National Gallery, London. (bot.) Museo del Prado, Madrid. 58 (top) *Iconographie générale et méthodique du Costume du IVieme au XIXieme siècle*, by Raphael Jacquemin. Paris, 1863–69. (bot.) Reproduced by courtesy of the Trustees of The British Museum.

La Bohème 59: Victoria and Albert Museum, London. 60: (top, c., r.) *Fashion in Paris*, by Octave Uzanne. Wm. Heineman, London, 1898. (bot.) By courtesy of Hachette Photo Service, Paris. 61: (l.) *Un siècle d'élégance Française*, by Nicole Verdès. Éditions du Chêne, Paris, 1943 (r.) *Petit Courier des Dames*, Paris, 1834. 62: (l.) *Daumier*. Manesse Verlag Conzett & Huber, Zurich (n.d.). (r.) *Fashion in Paris*. 63: *Die Mode. Menschen und Moden im 19ten Jahrhundert*, by Max von Boehn. F. Drückmann, Munich, 1924. 64: (top) *Die Mode*. 65: (top, l.) *Fashion in Paris*. (top, r.) *Daumier*. 66: Achille Devéria, *Les heures de la Parisienne; dix heures du matin*. Éditions Rombaldi, Paris (n.d.). 67: (bot.) *L'Imagerie Parisienne*, by P.-L. Ducharte and René Saulnier. Librairie Gründ, Paris, 1944. 68: (bot.) *Fashion in Paris*. 69: (bot.) *Album Historique de l'Armée et de la Marine*. J. Leroy. Paris, *1905–1906*. 70: (top) *Modes de Paris*. (bot.) *Die Mode*. 71, 73 (top): *Les heures de la Parisienne*. 73: (bot.) *Die Mode*.

Carmen 76: The Museum of Modern Art/Film Stills Archive, New York. 77: (top) *El traje Español en la época de Goya*. Gustavo Gili, Barcelona, 1962. (bot.) *España. Tipos y trajes*. Publicaciones Ortiz-Echagüe, Madrid, 1963. 78: *España. Tipos y trajes*. 79: (top, l.) *El traje Español en la época de Goya*. (r.) *Costumes of Andalusia*. 82: *La Magazin Pittoresque*, Paris, 1833–1909. 83: The Museum of Modern Art/Film Stills Archive. 84: *España. Tipos y trajes*. 86–87: *El traje Español en la época de Goya*.

Così fan tutte 89: Private collection. 90: Topkapi Palace, Istanbul. 91: (top) Theatre Museum, London. (bot.) The Metropolitan Museum of Art. Gift of Mrs. Thorneycroft Ryle, 1957. 92: (r.) *Military Uniforms*, Orbis, London, 1923. 93: (top) *Agenda E.N.I.T. 1957*. A. Pizzi, Milan, 1957. (bot.) Victoria and Albert Museum, London. 94: (top, l.) Victoria and Albert Museum, London. (bot.) *Il Presepe Napolitano*. Unedi, Milan. 95: (top, l.) Musée Carnavalet, Paris. (r.) *Il Presepe Napolitano*. (bot.) Victoria and Albert Museum, London. 96: *Costumes de Théâtre de 1600–1820*. Library of Brooks Van Horn Costume Co., Inc., New York. 97: *Tiepolo a villa Valmarana*. Unedi, Milan.

Don Giovanni 100–101: Amsterdam Rijksmuseum. 102: (top) The Metropolitan Museum of Art, Rogers Fund, 1932. (bot.) Victoria and Albert Museum, London. 103: (top, l.) Victoria and Albert Museum, London. (r.) Baltimore Museum of Art, Bequest Jacob Epstein. (bot.) Victoria and Albert Museum, London. 104: Galleria degli Uffizi, Florence. 105, 106 (bot.), 107 (bot.): Victoria and Albert Museum, London. 107 (top): Private collection. 108: Collezione Pallavicino, Genoa. 109: Librairie centrale d'art et d'architècture. Anc. Maison Morel. 110: The Metropolitan Museum of Art, Rogers Fund, 1960. 112: (top) The Metropolitan Museum of Art, Rogers Fund, 1912. (bot.) Courtesy of the Greater London Council as Trustees of the Iveagh Bequest, Kenwood. 113: (top) *Bringing Soprano Arias to Life*, by Boris Goldovsky and Arthur Schoep. Schirmer, New York, 1973. (bot.) Reproduced by permission of the Trustees of The Wallace Collection, London. 114: (top) Bavarian State Collection, Munich. (bot.) The Fine Arts Museum of San Francisco. Gift of Archer M. Huntington.

Don Pasquale 118: *Bringing Soprano Arias to Life*. 121: (top) Museo Civico, Venice. (bot.) Victoria and Albert Museum, London. 122: (top) Courtesy of the Fogg Art Museum, Harvard University. Bequest-Grenville L. Winthrop. (bot.) Collection Bonnat, Bayonne, France. 123: *Die Mode*. 124: *El traje Español en la época de Goya*.

Eugene Onegin 125, 127–29: *Ruskiy Kostyum 1750–1917*. Vserosiyskoe Teatralynoe Obshchestvo, Moscow, 1960. 130: The Metropolitan Museum of Art, Morris K. Jesup Fund, 1930. 131: (l.) *Petit Courier des Dames*, 1834. (r.) *Ruskiy Kostyum 1750–1917*. 132–37: *Ruskiy Kostyum 1750–1917*. 137 (bot. r.): *Down Memory Lane*, by Sylvia G. Dannet and Frank R. Rachel. Greenberg, 1954. 138: City Arts Gallery, Bristol. 139–41: *Ruskiy Kostyum 1750–1917*.

Faust 144: The Metropolitan Museum of Art, Fletcher Fund, 1919. 146: *Civil and Military Clothing in Europe*, by Frederic Stibbert. Benj. Blom Inc., London, 1968. 148: (top) *Civil and Military Clothing in Europe*. (bot.) Amsterdam Rijksmuseum. 150: Kunstmuseum Basel. 152: Kunsthistorisches Museum, Vienna.

Die Fledermaus 155: *English Women's Clothing in the Nineteenth Century*, by C. Willet Cunnington. Faber & Faber, London, 1937. 156: (l.) *Washington Past and Present*, by Chalmers M. Roberts. Washington, D.C., Public Affairs Press, 1950. (r.) *Victorian Fashions and Costumes from Harper's Bazar: 1867–1898*, by Stella Blum. Dover, New York, 1974. 157: (r.) *Victorian Fashions and Costumes from Harper's Bazar*. 158: (top) *Handbook of English Costume in the Nineteenth Century*, by C. W. and Phillis Cunnington. Faber & Faber, London, 1959. 160: (top) The Russian Museum, Leningrad. (bot.) The Hermitage, Leningrad. 161: The Hermitage, Leningrad. 162: (top, l.) *Un siècle d'élégance Française*, by Nicole Verdès. Éditions du Chêne, Paris, 1943. 162 (top, r.), 163 (l.), 164: *Victorian Fashions and Costumes from Harper's Bazar*.

Marriage of Figaro 165: Musée des Arts Decoratifs, Paris. 166: Bibliothèque Nationale, Paris. 167: Bibliotheek van het Rijksmuseum, Amsterdam. 168: *Costumes de Théâtre de 1600–1820*. Library of Brooks Van Horn Costume Co., Inc., New York. 169: *Die Mode*, by Max von Boehn. F. Drückmann, Munich, 1924. 170: *Costumes de Théâtre de 1600–1820*. 171: *Galerie des Modes et Costumes Français*. Librairie Centrale des Beaux Arts, Paris (n.d.). 172: (top) *Die Mode*. (bot.) Musée National du Château de Versailles. 173: (top) *Galerie des Modes et Costumes Français*. (bot.) National Historical Museum, Mexico City. 174: *Die Mode*. 175: Museo del Prado, Madrid. 177: (top) Hispanic Society of America, New York. (bot.) *Galerie des Modes et Costumes Français*. 178: Courtesy of the Fogg Art Museum, Harvard University, Portrait Collection. 179: *Galerie des Modes et Costumes Français*.

Tannhäuser 183, 184: *Richard Dadd*, by Patricia Allderidge. St. Martin's Press, New York, 1974. 185: *Costumes de Théâtre de 1600–1812*. 186: *Opern Typen*. Verlag G. Kölle, Berlin (n.d.). 187: (top)*Die Minnesinger*; Die Manessische Handschrift. Insel-Verlag, Leipzig, 1929. (bot.) *Bringing Soprano Arias to Life*. 188, 189 (top, l.): *Die Minnesinger; Die Manessische Handschrift*. 190: (top) *Richard Dadd*. (bot.) *Die Minnesinger; Die Manessische Handschrift*. 194: *Die Minnesinger; Die Manessiche Handschrift*.

Tosca 196–97: Sources unknown. 198: (l.) Musée Hyacinthe Rigaud, Perpignan. (r.) Musée Granet, Palais de Malte, Aix en Provence. Bernard Terlay, service photographique du musée. 199: *Incroyables et Merveilleuses*, by Horace Vernett. Éditions Rombaldi, Paris (n.d.). 200: (top) Musée Condé, Chantilly. (bot.) Galleria Santa Luca, Rome. 202: (top) Parma Galleria Nazional. (bot.) Private collection, Genoa. 204: (top) Musée du Louvre, Paris. (bot.) Musée National du Château de Versailles. 205: (top) Musée de la Malmaison, Rueil-Malmaison. (bot.) William Rockhill Nelson Gallery of Art, Atkins Museum of Fine Arts, Kansas City, Missouri. 206: (l.) *Le Costume de la Revolution a nos jours*, by Raymond See. Éditions de la Gazette des Beaux Arts, Paris, 1929. (r.) Scala Palazzo del Municipo Trento.

La Traviata 207: By permission of Harry Twynford Peters, Jr. 208: *Graham's Magazine*. 209: Musée de la Malmaison, Rueil-Malmaison. 210: *The Lady's Home Magazine*. T. S. Arthur & Co., Philadelphia, 1858. 211: *What People Wore*, by Douglas Gorsline. Viking Press, New York. Copyright 1952, © 1980 by Douglas Gorsline. 212: The Metropolitan Museum of Art, Harris Brisbane Dick Fund, 1936. 214: (bot.) *La Vie et l'Art Romantiques*, by Achille and Eugène Devéria. H. Floury, Paris, 1925. 215: (top) *Fashion and Reality*, by Alison Gernsheim. Dover Publications, Inc. New York, 1963. 216: (l.) *Victorian Fashions and Costumes from Harper's Bazar: 1867–1898*. 217: *La Mode féminine de 1790 a 1920*. Éditions Nilsson, Paris, 1926. 219: (r.) *Un Siècle d'élégance Français*. 220: *The Lady's Home Magazine*.